Running
Crazy

Running Crazy

Imagine running a marathon. Now imagine running over 100 of them. Incredible true stories from the world's most fanatical runners.

Helen Summer

JOHN BLAKE

Published by John Blake Publishing Ltd,
3 Bramber Court, 2 Bramber Road,
London W14 9PB, England

www.johnblakepublishing.co.uk

www.facebook.com/Johnblakepub   facebook

twitter.com/johnblakepub   twitter

First published in paperback in 2012

ISBN: 978-1-84358-756-9

British Library Cataloguing-in-Publication Data:

A catalogue record for this book is available from the British Library.

Design by www.envydesign.co.uk

Printed and bound by CPI Group (UK) Ltd, Croydon, CR0 4YY

1 3 5 7 9 10 8 6 4 2

Papers used by John Blake Publishing are natural, recyclable products made
from wood grown in sustainable forests. The manufacturing processes
conform to the environmental regulations of the country of origin.

Every attempt has been made to contact the relevant copyright-holders,
but some were unobtainable. We would be grateful if the
appropriate people could contact us.

DEDICATION

I have always considered myself a lucky person – not because everything in my life has always been rosy – I reckon I've had my fair share of thorns, but because every now and again something rather special happens unexpectedly.

Being given the opportunity to write this book was one of them. Meeting the gals and guys from the 100 Marathon Club was another. The two are, of course, inextricably linked and both have given me immense pleasure.

The first because it has long been my dream to be published; the second because occasionally we come across a person who is so uniquely special that we feel our lives have been enriched merely by meeting them. To meet over 30 such people within the space of nine short months as I have through the 100 Marathon Club, is more than lucky, it is a privilege and an honour.

It has also been humbling. Not least because these people are ordinary, every day people who have not been given any special privileges, in some cases quite the opposite – some have even had to fight quite literally for their lives, and yet they have achieved so much. And what is most admirable is that they have done it all by themselves.

For each of them set their own challenges – whether to raise money for charity, run faster or further or simply to add another marathon to their numbers, and each of them works hard to achieve them. Sometimes they succeed, sometimes they don't, but they never give up. They have the courage and determination to keep on trying, no matter what.

But it doesn't end with what they want to achieve for themselves. They also support and encourage each other in their endeavours and there is always a shoulder to cry on when things don't go to plan. Through their sport, they demonstrate all that is good in the human spirit and the most positive aspects of man's innate nature. They are also friendly, fun and a joy to know and I cannot thank them enough for the willingness and warmth with which they welcomed me into their remarkable 'family' and shared their stories and their lives with me.

I stand in awe.

Helen Summer

CONTENTS

ACKNOWLEDGEMENTS

I have to thank the following contributors who gave so generously of their time and their stories, even though they were out running marathons most weekends and in some cases, even training in between – and without whom there would be no book.

Roger Biggs, Martin Bush, John Dawson, Peter Dennett, Steve Edwards, Jerry Forde, Richard Fulford, Chris Heaton, Ron Hill, Adam Holland, David King, Gina Little, Dave Major, Linda Major, Jim Manford, Mike Marten, Brian Mills, Dave Moles, Janet Moles, Chris Monsey, Kay O'Regan, David Phillips, Naomi Prasad, Steve Price, David Ross, Mel Ross, Allan Rumble, Jill Rumble, Kio Vejdani, Paul Watts, Osy Waye and Sid Wheeler.

With special thanks to: Malcolm Hargraves of Running Crazy Limited, without whom none of this would have happened; my publisher, John Blake (whose brilliant idea this book was in the first place) for having such faith in me and making my writing dreams come true; my editors, Lucian Randall, Allie Collins and

Jane Donovan, who turned this book into something so much better than it would otherwise have been; Envy Design for coming up with such a fantastic cover; Gerry North for putting me in touch with one of the world's greatest athletes; my family and friends for listening and never once telling me to shut up and my son, Jack Matthew Archer, who brought summer back into my life and whose brilliant idea it was to divide the book into 26.2 chapters.

I dedicate this book to my son Jack, who never stopped believing this day would come and who is without doubt the best thing that ever happened to me. Also in memory of my beloved mum and aunt, who taught me how to be just a little bit naughty.

FOREWORD BY STEVE EDWARDS

L ooking back through my childhood I have vivid memories of
being bullied because of my deformed hand and forever
being told that I would find many things impossible. I could,
therefore, perhaps be forgiven for not having achieved my
potential by the time I left school in 1979. Not that I cared too
much at the time; I found a job, discovered beer, clubs and, of
course, girls. The world was my oyster. Or was it? Despite
being a naive young man, I started to question where my life
was going.

Two years later, I was drawn to a poster advertising the
inaugural Coventry Marathon (my home town). Although I was
only 18 and hadn't run since school, it was one of those special
moments when something sparked in my mind. I couldn't really
explain the feeling, not only did it seem the right thing to do,
but it somehow seemed to suggest an opportunity to take a new
path in life which could possibly lead to better things. After a bet
with some mates, my decision was made.

Of course I didn't know the first thing about training for a marathon and did everything wrong, from wearing inadequate footwear to not hydrating properly and certainly not doing enough miles in training. I reached mile 15 in the race and began to wonder what all the fuss was about, a mile later I found out! Something hit me and it was as if my legs had decided to just pack up. I learned some time later about 'the wall', but at the time I didn't know whether to walk, sit down or give up. In the end, I did none of these and struggled on to finish in a time of 3 hours 38 minutes. After crossing the line I experienced a feeling like I'd never felt before, one of accomplishment and sheer euphoria, it felt like I'd conquered the world!

Unfortunately, that feeling faded somewhat the following day when I woke up to discover I had legs like gateposts and after attempting to walk down the stairs, I swore I'd never run a marathon ever again! It was all I could do to go down the stairs backwards and a full week passed before I could walk normally again. Time, of course, is a great healer and several weeks later, I was back running again. I'd found something special that I enjoyed, something that made me feel confident about myself and something that felt good, not only physically but also spiritually.

I wasn't aware at the time, but this was the start of an incredible journey. Not only a journey of personal achievement, but a journey that in time would see my wife and I travel to many wonderful places where we would meet many like-minded people with a common goal and make many new friends. It would give me the opportunity to put something back into the world, to inspire others and learn a lot more about myself as a human being, not only in terms of my character but to realise what an amazing machine the human body is.

In a world where obesity and alcohol abuse are on the increase, where role models are created from appearing on reality TV programmes and where the greater media seem intent on focusing on all the gloom and negative aspects of life, this book is about an amazing group of people who, like me, have followed an incredible journey in the sport of extreme marathon running. They are not famous nor are they generally known to the wider public community, why would they be? What they do is healthy, positive and inspirational, attributes that sadly have perhaps been forgotten in some parts of modern society and all the things so often overlooked by today's media in favour of so-called celebrity and TV-manufactured idols who are then held up as role models.

Call me old fashioned, but I was brought up to realise that the world owed you nothing, there were no short cuts, if you wanted respect it had to be earned and you only achieved success with hard work and dedication. To run 100 or more marathons requires determination, courage and endeavour. For the 100 Marathon runners, the reward of achieving that goal is not one of fame or fortune, but a way of life that no one can buy and, sadly, not many will ever experience. It is well known that more people have climbed Mount Everest than have run 100 marathons or more. I therefore feel both proud and privileged to have discovered that way of life from an early age.

I left school with little ambition, only too ready to step onto life's conveyor belt of conformity and follow the masses that seem to be controlled by what comes out of the screen in the corner of the room. Thankfully, like the people in this book, I discovered an alternative life, that through doing something as simple as putting one foot in front of the other as quickly as possible over a long distance gave me the opportunity to feel alive. This book clearly demonstrates that with belief, hard work and dedication you don't have to be an elite athlete on the world stage to realise a dream and that ordinary people can achieve extraordinary things.

I would like to sincerely thank the author, Helen Summer, for allowing me the special privilege of writing this 'foreword'. Also, congratulations and thank you to all the members past and present of the 100 Marathon Club for who you are and what you have achieved. Lastly (but by no means least) I'd like to thank my wife, Teresa, the other half of 'Team Edwards', whose love and support has contributed greatly to all that I have achieved.

To all who read this book, remember one thing, we are all born athletes, what we do after is our choice.

Steve Edwards, the fastest person in the world to run 500 marathons

INTRODUCTION

When I was first approached to write a book about people who had run over 100 marathons, never having run one marathon myself, never mind 100, I wasn't convinced I was qualified. However, once it was pointed out to me that I had been involved in running for over 40 years (I started very young), that as a UK Athletics Level 3 endurance coach who had coached marathon runners of varying ages and abilities, and through my work with Running Crazy Limited (www.runningcrazy.co.uk) who arrange running trips abroad, I was constantly in the company of marathon runners, I realised maybe, just maybe, I wasn't totally *un*qualified. Plus, never having run one meant I could take an objective view of matters, and never having run 100, I wouldn't be blinded by my own obsession or my insanity, which, let's face it, if we're honest most of us would consider a prerequisite of anyone who has run a minimum of 100 marathons.

But what if we're wrong? What if, instead of being crazy they are just passionate? Perhaps instead of being obsessive they are just committed? And what if I told you that having met some of them, I can honestly say a nicer, friendlier, happier and more positive bunch of people you'd be hard pushed to find anywhere? So much so that in the end I forgot to feel unqualified and simply felt privileged to enter a world where people genuinely care as much about their fellow man's performance as they do their own, where they celebrate with total generosity of spirit one another's achievements, as well as sharing in their disappointments, comparing aches and pains and recounting the sheer bloody hard work that is actually a prerequisite of every marathon, whether it's your first or your 100th.

Okay, so maybe there is a hint of madness but where would be the fun in this book, both for me as the writer and you as reader, if there wasn't?

Of course while this book is predominantly about the people, it is also about the extraordinary, sometimes bizarre races they have run in, the places they have been to and the discoveries they have made, not only of themselves but also the world at large. It is also about the way running reflects life, testing, challenging and ultimately teaching us how to deal with both the good and the bad with grace and dignity.

And so, without further ado I urge you to follow me and meet the characters who make up the 100 Marathon Club, discover the uniqueness of the Addis Ababa Marathon, the perils of appearing at Trafalgar Square dressed as a polar bear and the horror in finding yourself mistakenly on the elite starting line of the London Marathon dressed in a bin liner and carrying a plastic cup of tea! Discover too what it's like to face the challenge of a marathon (or over 100 of them) when you are blind or in a wheelchair.

Share the laughter and tears, the pain and the glory, while reaping the benefit of words of wit and wisdom from those who have a wealth of knowledge and experience of marathon running – some stuff you can't learn from a textbook!

AUTHOR'S NOTE:

The total number of marathons run by each athlete was correct at the time of writing; however, due to the very nature of the sport, all numbers will have increased by the time this book goes to print.

MILE 1

A LITTLE BIT OF HISTORY, PLUS SOME OTHER STUFF

Before we get to the really interesting bit – the people themselves – let's start at the beginning. How exactly did a club for people who had run over 100 marathons begin?

I was lucky enough to be put in touch with one of the Club's founder members, David Phillips, a man who, by the time this book goes to print, will have run over 400 marathons in 25 years and raised over £50,000 for charity in the process.

I feel humbled. At least I did until he presented me with a car boot full of memorabilia.

I was further aided and abetted in the writing of this chapter by Saint Roger Biggs, current chairman of the 100 Club and patron saint of patience, and Steve Edwards, one of the youngest original members.

YESTERYEAR

During the running boom of the early 1980s, a number of runners kept bumping into each other at marathons around the country and they would tell each other what their totals were –

40, 50, 60 marathons. One of the most prolific was a man called Richard Bird, who ran 76 marathons in a 12-month period, setting a World Record.

'He was probably the biggest influence in setting up the Club and getting other people to do numbers. Everyone knew him, he was at every race,' Dave tells me.

However, it is believed that it was another man, Harry Martin, who was actually the first to reach 100, which he did at Blackpool in about 1987.

'He bought a bottle of cheap champagne to celebrate afterwards,' Dave recalls.

While the group of runners celebrated Harry's achievement, they decided to form a club exclusively for those who had run 100 marathons and to call that club the '100 Club'.

One of those most involved with the setting up of the Club was an Irishman called Brian Doherty, or 'The Ladder Man', as he was popularly known – because he was a window cleaner who ran every marathon carrying his ladder!

Initially, the newly formed Club decided to present each new member with a special medal to mark the completion of 100 marathons but a few years on, Brian purchased a silver trophy from a second-hand shop, which became known simply as 'The Cup'.

'Every new member had their name and details of their 100th marathon engraved upon it and would keep The Cup for a year,' says Dave, whose own name appears thereon as the 25th Brit to complete his 100th in 1991.

Others who ran their 100th in those early days, and whose names appear regularly in old newsletters, were Peter Sargeant, Andrew Radgick, Derek Appleton, Don Thompson (50K Walk Gold medallist in the 1960 Rome Olympics), Sid Morrison, Mike Olivera, Eddie Edmonds, brothers David and Richard Tann, and Steve Edwards, who at that time also took the World

Record for the greatest number of marathons run in 12 months to 87. There is also, among the names engraved on that trophy one Ron Hill, probably the most famous multi-marathoner in the world.

But the 100 Club didn't want to encourage only Brits to run marathons, they were keen to encourage everyone and therefore the Club and The Cup boasts the names of runners from all over the world, regardless of whether they are members of the Club.

Of course, once they'd passed the 100 mark there was only one place to go – and that was *200*! It is believed two men, Edwin Bartlett and Colin Greene, were among the first to notch up a second century.

And then there were the ladies.

Rita Banks of Staffordshire is believed to have been the first woman to complete 100 marathons, which she did at Nottingham in 1990. She also set a new World Record for Most Marathons Run in One Year By a Woman (52). At the time she was 45.

'After her 100th, she had a party to celebrate in the car park,' Dave recollects. 'She set up a table and we had cakes and coffee.'

Trust a lady to do it properly!

'That was the real start of the tradition of partying after your 100th, and if you didn't have a table, you just did it out of your car boot!' Dave adds.

'Sue Goddard from Luton was another one of the original ladies,' he continues. 'She liked to write about the races and was a regular contributor to the newsletters and early magazines we used to produce.'

Dave should know. With his accountancy background, the club very quickly utilised his particular skills in making him their first treasurer, not to mention first secretary and magazine editor/printer.

'In those days,' he remembers, 'we weren't affiliated to the AA

(Athletic Association) or anything. It was just a matter of us all meeting up at races, celebrating our centuries and forming friendships. It was all very informal, but also very positive.

'It was also seen as a way to promote marathon running in England as a whole. In fact, the 100 Club were responsible for setting up 79 new marathons in the UK during the 1980s. Unfortunately, that number dropped to around 30 during the 1990s as the popularity of marathon running decreased.'

However, it's now back on the up again to around 50, with a running boom being reported right across the land, no doubt fired by the impending London Olympics in 2012.

At some point, though it's not clear from the records exactly when, there was the introduction of 'wannabes' to the Club. These were runners who had run 50+ marathons and were now working towards their century.

YESTERDAY

Probably the biggest change the 100 Marathon Club has faced in recent times is the formalisation of its constitution, which includes becoming affiliated to the South of England Athletics Association and the engagement of an official chairman in the shape of Roger Biggs.

'Roger has really brought the Club into the 21st century,' declares Dave.

By his own admission, Roger is 'a bit of a stats man' and as such, had been collecting and collating results, as well as keeping members informed of races, results and any other newsworthy matters in an unofficial capacity for some years prior to becoming chairman in 2005.

With Roger at the helm and following lively discussions among its members, the Club finally settled on its constitution, which was primarily to provide a focal point for runners in the UK and Ireland who had completed 100 or more races of marathon distance or longer, to share knowledge and experience and encourage newcomers to the sport of marathon running and to promote road marathons in the British Isles.

It was further agreed that only official races with at least three participants and official results could be included in a member's total number of marathons run, and that the runner must have completed the whole race entered (e.g. if it's an ultra-marathon – a race longer than marathon distance – the full race distance must be completed but this would only be counted as one marathon). All road races must also be officially measured and stated to be 26 miles 385 yards or 42.195 km by the race organisers; for trail marathons, where accurate measurement is not always possible, the distance must be rounded down to those distances.

Consideration was also given to making comparisons between marathons run on road, trail or as part of an ultra-marathon event. Eventually it was decided to split these statistics into three separate groups (road, trail and ultra), so allowing like to be compared against like.

Of course, the UK is not the only country to have its own 100 Marathon Club. Such clubs also exist in Australia, New Zealand, Japan, USA, the Czech Republic, Germany, Slovenia, Netherlands and Finland. Unfortunately, not all of them are governed by the same rules as the UK Club. For example, in Germany it is acceptable to step outside your front door, take yourself off on a 26.2-mile run and include this in your total number of marathons run.

This in turn makes it impossible to compare world performances or to accord performances World Record status – unless, of course, they are verified by the *Guinness World Records*. Therefore, unless otherwise stated, all national records within this book should be viewed as potential World Records.

Two other important changes Roger has brought to the

Club are the introduction of a website (originally designed by his son) and the more recent addition of Facebook. For a club whose members live the length and breadth of the British Isles, this is vital for keeping members informed and in touch with each other.

'It is also the Club's window for the world,' says Roger. 'As such, it is essential that any performances should be officially ratified and recorded as accurately as possible before being displayed on the site as any false claims or mistakes would be instantly picked up and could discredit the Club's reputation and credibility.' The address is www.100marathonclub.org.uk.

To that end, anyone applying to join the Club or existing members wishing to update their performances must provide a list of all the races they claim to have run, complete with dates and times. Roger will then check the validity of such races, making sure they have been run in accordance with Club rules and verifying the results.

There are a few things that haven't changed, though, such as the engraving of new centurions' names on a cup, although The Cup soon became full and a special plinth has now taken its place; a medal (bronze in colour and inscribed with the Club logo on one side and a personal inscription including name, place and date of the individual's 100th marathon on the other) is still awarded to each new member; pins are also awarded for the first 100 and every subsequent century.

There is also the Club kit. Only full members are entitled to wear the Club colours – royal blue with a luminous yellow side panel and the Club logo, '100 Marathon Club', the '100' set within a laurel wreath and displayed quite modestly just below the shoulder strap. The back of the shirt is a different matter, though – get behind one of these guys in a race and you'll know it, for here the Club logo is proudly – almost arrogantly – displayed in large, bold, luminous yellow letters that could only be missed by a short-sighted, illiterate mountain goat. Becoming the owner of the kit is understandably a matter of great pride.

'It cannot be bought like a university T-shirt – there is only one way to attain it and that is to have completed 100 marathons,' says Roger.

TODAY

Five years on from its inception and the website reflects not only the progress of a successful club, but the steady growth in membership of a club that people might be forgiven for thinking would attract only the clinically insane! However, with full membership currently standing at over 200, as well as the Club's 50+ 'wannabes', either the world is producing more than its fair share of madmen or more and more perfectly sane, intelligent people have found something that not only keeps them physically fit, but perhaps more importantly and maybe somewhat conversely, keeps them mentally well balanced, as well as giving them a real sense of wellbeing.

It also offers them a lifestyle they might not otherwise have enjoyed. With many running every weekend, there is a need to look further afield than the UK for races and it's not unusual for Club members to finish work on a Friday, jump on a plane on Saturday and run a marathon on Sunday before returning to work on the Monday.

'When you tell people what you do they react with shock and go away shaking their heads, clearly thinking you are mad,' explains one member. 'But it's a great life, a great way to stay fit and see places you wouldn't see, if not for the marathon.'

Put like that, it certainly sounds rather more fulfilling, not to mention exciting, than many people's weekend ritual of car washing, shopping and drinking at the local pub! Not that those who run multiple marathons don't drink or know how to have fun either. You won't find many of them tucked up in bed at six o'clock on pre-race night, they are more likely to be found in some hospitable hostelry, making friends with the locals and sampling the ales.

'It's a great way to see the world, meet new friends and try the beers,' says another member.

It would also seem that while running is often cited as an individual sport, conversely, it is actually a great way to make new friends and keep in touch with old ones. Often members of the 100 Club collectively arrange trips away, both at home and abroad, flying out from various UK airports before meeting up in some foreign city, from whence they will eat, drink and explore together as a group.

To keep life interesting, the Club constantly issues fresh challenges to its members, such as running a marathon in the most different countries, or counties (a potential total of 103, including Ireland), or running the most marathons in a year. As well as meeting such challenges and setting records within the Club, several members hold world and nationally recognised records, such as the first Brit to have run a marathon in all 50 American States, the person to have run the most marathons in a career (780 and counting) and the youngest person in the world to have run 100 marathons (23).

Indeed, perhaps one of the most surprising things about the Club is that its members are not all in their dotage, with ages ranging from 23 to 76. Naturally, there are women as well as men and several couples listed as members. One married couple have completed over 600 marathons between them.

Add to that honorary life members in the form of two wheelchair racers and a blind runner, who is guided round races by sighted members and you begin to appreciate that this is a club with no prejudices and only one prerequisite to membership – the completion of 100 marathons. It makes no distinction between race, colour, creed or ability. That in itself must be considered a worthy achievement.

As such, it is a club that is full of colourful, contrasting characters, distinct individuals with idiosyncratic personalities and diverse lifestyles, creating a gargantuan melting pot of humanity. Yet, despite such diversity, one common desire links them all together: to run, and run and run.

TOMORROW

Who knows? 1,000 is possible, even probable. But maybe the best thing that could happen would be the formalisation of a worldwide constitution so that proper comparisons might be made on an international level.

MILE 2

VIRGINS AND SLUTS

Virgin – someone who has never run a marathon before.
Slut – someone who, while running one marathon, is thinking about another. Commonly a 100 Marathon Club member.

You never forget your first time. Whether you only ever do it once or you end up doing it 100 times, the first time remains with you always. You'll be able to recall with clarity the weather, the people you met, how many drink stations you stopped at along the way, at what mile you felt your best (and your worst), how your nipples fared and what underwear you wore – and despite those last two references you'll have guessed by now that I'm not talking about sex.

You will also be able to recall that magical moment when you stepped across the finishing line after covering 26.2 miles on foot, unaided, with only your mind and body for company. That's not to discount the thousands of other runners who ran it with you or the crowds cheering you on along the way or the countless officials, who handed you water and gels or placed a medal around your neck. There was only one person who got you from the start to the finish, and that person was you.

It was you who kept going despite the burning pain of a blister on your little toe that rubbed against the side of your trainer with every step you took, it was you who kept going when your legs screamed at your brain to tell you to 'STOP, STOP NOW!', and it was you who kept going when your heart banged painfully inside your chest and your lungs tightened and had you gasping for air like a fish out of water.

And it is because of those things that when you finally cross the line and feel the soft brush of a warm hand placing a ribbon around your neck and the contrasting cold, harsh metal that almost knocks your teeth out as you bend over in an effort to locate a pocket of air in your chest, making you take the medal in your hand as you straighten up, you cast your eyes downwards and stare almost in surprise at the gong in your hand confirming what you have just achieved. You study the inscription, move your fingers around the rough edges, caress the solid piece of metal and slowly a smile spreads its way across your face, despite the fact that you have never felt worse in your entire life. And you know a moment of pure, unadulterated joy, the joy that comes with the knowledge of all you have suffered yet never given in to, of the months spent training alone on cold dark nights, of revelling in the aches and pains in your body that are part of your achievement and make it real.

And as you look around, you see others – total strangers, their faces mirroring your own emotions and that same slow smile spreading its way across their faces – so that when eventually your eyes meet, you smile at one another like old friends with a shared history. Such is the experience of running marathons, whether your first or your 100th.

I know this to be true not from personal experience but from talking to those who have run anything between 100 and 800 marathons. It would seem not only is there always the pain and suffering during a marathon, no matter how experienced you are, always there is the joy, too. It also appears to be the case that no matter how many marathons a person runs, perhaps not surprisingly the first is the one that stays most clearly in the mind.

Take current chairman of the 100 Marathon Club, Roger Biggs. To date, he has 635 marathons under his belt and holds several records, but can still recall his first marathon with clarity.

'Like many others, I'd watched the London Marathon on TV and was inspired to run one myself,' he explains. 'I failed to get into London, but in 1984 my hometown of Stevenage was having its first marathon so I decided to give it a go there.

'I trained on my own and with a friend, and also ran three or four half marathons leading up to my debut. I remember in the race itself, I walked for the first time at 18 miles on a downhill section. By the time I entered the finish area, my calves were on the limit and I actually ground to a halt about 100 metres from the finish. A spectator helped me with a quick calf massage and believe it or not, I was warned for getting outside help! I finally got going again and limped over the line in 3 hours 58 minutes and 11 seconds.'

And then there's Gina Little, who has run 400 marathons – the most marathons ever run by a female. She too has no difficulty in summoning up her experience of that first time.

'It had to be London,' she remembers. 'The course passes the end of my road and I'd seen the runners in the second London in 1982 and promised myself that I would do it the following year.'

Sure enough, in 1983 Gina was on the start line.

'On the morning of the marathon I walked up the hill towards the start. As I got nearer, I could smell the liniment runners were rubbing into their legs. The nearer I got, the stronger the smell! That smell still brings back great memories of that very special day.

'I also remember that the friend I was running with was very nervous and had an upset tummy, so all through the race we had to keep stopping for the loo. One stop was in a pub and the loo was all the way downstairs. We must have lost so much time in the different loos we visited!'

Another prominent 100 Club member, Steve Edwards, who has completed over 550 marathons and has a selection of past and current national and world marathon records under his belt, gives an account of his first experience.

'I did everything wrong,' he admits. 'It was 1981, I was 18 years old and I entered the Coventry Marathon with six weeks to go. I did no proper training, had no dietary preparation and wore the wrong shoes.

'Back then there was no internet or ready advice about training, so I decided to run five miles a night for five nights a week. However, I had no idea how far five miles was, so I went down to the school running track and ran 20 laps of the 400-metre track to cover the five miles and did that every night leading up to the race!'

Race day dawned and Steve set off in his old, barely-there football boots, in which he'd done all his training and which had less support than a school football match.

'I remember with about 10 or 11 miles to go thinking everything was okay – I was running at around 8-minute mile pace, which meant I would finish in around 3 hours 30, which I would have been really happy with. I even started to wonder what the wall thing was that the Americans were always talking about!'

Just over a mile later, though he knew exactly what they meant. Not so much hitting the wall as running smack-bang into a concrete edifice.

'I no longer owned my legs, they wanted to stop and I was trying to make them move. I knew if I wanted to finish I had to stop but that only resulted in me stiffening up, so I started to walk and then tried a little jog and eventually ended up doing alternate jogging/walking until the last mile when, somehow, I was able to run again.'

Steve eventually crossed the finishing line in 3 hours 38 minutes.

'The next day and for several days afterwards I could barely walk. My legs felt like gateposts and I had to walk backwards down the stairs.'

In fact, this is such a common experience for first-timers that there is actually a T-shirt available to purchase with the logo 'I'm in the Downstairs Backwards Club'!

Steve clearly recollects his first words after finishing, 'I am never doing that again!' Those words are probably the most common ones spoken at the finishing line of a marathon, particularly when it comes to those who have just lost their 'virginity'. It would appear that the members of the 100 Marathon Club are no exception. Indeed, only one of the guys and gals I spoke to admitted to setting out on that first marathon with the intention of running at least another 99 – you have been warned.

SLUTS' TOP TIPS FOR VIRGINS

Roger Biggs (635 marathons)
'It will always hurt at some point in a marathon, but believe that you will come out the other side.'

Gina Little (370 marathons)
'Don't worry about time, try to relax and enjoy the experience. It doesn't matter how many more marathons you run, the first is something special.'

Steve Edwards (550 marathons)
'Do the training, there are no shortcuts; you'll only get out what you put in. Start off steady at the pace you are intending to try and complete the marathon. Don't think that by going quicker at the start you'll have time in the bank, it doesn't usually work like that and will generally do the exact opposite. If you've done the training, you'll maintain the same pace and finish on time, perhaps slightly quicker. If you haven't done adequate training for the marathon in that time it was never going to happen anyway.'

Brian Mills (771 marathons)
'Enjoy the day.'

Naomi Prasad (103 marathons)
'Leave your watch behind! It isn't about time for your first race, there are plenty of other future races if you want there to be when you can worry about that. Just go out and finish with a smile on your face.'

Mel Ross (151 marathons)
'Don't start off a marathon too fast, ensure you drink enough.'

Dave Ross (206 marathons)
'Take time to build up the distance that you intend running, increase the mileage off-road as much as possible and eat well. It's worth having running gait analysed, too – to ensure that the correct shoes are used prior to commencing a training routine.'

Paul Watts (220 marathons)
'Don't let the euphoria of race day get to you and send you off too fast as you could end up regretting it later in the run.'

Dave Moles (376 marathons)
'Don't do anything on race day that you haven't already tried in training, e.g. drinking sports drinks.'

Martin Bush (562 marathons)
'Don't worry about times, it's more about completing the distance.'

Richard Fulbrook (131 marathons)
'Go out and enjoy the experience.'

Osy Wayne (115 marathons)
'Forget your watch and take it easy. Start with a big city marathon so you will never be alone.'

Mike Marten (141 marathons)
'Enjoy this one as much as possible, but more importantly, when you do the second marathon, don't automatically assume you will better the time set in your first and for heaven's sake, don't be disappointed if you don't. Enjoy!'

Adam Holland (103 marathons)
'When doing your first marathon, don't think of it as a race but a long training run, but with more people around. Just enjoy the first one to see what it's like.'

Allan Rumble (130 marathons)
'Follow your training plan to the letter, Vaseline between your toes and smile for the camera when you cross the line.'

Jerry Forde (180 marathons)
'Allow 12 months before you do a marathon and build up to as high mileage as you can.'

David King (201 marathons)
'Don't try to run too fast at the start. If, during the course of the marathon you run a PB [Personal Best] at 10K, try to make it the last 10K rather than the first! Don't get swept along at other people's paces.'

Dave and Linda Major (436 and 291 marathons respectively)
'Don't run before you can walk; set yourself goals that are attainable and get to know your limitations.'

Kio Vejdani (140 marathons)
'Don't stop running until you have finished, don't walk (keep running to the end, no matter how slowly); hold back until you get near to home then you can pick up the pace because you know you will finish. Do your first marathon somewhere special with good atmosphere and lots going on, such as London. Then do the next one somewhere with a lower profile.'

Jim Manford (154 marathons)
'Treat the distance with respect. Be realistic in the time you want to run and follow a recognised training plan based on your previous performances. Use your first marathon as a learning experience, just enjoy the day and don't be disheartened if you don't get the time you intended – there's always another one in which to get it right!'

Sid Wheeler (203 marathons)
'Learn pace judgement – don't go off too fast!'

Chris Monsey (130 marathons)
'Respect the distance but don't be overawed by it. If you have an inclination to stop and walk, just try to keep jogging no matter how slowly you feel you are going: you will eventually run through

the wall and feel better. Envisage the finish and remember pain is temporary, achievement is permanent.'

Steve Price (197 marathons)
'Go slow for the first few miles, or suffer the last six!'

John Dawson (383 marathons)
'Make sure your body is balanced and that you get good advice when buying shoes – and don't wear them until they wear out.'

Kay O'Regan (102 marathons)
'Forget about the time, enjoy the experience.'

David Phillips (393 marathons)
'Get your body and mind ready for running; run every day.'

Liz Tunna (wannabe –84 marathons)
'Cherish the experience and the atmosphere. Wear comfy kit and trainers, and make sure you're well hydrated and fuelled. Don't put pressure on yourself to get an amazing time, just enjoy the day and feel proud upon crossing that finish line.'

Peter Dennett (wannabe – 81 marathons)
'Try a half marathon race before a full one to get the experience of racing, as opposed to just training.'

SUMMER SHORTS

Taper (reduce) your training about 2–3 weeks before the race (i.e. run shorter distances the nearer you get to race day). Rest more or risk running tired. Forget the time, but do remember the Vaseline.

MILE 3

VITAL STATISTICS, CONTACT LENSES AND A HANDKERCHIEF

For Roger Biggs, chairman of the 100 Marathon Club, running marathons is a way of life.

ROGER BIGGS

Born: 1948

635 marathons:

- 1st marathon: 1984 – Stevenage
- 100th marathon: 1996 – Boston

Records:

- UK record for the longest set of sequence marathons (111)
- Only Brit to have run a marathon on all seven continents and in all 50 American states
- Most counties of UK/Ireland (58)
- Most countries (50 = with the late Ted Lancucki)
- Most continents in the same year (7)
- Most northerly and most southerly.

Roger Biggs, current chairman of the 100 Marathon Club and self-confessed statistics anorak, does not have the appearance of a man who has run over 600 marathons. Of average height and build, with greying hair and reactor-light glasses, he looks as though he'd be as much at home in a suit and loafers as tracksuit and trainers.

But, as we all know, appearances can be deceptive. For this is a man who describes running marathons as 'a way of life'; the tracksuit and trainers as much a part of him as his teeth – which are all his own. I have checked. Not by sticking my hand in his mouth and waggling each tooth around to see if it will come free on a plate, obviously, but by asking, politely.

Nobody gets to do 635 marathons by good dental hygiene alone, though. No, indeed, there is only one way to increase the numbers of marathons run and that is to run them. Which is just what Roger did.

'I did 65 in 2010, 58 in 2009 and around 45 for the previous five years to that. I need to peg it back a bit, maybe to 45 again,' Roger says.

Forty-five is pegging back?

'It's all relative,' he insists.

Yes, sure, of course it is – to the number of hundreds and thousands in a packet, perhaps.

'It happened really because of the sequence running…'

Sequence running?

'Running a marathon or ultra-marathon at least once a week, every week,' he explains.

Until…? Death, perhaps, or the cows come home? Or, dare I suggest, until the return of sanity?

In Roger's case it was none of those things; instead it was that impudent Snow Fairy arriving at Gatwick Airport only to dump an entire year's supply of the white stuff on the ground at once, thus preventing him or anyone else flying anywhere.

'I managed 111 before the snow grounded me and stopped me continuing the sequence,' he continues and there's no mistaking the rumble of annoyance in his voice.

'That must have been very frustrating,' I tentatively suggest. (Personally I'd have found it something of a relief and given thanks to the Snow Fairy before showering her with suitable gifts.)

'It was, *very*,' Roger readily agrees, letting out a long sigh as if to relieve all that pent-up frustration.

Despite this, and despite being prevented from breaking the World Record, Roger's 111 marathons did set a new British record – as far as he is aware.

As far as he's *aware*? If I were to put myself through something like that, I would definitely want to know for sure. I guess that's what he means about running being a way of life. I mean, you don't consider whether brushing your teeth an extra time each day makes you a World Record holder in teeth cleaning, do you? You just do it. Just as Roger completed 111 marathons. It's much the same really.

'People are doing all sorts of things these days,' he explains, 'it's hard to keep up with it and if people don't belong to the Club, we have no way of knowing what they may have done.'

Given most centurion marathon runners are members of the Club, it seems fairly certain that Roger's efforts are indeed a record.

But what on earth gave him the idea for such a challenge?

'Statistics, of course!'

Naturally.

'I just realised I was running most weekends and thought I might as well turn it into a more structured challenge. I started off thinking I'd do 52, which would be at least one every week. One thing led to another and I thought I might as well go for 100.'

As one does, Roger, as one does…

Apart from not knowing whether or not he had set a new British record, something else Roger didn't know until his physiotherapist told him was that he was in fact treated for four different injuries throughout the 111 marathons.

I'm pretty impressed by this – I've known people treated for four injuries during *one* marathon, never mind 111. So, does he suffer generally from injuries?

'Of course,' he readily admits. 'Luckily, they're mostly minor ones when you miss a week or two. The worst I've had was when I had a couple of stress fractures back in my earlier days. It took me about two years to totally get over the first one, back in 1986.'

So, returning to the sequence, presumably with four injuries he needed to take some time out?

'I missed one race on the 19th December,' he tells me, 'and then did my next one on the 27th December, so it wasn't too bad.'

Not bad at all. And there was me thinking he might not have done anything until I met him in Malta in February. Silly me. Of course he was not only there in a running capacity, he was also in Malta as chairman, presenting some of the 100 Club members with various awards. I watched in awe as this apparently ordinary man made speeches, presented medals and socialised with club members, as well as speaking to me, introducing me to various people and giving me heaps of further information about the Club – and that was after he'd run a marathon!

Doesn't he ever get tired? I mean, running marathons, travelling, socialising, it's a fairly heavy workload for anyone, never mind for someone who, while not yet in plaid dressing gown and slippers, is probably not in floral print shirts and flip-flops either – even if he does still have all his own teeth.

'Yes, of course I do,' he freely admits, 'but the body is very resilient. And then there's the endorphins that kick in!'

Ah, so that's where I went wrong; I should have run and produced my own endorphins. As it is, from my vantage point sitting with a group of the 100 Club, feeling pretty tired just from having left home at four o'clock the previous morning and merely observing others running a marathon, I see a man who is both inspired and inspiring, enthusiastic and encouraging to others and clearly much at home with his 'running family'.

He says other people are often surprised to find that members of the 100 Club know how to enjoy themselves over race weekend.

And I can vouch for that.

'We party, drink and stay out late after the marathon – and in some cases before as well!' he tells me. 'We are certainly not all in bed by six o'clock! Some drink more than is good for them,' he adds with a small smile, sounding rather like a slightly over-indulgent father.

'Often we will go away as a group, large or small, sometimes as individuals, sometimes for a couple of days, sometimes a week. It depends upon the individual runner's circumstances – some who are working need to get home, others, like me, are retired and can afford to spend more time away.'

And he does. Since retiring from his job in IT in 2007, Roger has been running all over the world.

'I've travelled to the States so much, I'm expecting to get an upgrade from American Airlines any day now! Running marathons isn't just about the running, though,' he says. 'You're always meeting up with people you've met before at other races in other countries and meeting new people, making new friends, experiencing new countries and cultures.

'I remember when I was in Seattle,' he continues, his speech now gathering speed, enthusiasm tripping off his tongue, 'I'd been running about seven miles, wearing my 100 Club shirt and my Christian name on my number. A lady runner came up from behind and asked me if I was Roger Biggs; she was from Australia and the only female Australian to have run over 100 marathons. We ran together up to 16 miles, then she stopped and I carried on.

'And in Tokyo,' he goes on, unprompted, 'I stayed with the family of a Japanese runner I'd met through running. He belongs to the 100 Marathon Club in Japan.

'Running in Spitzbergen, which, at 78°N, is geographically the most northerly road marathon in the world was simply amazing. It has the strangest light, with the sun just above the horizon all the time. Despite being June, it was very cold and there was a possibility of polar bears.

'Then there was Everest…' At this he shakes his head and blows out his cheeks at the memory. 'You started at 17,000 feet and it was way below freezing, not the most pleasant of conditions. Mind you,' he goes on, a smile tugging at his lips. 'I've got a funny story for you, if you want one…'

Always, Roger; *always*.

'Well, I'd spent three weeks trekking up to just short of Everest Base Camp. For the whole trip I'd tucked my contact lenses inside my sleeping bag to stop the fluid freezing. One night I didn't do it very well and my contacts froze. At just the right time hot tea arrived at our tent and my friend suggested I try floating my contact lens case on the tea. I did, and soon all was well!'

Ah, what a lovely, contact-lens warming story.

'The easiest marathon I've ever run,' he goes on, now seemingly unstoppable, like a rising tsunami, 'was the Tyrol Speed Marathon, which started in the mountains just inside the Italian border, then ran down all the way into Innsbruck.'

Wheeeeeee! (Or maybe that would only work on a sledge?)

I can see that Roger could probably fill this whole book with the marathons he has run, so I decide to rein him in a little and ask if he has a favourite.

'Tough one,' he says.

As he's rubbing his chin and frowning slightly in a thoughtful way, I assume this is merely his response to my question rather than the name of some hideously testing marathon to which I should have accorded capital letters.

'I do still like London,' he eventually says, 'and have especially fond memories of the 1995 one – which I did with my son – but my favourite trips were to Everest and Antarctica. Others worthy of mention are Capri, Night of Flanders, Barcelona, Comrades and lastly, and maybe the best, the Yakima River Canyon in Washington State. My best American friends are the race directors.'

The best of both worlds, I guess – people *and* places.

So, was it the idea of all that travel that initially got him started on the road from 0–100?

'Not at all,' he says, 'It all began when I watched the London Marathon on TV and saw a woman in her 70s doing it. I thought, if she can do it, so can I.'

That woman has a lot to answer for – a lot.

'Do you know 50 per cent of runners start running marathons because of London?' he asks, interrupting his own story to throw in this apparently vital statistic.

I didn't, and obediently jot this down with an additional note to self not to watch the London Marathon.

'I applied for London for two years but didn't get in, so settled for running in my hometown of Stevenage instead. I remember that first race well,' he continues. 'I walked for the first time at about 18 miles on a downhill section, something I tell my training group never to do. Mind you,' he adds, 'I always make them warm up and cool down too, but I don't necessarily do it myself!'

Do as I say, not as I do, eh? But I'm in no position to be casting first stones about the place, so I encourage him to tell me more.

'I was going okay until the last 100 metres and then I got cramp in my leg and came to a halt. A spectator helped me with a quick calf massage and believe it or not, I was warned for getting outside help!'

So, was the spectator by any chance female?

'Well, yes, actually, she was,' Roger admits, with feigned innocence. 'How did you know that?'

Ah ha! So that's why he's run so many marathons!

He laughs, reading my not-so-subtle smug smile all too well.

'Unfortunately, of all the marathons I've run, that's only ever happened the once!'

Oh.

So what, pray, made him decide to run 100 marathons?

'It just happened over time. It took me four years to get into double figures,' he replies, as if he can't quite believe it himself. 'Then you just get used to doing them. And who wants to do long training runs? Gradually all your friends become runners, so that's what you talk about.'

The statistics, however, are never far away.

'Statistics definitely led me to the choice of where and when to do my 100th,' he tells me with a commendable lack of embarrassment on his part. 'I ran my 100th marathon at the 100th Boston Marathon in 1996. I actually ran my 100th 10-mile event, my 100th half marathon and my 100th marathon in consecutive races!'

That was over 15 years ago, but Roger still sounds quite excited.

'I like statistics, you get carried away,' he explains.

So it would seem.

'I think it's important for everyone to have goals to aim at,' he goes on.

Not least himself, it would seem for apart from the sequence running record, Roger is the only Brit to have run a marathon in all 50 American States as well as on all seven continents of the world, while within the 100 Club, he's the only person to have run all the continents in the same year as well as the most northerly (Spitzbergen, North Pole) and the most southerly (Fin Del Mundo, Antarctica) marathons in the world.

'People will always be chasing something or someone else's record – it's good for motivation. That's why the 100 Club are always trying to think up new competitions!' he adds, with a twinkle in his eyes.

'What sort of competitions?' I ask suspiciously, though I've no idea why I should be suspicious. I mean, it's not as though I'm planning on entering any of them, is it?

'Oh, things like who can run a marathon in the most countries; who can run the most northerly, southerly, easterly, westerly marathons and we're currently doing one for a marathon run in the most number of counties in the UK, including Southern Ireland. That's a potential of 103 counties,' he informs me, easily spotting the geographical flaw only marginally less than the mathematical flaw in my otherwise incomparable intelligence.

'Sometimes, though,' he adds, a worried frown creasing his brow, 'I do worry that encouraging people to run lots of marathons means you produce slower runners who run a lot of races, rather than people who run fast.

'I mean, I honestly believe if I hadn't been running 30–40 marathons a year when I was younger, I could have gone under 3 hours,' (Roger's personal best is 3 hours 02 seconds, at the age of 42). 'It's too late now, of course, but I don't regret it,' he insists, almost defiantly.

'Running every week is not a good idea if you want to get your times down, as you get no rest so do little training and actually end up running/training less mileage than guys who race only a few times a year.'

So, how much training does he do then?

'Assuming I race on Sunday, I'm usually in the gym on Monday morning, quite early. I weight train most weekdays; this includes some light CV work. I also do a lot of stretching in the gym. Then normally I would run on the Tuesday evening, usually doing two 5–6 mile runs.'

Presumably he recovers fairly quickly from his marathon efforts?

'Yes, you could say I recover quickly. Getting out of a car, though, is another matter!'

No good blaming that on marathons, Roger. I have the same problem: it's called 'ageing'.

Roger gives me a look that acknowledges the veracity of this. 'You know,' he continues, 'I used to think when I looked at the times of older runners that I would be winning titles all over the place by this age, but I realise now those people who won at an older age won because they were very good runners for their age.

'My performances at 60+ within the age category are better than when I was in the 50+ age category, but I think this is more down to less people participating due to health, injuries, old age, etcetera rather than me getting that much better.'

Talking of which, does he see a day when he will pack it all in?

'I don't know whether I'll make that decision myself or whether it will be made for me through injury or illness, or some other unforeseen circumstance. You know, in the Club we have a husband and wife whereby the husband has run 400+ and the wife 200+, and the husband says one day he thinks he will just decide that he's had enough and won't run another one ever again but I'd don't know that for myself yet.'

So, if other people are giving up due to age, what will keep him going?

'The Club,' he says simply, 'the friends I've made, the after-race camaraderie – comparing notes on the day's race, that awful hill, previous races, those yet to come…'

And is there anyone who inspires him?

'Rob in my local club has been a great friend over the years, although he doesn't do too many these days. We still go for a training run together most weeks.

'Myself & Jack [Brooks – fellow 100 Club member] go on a lot of events and trips together, and of course there is the Basher versus Dasher stories…' (humorous reports on the Club's website reporting the latest in a long-running, light-hearted rivalry between the two – Roger 'Basher' Biggs and Jack 'Dasher' Brooks – at various races).

'And then there's Gina [Little – 100 Club], who picks up a trophy most weeks and doesn't think she is competitive. Not much!

'There's also our two wheelchair athletes, Mike [Marten] and Jerry [Forde] and Blind Paul [Watts] – they're always an inspiration to the rest of us. Various people from the Club run as Paul's guide, as and when they are available,' he tells me.

So, does the Chairman have any advice to give to aspiring 100 Marathon Club members?

'Don't do too many doubles [two marathons in two days] and be very careful with shorter distance events. Shorter events can be very good training, but you hit the ground a lot harder. They're probably okay normally but if you're just building up the miles, the body is fatigued and then you hit it with some fast stuff.'

What about lucky charms or superstitions?

'No lucky charms, not me, although I do like to make sure I have a hankie with me.'

Er, why?

'It just seems a sensible thing to carry.'

Now he sounds like my mother!

'In case I get a sudden cold or need to wipe my brow or, er, other problems,' he expands.

Enough information, thank you!

'As for superstitions, I never wear the race shirt before the race except for trying it on for size. I don't usually pin the number on until I get to the race and I always try to keep the race number afterwards, for posterity!'

And what about food and drink?

'I try and get some pasta the night before a race. I will sometimes have breakfast to be sociable but more often than not, it's a "food bar" and a cup of tea. I really believe in gels [these are similar to sports drinks, but can be taken without water on the run to boost energy and promote recovery]. For a road marathon I would usually take one before and five during the race. It doesn't make me run faster, but I don't slow as much in the second half.'

As for any favourite clothing, Roger says he likes to be warm and recommends a zip-fronted, long-sleeved top for the season fringes. Of course when racing, he takes great pride in wearing his 100 Club top.

So how do others react once they know how many marathons he's run?

'One hundred is not too bad but when you say 635, they are somewhat surprised.'

As in I am 'somewhat surprised' to find that I'm feeling slightly nauseous after a double helping of Death by Chocolate with Cornish clotted cream, perhaps?

So, does he think he's obsessed with running marathons?

'I guess I am,' he answers without preamble, 'but it's just as much about ticking boxes as well. A box can be a different state or country or whatever, or maybe just somewhere you want to visit, and the marathon is the excuse. For example, when we completed the six marathons in six days in Northern Ireland, we were taken to see the Giants Causeway afterwards.'

Whether or not he's obsessed with running marathons, one thing is clear. With his passion for the sport and the generous giving of his time, knowledge and experience to others (as a UK Athletics qualified coach Roger can be found most Tuesdays at his local athletic club, Fairlands Valley Spartans, coaching adult road runners), not only is he ideally suited to the role of chairman, he also epitomises what the 100 Marathon Club is all about.

Certainly, I can't help but notice that the entire interview has been peppered not only with statistical references but references to other members of the 100 Club, almost as much as to himself.

As we approach the end, I ask if there are any other comments he wishes to make.

'Just one,' he tells me, brown eyes twinkling behind his spectacles, the corners of his mouth twitching.

'Go ahead,' I encourage, pen poised for still more pearls of wisdom.

'That was harder than running a marathon!' he concedes and explodes with mirth.

Coming from a man who likes nothing better than fresh challenges, I shall take it as a compliment.

SUMMER SHORTS

As Roger mentioned, it's hard to combine running multiple marathons with fast times. Indeed, there's a well-known adage in the running world that says if you want to run fast, train fast. However, if you run too fast you may not find time to discover the compensations of running more slowly, such as making new friends along the way. 'Personal Bests' come and go; friends may stay forever.

They say if you want something doing, ask a busy man. For best results, promise to buy him lots of beer!

MILE 4

BUTTERFLIES AND BASHFULNESS

Despite having a tendency towards shyness, Brian Mills has run almost 800 marathons and travelled all over the world.

BRIAN MILLS
Born: 1955
791 marathons:
- 1st marathon: 1989 – London
- 100th marathon: 1993 – Dublin (trail)/New York (road)
Records:
- Most Marathons Run by Anyone in the UK.

Fifty-six-year-old carpenter Brian Mills is something of a legend in the running world – not just for completing the greatest number of marathons ever run by a Brit (791 and counting), but also for having a butterfly tattooed on his body for every marathon he has ever run! At least that's the rumour.

I first met Brian at a hotel in Mallorca – I was helping out on a Running Crazy trip and he was there with the 100 Marathon

Club. At that point I hadn't been asked to write this book and had no idea who Brian was. We had one brief conversation at breakfast the day after the race when we both reached for the orange juice at the same time.

'Go on,' said Brian politely, indicating I should help myself to the juice first.

'Thank you,' said I, trying to ignore the sight of a brightly-painted butterfly crawling out from beneath the collar of his 100 Marathon Club sweatshirt.

'Did you have a good run yesterday?' I enquired, the giveaway sweatshirt lending confidence to my line of questioning.

'Not really,' he replied, with a nervous smile.

'Oh, I'm sorry,' I said, forcing my eyes away from the colourful creature adorning his neck to look him in the face and offer some sympathy.

But Brian had already turned and was walking away from me, which took me by surprise because most runners when asked how their race went are only too happy to regale you with all the details (and I do mean *all*) – the highs, the lows, the aches, the pains… They don't care who you are; if you have asked the question, they will give you a mile-by-mile account so that in the end you feel as if you have run the whole thing with them.

Not Brian. Unbeknown to me back then was the fact that behind the longish, greying, wispy hair and tattoos, which might suggest a certain kind of character, lies an entirely different type of person, a quiet, retiring man. So much so that when people who knew him heard I was planning on interviewing him, they wondered how I'd get on with someone so reluctant to talk about his achievements. And if I'm honest, so did I.

Passion, however, is a remarkable thing: it can bring out the shyest of people, and so it proved with the quiet and diffident Brian. Almost as soon as we got chatting, he got into his stride, talking quickly, almost gabbling. His words came tumbling out so fast, they almost fell over one another, exuding passion and enthusiasm and beating shyness hands down. Soon it was evident that his passion is not just restricted to running itself but extends to those he has met as a result of the sport. That friendship and camaraderie has meant a lot to a man who lives alone in a town only a short distance from where he was born and bred.

So, how and when did it all begin?

Well, Brian did cross-country at school, as well as the 1500 metres. He also threw the discus (because no one else would do it), but it wasn't this that led him to start running marathons. After finishing school, he took up squash but it wasn't this that led him to start running marathons either: it was watching the London Marathon on television, knowing other people who had done it and deciding he wanted to do it, too.

And so he did, in 1989, aged 33.

'It was okay,' he says, before expanding quietly, 'I didn't intend doing any more although I had enjoyed it, but somehow I ended up doing four that first year.' He still sounds slightly surprised by this, almost as though he somehow ran them by accident.

'And then the numbers increased as the years went by,' he goes on, unprompted, sounding more as if he's referring to his age and birthdays rather than marathons run.

'Then I met some people from the 100 Marathon Club and decided to go for the 100. I think I did my 100th in Dublin, but I can't remember now for sure.'

He can't remember? I'm certain if I ran 100 marathons, each and every one of them, but most especially the 100th would be forever etched on my mind, like a permanent scar. Then again, perhaps when you've done something so many times, it may be difficult to remember exactly what number went where?

'But I do know I did my official one – one run on road as opposed to trail – in New York that same year,' he suddenly adds, rather more positively.

Thank goodness for that! Brian is not a robot after all.

These days, Brian averages around 40 marathons a year, although when we spoke he told me his total for 2011 would be more.

'In fact,' he said, 'it will be the most I've ever run as I want to get my total up to 800 by Christmas.'

The mind, not to mention the body, boggles.

Does that mean he's heading for the 1,000 mark?

'I don't think that far ahead,' he tells me, coyly. 'I will aim for the 800, then 850, then 900, and so on.'

Beneath the softly spoken words I sense a quiet determination to keep going and would dare to suggest Brian does want that 1,000th run and he doesn't want anyone to catch him – certainly not in his lifetime. It's the curse of the front runner: the rest of the pack are forever chasing, baying for blood, breathing down your butterfly-tattooed neck. As soon as you slow down, you risk being overtaken.

(As if to prove my point, a couple of months after this interview I discovered that Brian would be running his 800th marathon in September 2011, three months earlier than originally planned.)

Will any of those numbers take him to the World Record?

'No,' he answers flatly. 'That record is held by a German who claims to have done something like 1,700, although they haven't all been run in official races.'

We are back to that sensitive issue of what can count towards your total number of marathons.

'It's impossible to make comparisons,' he continues. 'The Germans can just take themselves off on their own, run what they consider to be 26.2 miles, return home and count that as one of their total. In the UK every marathon must be run within an official race and properly ratified for it to be counted.'

How very English and, in my totally unbiased view, fair.

However, I guess that unless an international body is set up to start governing such matters, the issue will remain a thorny one.

So, does the man who has run approximately 21,000 miles, just 4,000 miles short of running all the way around the world, hold any other records apart from the one for having run the most marathons in the UK?

'Not so far as I know,' he tells me and if it's possible to hear a shrug in someone's voice, I hear it in Brian's. He sounds totally unconcerned.

So, apart from the numbers, what keeps him motivated?

'I love running marathons and the social element to the 100 Club,' he explains. 'I live alone, so am glad to socialise at the weekends. I also like the travelling. If it wasn't for running marathons, I wouldn't have been to half the places I've been to.'

His favourite place to run is Holland.

'Not because it's flat,' he says as if to read my mind. 'In fact,' he goes on, 'some of the races there do have some ups and downs but I just love the country, the people and the scenery. I could see myself living there.'

Barcelona is also a favourite.

'I love the city and the course around it,' he says.

Not so popular with Brian is the Jungfrau Swiss Mountain Run.

'The Jungfrau is actually higher than the Eiger,' he informs me with all the authority that can only come from having run up said offender. 'It's the highest in that range,' he goes on, as if to drive the point home. 'It took me five-and-a-half hours to complete it. That was a tough one.'

I can almost hear the tired sigh in his voice as he undoubtedly recalls the mountainous challenge.

Not all marathons have to be abroad though, for Brian to give them a go.

'I enjoy home marathons as well,' he continues, 'although I don't like running in the rain.'

Rain, in England? No worries there then.

'I'm running a new one in Sussex next weekend,' he tells me. 'It finishes at the site of the Battle of Hastings, which I'm very interested to see.'

Fitness, friends, travel and culture… is there no end to the advantages of running marathons? Well, actually, I can spot one disadvantage – if my knowledge of British geography serves me at all well, that's quite some journey Brian will have to make.

'Two hundred and forty miles,' he concurs. 'I'll drive there on the Saturday, stay in a B&B on Saturday night, run on Sunday and then drive back after the race before returning to work on the Monday. It's the same if I'm running abroad, except obviously I'll fly rather than drive and take a day off work if necessary to fit it in.'

'I guess you go back to work for a rest!' I joke.

'Not really,' he says, seriously. 'As a carpenter I work full time, from six in the morning till six at night.'

I wonder how he has the energy to do a manual job and run so much.

His answer is simple: 'I don't train at all in between races.'

As a coach that's hard for me to get my head around. At best, I can accept that at least he is giving his body a chance to recover between races.

And he agrees: 'I've been very lucky with injuries. I do get back pain occasionally and I had shin splints for just over a year once but I carried on running, apart from two weeks off, and they just eventually got better.

'At the moment,' he adds, 'I'm in very good health but you never know what's around the corner – that's why I just want to do as much running as possible while I can.'

And that's also why he's recently gone on a diet.

'I was actually overweight and had slowed down a lot,' he concedes, although personally, I would have to say that the man I met, while maybe not a skinny latte, could in no way be described as overweight.

'I wanted to speed up again so I went on a diet last December and I've now lost two and a half stone in just 14 weeks. Last Sunday I ran my quickest marathon for years in 4 hours 04 minutes. Now I want to get down below 4 hours again. I feel so much better running lighter.'

He has dieted by cutting out all sugar as he believes it's a really bad thing for putting on weight and has been eating sensibly, with lots of salads and yoghurts.

'Today, for the first time ever, I tried mackerel with salad and really liked it,' he says, 'even though I would say I'm not a great fan of fish, but then I'd never tried mackerel before.'

Despite changes to his everyday diet, come race day Brian still tends to eat the same things he's always eaten.

'I usually have something to eat about two to three hours before the race, anything that's going, really – including a cooked breakfast, if available! And I'm always starving after a race and will have something to eat almost straightaway. I take ready-meals with me and eat them while watching other people coming in at the finish.'

Rather unusually, he always sucks a Halls Mentho-lyptus Lozenge at the start of a marathon.

'I find it helps with my breathing and stops me getting thirsty before the first water station. After that, I'll take a drink every five kilometres, preferably a sports drink rather than water, and I'll also eat bits of banana from feeding stations if it's available.'

I shut out the image of marathon-running monkeys and turn my attention back to Brian, who is now telling me how much he hates carrying anything when he's running.

'It's a real pet hate of mine,' he says. 'I won't carry water or any other kind of drink or food. I once carried a camera, but got so annoyed carrying it that I threw it away!'

His one piece of advice for aspiring 100 Club members, though, is simple: 'Never give up, just keep going; you can do it, you just need willpower. It doesn't matter what anyone says, thinks or does, it is your own challenge and you can do it if you really want to.'

So, does he see a time when he will ever give up?

'Not unless I am forced to stop.'

It's an obsession, then?

'Yes, I think it is.'

So, does that mean he considers himself to be, how can I put this politely, a little crazy perhaps – when it comes to running marathons, I mean?

'No, I don't think so,' he replies. 'Other people may think so, but not me. Breaking it down, I enjoy the physical activity, the camaraderie and socialising at races and the travel to new and different places. What's crazy about that?'

Well, when it's put like that, nothing really.

And what of the butterfly tattoos?

'I like the colours,' he says, simply. 'They're all based on different species of real butterflies and the guy who does them for me checks them for authenticity.'

And does he really have one done after every race? I mean, are there that many species of butterfly in the world?

'That's what they say,' is the only comment he's prepared to make.

So, what of the future?

'I will just carry on running until I can't go on,' he repeats his earlier assertion. 'I would have liked to run London again as it's one of my favourites (isn't it everyone's?) but I can't because you can now only enter online and I don't own a computer, nor can I get to the library to use one as I'm out at work all day and the nearest library is in Gloucester.'

Now that just doesn't seem right: London Marathon organisers take note.

SUMMER SHORTS

Running can be whatever you want it to be – a race to be won, a distance to be completed, a time to be beaten, a cause to be helped. You set your own goals, put in your own effort, celebrate your own achievement. Through such endeavour and achievement you will gain confidence and self-esteem. You also gain fitness and health, friendship and camaraderie, while meeting like-minded souls with whom to explore the world, however quiet you might be.

MILE 5

FROM ANOREXIC TO UK/WORLD NO. 1

At school, Naomi Prasad was so skinny she was banned from doing any sport because her teachers feared she would collapse. Today she holds the UK/World Record for being the youngest female ever to have run 100 marathons.

NAOMI PRASAD
Born: 1981
104 marathons:
• 1st marathon: 2003 − Paris
• 100th marathon: 2011 − Malta
Records:
UK/World Record Holder for Youngest Female to run 100 Marathons.

At 29 years old, Naomi Prasad's enthusiasm for marathon running bubbles over like a glass of champagne poured by an inexperienced wine waiter but she hasn't always been quite so enthusiastic about sport.

'When I was younger, I was anorexic,' Naomi tells me. 'At school, I was five feet eight inches tall and weighed six stone five ounces. The teachers wouldn't let me do any sport because they were afraid I would pass out, so I had to sit with the chemistry teacher in her office drinking tea! She was supposed to talk to me about why I was so skinny, but instead we chatted about decorating (I think she'd just bought a flat or something and was into interior design). I hated sport and exercise and thought it was great!' So says Naomi, just prior to becoming the youngest woman in the UK/World to run 100 marathons.

This is what they call irony, I think.

I ask Naomi if she's comfortable with talking about that time of her life and whether she minds if I include it in the book.

'No, I don't mind,' she says, 'maybe it will help someone else.'

So, I ask her to tell me all about it and here is her story:

'The eating disorder began when I was a teenager with the usual teenage angst, parents divorcing, et cetera. I felt I couldn't control anything, but I could control what went into my mouth. I didn't have a period for 18 months and I started growing downy hair all over my body. Then I moved to a new school and knew I would have to start to eat lunch if I was to fit in, even though it made me feel sick.

'My mother never spoke to me about it, though she must have known and I'm sure she was concerned – I think she simply didn't know how to. My father wasn't around after the divorce. I was the youngest by four years and my older brother and sister were away at university at that time, so I was on my own with it.

'I ate nothing but started drinking lots of wine. I thought I had huge thighs and a big bum, and felt guilty if I ate. I felt I was letting myself down, losing control.

'I would feel hungry a lot of the time but that was perceived by me as a good thing because it meant I was in control.'

For someone like me, who has never suffered any kind of eating disorder – unless you count a marshmallow fetish that once saw me in the garden at a friend's eighth birthday party, hands tied behind my back, scoffing all the mallows that dangled tantalisingly on pieces of string attached to a washing line while the other party-goers were distracted (foolishly in my opinion) by the party-giver's male relatives prancing around in white sheets pretending to be ghosts, it's hard to imagine what it must be like to believe that feeling hungry is anything other than bloody annoying.

These days, thankfully, Naomi has her eating disorder fully in hand so that when I travelled to Malta to watch her run her 100th marathon, I met a tall, slender, attractive young woman with jet-black hair, enormous expressive dark eyes and a wide smile.

'I eat normally these days,' she says, 'although I am very aware of it, but much more relaxed now. Funnily enough last year when I was running so much, I was having real problems eating enough – I couldn't keep the weight on at all and was worried. It turned the whole thing on its head.'

So, how did an anorexic, who hated exercise, turn into a marathon mogul?

'It was 2003,' Naomi begins, 'I was 20 and at university, and decided to run the Paris Marathon to raise funds for an expedition to Borneo. In those days I was still not eating much and drank lots and was very skinny. I wanted to do the trip to Borneo, but I also thought that if I ran a marathon, everyone would be impressed. And they were, even though it took me 5 hours 10 minutes to finish! They couldn't believe someone like me could do it. It was great. I really enjoyed it; it was an incredible experience.

'Also, after too much boozing in the first year, I really enjoyed the feeling of being fit. It was good for my weight management, too. I hadn't put on weight but this enabled me to have a healthier approach as to how much I ate. Having gone through a phase of eating half a baguette for lunch and the rest of it for dinner, I thought it was time I grew up a bit!

'As far as I was concerned, after that first marathon, that was it: I had no plans to do another one and certainly no plans to do *100* of them,' she says, laughing.

So, what happened?

'In a word, London,' she tells me. 'I wasn't interested in doing another marathon for the sake of it, but I did want to do London. Like many novice runners, London seemed to me to be the ultimate race – the biggest, the best, the most fun and the best atmosphere. So I entered the ballot and it took me four years to get in.

'At that time I was working in Jakarta as an equities analyst. The roads out there are dire, so all my training had to be done on a treadmill. Plus, there are no trails and next to no running culture, even amongst the ex-pats. I've never seen a gym before or since where all the treadmills are taken by people walking!'

Training four times a week, doing three shorter runs and one long run of up to three-and-a-half hours each week on a treadmill brought with it some unique difficulties.

'Running for that length of time on a treadmill is guaranteed to give you jelly legs,' Naomi says, laughing at the memory. 'And it's very boring – I watched lots of *CSI*!'

She also found that treadmill training was not good preparation for the impact of running on a hard road.

'I suffered a stress fracture on my first post-marathon run a few days later, which put me out of action for about six weeks. Consequently, I didn't run my next marathon until October 2007.'

The mathematical part of my brain (the smallest part) kicks in. If it was four years before she did her second and third marathons, then she must have run 97 marathons in just four years! That's some running. However, I'm wrong. Not, surprisingly, because my maths is rubbish but because, in actual fact, Naomi didn't decide to go for 100 until another two years later, in 2009.

'I ran the two marathons in 2007 and then I did seven in 2008,' she explains. 'Again, I really enjoyed them. I even did a back-to-back [two marathons in two weeks] and had no problems. And then a friend in the pub told me that a woman called Melanie Ross held the record for being the youngest woman in the UK to run 100 marathons and she was 34. He said I had loads of years on her and that I could take the record.'

And she believed him?

'Oh yes,' she replies, 'I did. When he said, "You could do this," I thought about it and realised that I could.'

And he's still a friend?

Naomi laughs surprisingly heartily for a woman of such slender frame and confirms that he is.

'I really enjoyed it,' she reiterates. 'I don't see the point in doing any of it if you don't enjoy it, although when I'm halfway round a marathon, I nearly always tell myself never again!'

I feel something akin to relief that this delightful, bright young woman is not, after all, suffering masochistic tendencies and I wonder about her views on training.

'I think training is really important – I want to run faster as well as doing the numbers,' she explains. 'It's easy to fall into the trap of doing a marathon at the weekend and then doing a four- or five-miler a couple of times in the week, but that won't make you any faster.'

The coach in me would have to agree with that sentiment, which begs the question whether Naomi belongs to a club and if she has a coach.

'No, I don't have a coach or belong to a club, apart from

Fetch.' (Short for 'Fetcheveryone' – a web-based club where runners, cyclists, swimmers and triathletes can exchange news and views, discuss races and maintain training blogs: www.fetcheveryone.com).

'Although as soon as I've done my 100th, I'll become a member of the 100 Club, I can't wait to get my club shirt!' she adds, excitement lending a quiver to her voice and reminding me of my own excitement when I went with my mum to buy a new Girl Guide uniform and ended up with a size 0 hat because my head was pea-sized. Not that that's important right now, or indeed relevant. However, I can empathise with Naomi's excitement.

However, both Naomi and I seem to have digressed somewhat. Donning my size 0 coach's hat, I am interested to learn what sort of training she does without a coach to advise her.

'When I first started training at university, I became a gym-rat! I was doing an hour's cardio session on a cross-trainer, plus a session on the treadmill and the rowing machine followed by lots of strength training, four or five times a week. I still train five times a week,' she tells me, 'but out of the gym with two or three mid-week runs, one or two steady, plus a tempo run of between 1 hour and 1 hour 20. My favourite session is fast 800 metre/1 mile interval runs.

'Sometimes I train with my boyfriend, but not often as he's too fast for me and I feel pressured to try and stay with him, not wanting to slow him down so I mainly train on my own, which I'm totally happy with.

'Running is a solitary sport, which suits me,' she goes on. 'I like the time out to be free with my thoughts – I see it as down time. I'm very self-motivated and have no problem getting out to train, no matter what the weather. I enjoy being in touch with the seasons, seeing the first snowdrops and crocuses, the feeling that my mind and body are at one with nature.

'I have definitely over-trained in the past, but I'm now much better at listening to my body and pulling back when necessary.'

Coach Summer is glad to hear it.

Despite this admission, Naomi tells me that she's never had any real injuries and thinks she is lucky in this regard.

'Although, actually,' she admits, a moment later, 'I did suffer from an overuse stress injury after the Brathay 10-in-10 at Windermere [10 marathons in 10 days], but rested for two weeks and was then fine again. And I had Achilles tendonitis after running on Chesil Beach for three and a half miles, but I think this was peculiar to the surface I was running on as I haven't had any trouble with my Achilles since then. And now and again I suffer a bit from ITB.' (Iliotibial Band Syndrome – a thigh injury often affecting the knee.)

'I actually had to have two weeks off last January,' she complains, 'but normally I train all the time. I get scared that if I have time off, I will lose my endurance.'

My coaching voice just will not keep quiet.

'Sometimes,' I venture, 'it's a good thing to rest. You won't lose a good build-up of endurance that quickly. In fact, quite often if you have already built up a good endurance base over a long period of time, a rest will allow your body to re-energise itself and you may even find you run better immediately after a short lay-off or a reduction in training. Remember, your body gets tired and if it gets too tired, you will just run tired.'

There's a moment's silence and I wonder if I've said too much, but then Naomi's back again.

'Actually,' she admits, 'I did have a week off at one point and then ran a personal best in my next race, knocking six minutes off my previous half marathon time.'

I feel vindicated.

As if marathon racing, training and a full-time job doesn't

keep her busy enough, Naomi has also recently taken up Dynamic Pilates, which apparently involves strength training and stretching, once a week.

'I don't have the patience for yoga or meditation,' she explains. 'Dynamic Pilates is hard work, it uses resistance and makes you sweat.'

I ask her to elaborate further as I have never heard of it.

'It's supposed to help alleviate stiffness and stretch out the muscles, helping to lengthen them,' she advises me.

Hmm, maybe this is something I should look into myself. My muscles could definitely do with a good stretch. I'm not so sure about the hard work and sweating bit, though.

As a coach I can't help but be impressed by Naomi's intelligent approach to her training, a lot of which she says she has picked up from various books on the subject.

'I particularly like the American writer Sam Murphy and *Runners World* magazine,' she says. 'I just apply what I like to myself and keep a blog of my training and racing – it's a good way of looking back and tracking my progress.'

Of course I shouldn't be surprised by Naomi's approach. This is a woman who read classics at Oxford, studying Latin and Greek literature, as well as some history, philosophy, art and philology (the science of language, according to the *Oxford English Dictionary*, when I look it up).

These days she works as an investment analyst for an insurance company, handling deals worth millions.

'It's a challenging job,' she says, 'but I do enjoy it.'

With over 100 marathons, training five times a week plus a challenging job, does she ever sleep?

'I *love* sleeping!' Naomi responds enthusiastically, sounding like Pollyanna. 'I like eight or nine hours a night and I sleep like a log!'

Hardly surprising given that she gets up every morning at

six o'clock, or earlier if she has meetings at work or needs to run longer.

'I always run in the mornings,' she explains, adding rather reassuringly, 'evenings are for drinking wine. I'm hopeless at waking up; I have a cup of tea and half a bowl of cereal. I can run on empty but I get more from training with a kick-start, especially for harder or longer sessions.

'I have a fast metabolic rate, which means I can't eat earlier than 45 minutes prior to running as I get too hungry,' she explains. 'During the 10-in-10 eating was difficult – obviously the amount of food you need is so different to the amount of food you want to eat, or would normally eat. I ate jam sandwiches – they were fantastic – and ginger cake; I had no problem digesting them. My mum actually fed me sausages and chips, which I managed to eat but they were a bit harder to get down.'

Whereas marshmallows would have been perfect!

'During races, I don't take on gels as I don't like them and only drink water or sports drinks. Cups of tea are good, too,' she adds, 'I love a cup of tea. At the 10-in-10, my mum made me tea to drink with my jam sandwiches!'

So, what does her mother think of her daughter's running exploits?

'My family are really supportive,' Naomi says straightaway. 'They came out for my early marathons in Paris, Dublin and Barcelona, and the 10-in-10. They were unbelievably wonderful, making the tea and jam sandwiches, and giving me their support. They are very proud of me – I find it very touching. It makes me feel a bit guilty about the amount of effort they expend. I wonder why I deserve it, I guess.'

Because you are family – unconditional love and all that, Naomi! It's so much a right as a living inheritance.

'My friends are also very supportive,' she continues. 'Many of them are runners of course, so they understand my motivation.

Many of them run faster than me or do ultras [races further than marathon distance] and juggle lots of other commitments, so you never feel like you're on a pedestal. You all have your own challenges. They're good, too for pulling your leg as much as celebrating your successes,' she adds, with a soft chuckle that speaks clearly of her fondness for them.

'Work are the most baffled. Most of them are not runners and find it hard to understand why I run so many races. It's amusing how they adapt to the idea, though. Once you've run a few marathons on consecutive weekends, they wonder why you have a weekend off!'

Surely they must also envy Naomi's impressive race travelogue, from which I ask her to select a few favourites.

'There are many,' she says, 'but Rome is definitely one of them. It has a really good atmosphere, beautiful scenery and is a fast course. Also, it's held in March, so it's a good time of year weather-wise, too.

'Marrakech last January was also very enjoyable and Mauritius is also worth mentioning. It was the first time they'd held a marathon and it started at six in the morning to avoid the heat. It almost succeeded,' she adds with a laugh, 'it was about 20 degrees when we finished, but we finished on a beach and ran straight into the sea at the end. It was beautiful!'

It sounds like it – apart from the 6am start and the 26.2-mile run, that is.

I wonder whether Naomi has any interest in running ultras and off-road races.

'I do at this time of year [February],' she tells me, 'just because there aren't that many road marathons and I want to keep the pressure up. In fact, I'm doing a 50-kilometre race this weekend [a week before Malta].'

Coach Summer rises to the surface and can't help but ask if Naomi really thinks this is a good idea.

'I wanted to do something that will keep me working before I do the 100th next weekend,' she offers by way of defence.

Well, by my reckoning, a 50K run should just about do it. I push the coach in me away. After all, this woman has run more marathons than I've watched so she must know by now what suits her.

And if Naomi is someone who is not afraid to push herself, she is also a person who likes to do things properly.

'I'm a bit of a purist when it comes to counting marathons,' she explains. 'I like them to be run on road in a proper marathon race as opposed to part of an ultra or off-road race, where it's difficult to measure the course accurately.'

Regardless of this approach, she tells me that she prefers road races anyway as she finds off-road/trails more difficult.

'They are much more tiring, heavier on the legs. Plus, you can't allow your mind to roam free as you have to concentrate on the uneven terrain.

'I can only get into my running rhythm in road races and can run faster times because of it. The time also goes more quickly. I find I can switch off and let my mind go wherever it likes, then I look at my watch and 40 minutes have passed. Running on the road it can feel effortless – you don't have to consciously think about where your feet are going, you are free to enjoy the movement, the surroundings and lose yourself in your own thoughts.

'Last year I ran loads of races – 52 in all, including the Brathay 10-in-10 and four or five doubles [two marathons in two days] but I've eased off a bit since then. My last race was four weeks ago.'

It's lucky I'm doing this interview over the phone and she can't see me at this point because my mouth has flopped open and my chin (of which, by the way, I'm pleased to report at this stage in my life there is only one) has just landed on my chest.

I can't see myself, of course as I'm not conducting this interview in front of a mirror, but I know that if I could then it would not be pretty.

'I think it's possible to do lots of marathons so long as you listen to what your body says,' avers Naomi.

As a runner from the days of yore when heart rate monitors and Garmins [sports watches that measure distance, speed, altitude, heart rate, time and pace and whose data can be uploaded to a computer for recording purposes] hadn't been invented, yet we were able to tell to the metre exactly how far we'd run just because we knew what it felt like and had learned to listen to our bodies, I find myself in total agreement.

So, moving on to the future. Where does she see herself going once she's completed the 100?

'Originally,' she says, 'I thought that when I'd completed 100, I maybe wouldn't run any more marathons but now I intend to carry on.

'I enjoy it too much,' she expands, 'the European cities, the travel, the weekend away in the sunshine, seeing different places… I will keep doing it but run fewer, hopefully faster.'

Interestingly, a few months after Naomi's 100th, I caught up with her again and asked how she now felt about running marathons: had she made any changes or set herself any new goals?

'My attitude is totally different now!' she says. 'I categorically won't run a marathon I don't like – for example, if they're badly organised or have a horrible route, or are over-priced or off-road and you have to find your own route with just a set of printed instructions. Before, the motivation was to get to the 100th – it was part of a bigger picture. Now I have to want to finish each race or the motivation isn't there.

'I've decided to do far fewer races, bag a few more "destinations" and target some fast times. I'm hoping to run 3 hours 30 in Stockholm this weekend, which would effectively take six minutes off my current personal best, so I've been doing more structured speed work under the guidance of a coach – running faster intervals, faster tempo pieces and more progressive runs.

'I am also enjoying the chance to do shorter races. They are a different test; it's nice to know you can finish a race without going anywhere near the wall.

'Overall, I am leaving things open for a while as I want to go back to really enjoying running, with no pressure rather than it being a task I have to complete. I have no more marathons in the diary after this weekend but will probably end up doing a few more this year. I have got my eye on Helsinki, Bilbao and Frankfurt, and would like to do a couple in the US, maybe the Big Sur next year.'

And what do her work colleagues think now that she's completed the magic 100?

At this she laughs heartily. 'They were very impressed when they read on the intranet a published article about the 100. It went to the investment staff in the USA, too and I was swamped by congratulatory emails. It was lovely to have my efforts recognised, though I do feel slightly fraudulent. If I have done it, it can't be that hard,' she adds, modestly. 'You just need to want to do it, have the time and a bit of cash, and some luck to avoid injuries.'

She doesn't mention dedication, commitment, self-motivation and a willingness to work bloody hard, I notice. Maybe that's because these qualities are such an intrinsic part of her nature, she isn't even aware of them.

SUMMER SHORTS

If you're hungry before a race but can't face sausage and chips, try eating a chocolate eclair! I did this once when I was waiting to run the last leg in a road relay race – the race was running late and I hadn't eaten for three hours. I told my coach I was feeling dizzy and couldn't run. She disappeared and five minutes later returned with a chocolate eclair. I ran the fastest leg I'd ever run on that course. I don't know to this day where she came by a chocolate eclair when we were in the middle of nowhere, but boy, did it taste good! I guess, too that it was light, easy to digest and gave me the sugar boost I needed.

Marshmallows would probably work just as well...

MILE 6

OUT OF AFRICA

C hris Monsey discovered racing in Africa brought some unusual challenges.

CHRIS MONSEY
Born: 1962
130 marathons:
• 1st marathon: 1981 – Scarborough
• 100th marathon: 2005 – Berlin

When Chris Monsey set off from home one day in 2003 on a business trip bound for Africa, little did he know that he was about to participate in the strangest marathon race of his life.

'I was on an Ethiopian Airlines flight when I had a chance encounter with the manager of a group of Ethiopian athletes,' he explains. 'He invited me to take part in a marathon that was being held that weekend in Addis Ababa and gave me the telephone number of the race organiser.

'I should have known something wasn't quite right because after

I'd rung him and arranged to enter the race, the race organiser actually delivered my race number to my hotel in person!'

For the uninitiated, it is normal practice for race entrants to have to go through the tedious process of collecting their own race numbers from an expo, involving lengthy queues in draughty buildings and single-minded salesmen trying to tempt you with the latest in designer sportswear and must-have, yet totally unnecessary techno gadgetry. In other words, Chris got lucky – or at least he thought he had.

'The race was due to start at eight in the morning at the national stadium in the centre of Addis Ababa,' he continues, 'the third highest capital city in the World, but it was actually delayed two hours and started instead at nearby Meskel Square.'

Uh-oh! Warning bells are beginning to chime.

'Along with the majority of the field, I'd purchased the Ethiopian national kit from a local sports shop and lined up at the start in red shorts and green vest with "Ethiopia" emblazoned in white letters across the front, a thick layer of sun block and shades!' he recalls. 'There was a small field of under 300 entrants and a few fun runners, but I was the only foreigner.

'The course contained scarcely any flat terrain and went through the outskirts of the city southwards towards Debre Zeyt. At the halfway point, we were to turn around and return the way we had come.

'The race was not the best organised – there was only one set of drinks laid out on a table at about the 10K point and there were no marshals, clocks or mile/km markers to indicate the distance covered. It was simply a case of following the stragglers.'

Hmm. Ding-dong (but not in a David Niven kind of way)!

'I'd done some training runs in Ethiopia, but at a much lower altitude,' he adds. 'From the outset I felt as though the thin dry air was scorching my lungs and the traffic fumes were also very uncomfortable. There were no spectators as such, just passers-by on a Sunday stroll, who gave cries of "Haile" – a reference to [distance runner] Gebrselassie – and "eye-zoh", meaning literally "be strong" – a refrain uttered to anyone facing adversity. The sight of a foreigner running in Africa seemed to excite at best mild bemusement and at worst, ridicule.'

Oh dear. Not quite London, was it?

'Then the stragglers began to accept lifts from passing vehicles.'

Ding Dong merrily on high! But he's kidding, right?

'No, I'm not,' Chris avers. 'I was running along with a youth in cut-off jeans. He had a ridiculous loping stride and was barefoot with huge splayed leathery feet. He jumped into a pick-up truck and I saw him dropped off 500 metres up the road. As I caught up with him, he accepted another lift and that was the last I saw of him.'

Ding Dong Merrily on High, with Tubular Bells!

'At another point I found myself running beside an oldish-looking fellow in a yellow vest, who bore an astonishing resemblance to the late Emperor Haile Selassie. We encouraged one another with "eye-zoh", but encountering a particularly steep hill at what I later estimated to be at around 21 miles, he too accepted a lift! This proved a devastating psychological blow to me and I began to walk.

'By the time I re-entered the southern outskirts of the city, there were no other runners in sight for me to follow. Consequently, at each junction I had to ask passers-by which way to go. Fortunately, I knew the words in Amharic for left, right and straight ahead, but it would only have taken one wrong direction and I would have been hopelessly lost and unable to finish.'

Now that is truly scary, especially for someone like me who can get hopelessly lost trying to find my way out of a paper bag

– not that I've ever tried it, never having found a bag large enough to get into.

'Aside from these difficulties,' the intrepid Chris continues, 'the broiling African sun was also taking its toll and in the absence of any proper provision of water, I took to stopping at roadside cafes to request "wuha" – water. A hush would normally fall upon the cafe as a sunburnt Englishman staggered across the threshold in vest and shorts, but they gave me what I asked for readily enough. I was even offered ice and a slice!

'After one such stop and mildly refreshed, I made an attempt to jog again. As I did so, I passed a boy herding an ox.'

Dehydration perhaps, or maybe a spiked lemon slice?

'It's true,' Chris assures me. 'To my surprise the boy began to jog beside me, spurring on his ox with a stick.

'"Haile, Haile!" the boy shouted to me,' says Chris. '"Eye-zoh!" I shouted back to him. I must have jogged 500 metres with the boy and his ox. Passers-by viewed our approach with some alarm and anxiously shepherded their children into doorways. I thought that this was almost as good as having a motorcycle out-rider!'

That's one way of looking at it.

'Somehow, though, running with the ox had helped me through a wall and I mysteriously found a second wind.'
There's nothing like a bit of oxen distraction to make you forget your troubles.

'I was also pretty sure I was getting closer to the city centre as I'd started to recognise some landmarks and at last I saw Meskel Square in the distance and could clearly make out the race director resplendent in his yellow tracksuit,' he continues.

Has the man no shame?

'But first I had to cross some traffic lights at the busiest intersection of the city. I closed my eyes and launched myself across eight lanes of traffic, hoping the lights would remain on red. Luckily they did!

'And then I saw the finish – or at least what remained of the finish. Originally it had been marked by an arch of balloons and a bouncy castle, but by the time I crossed the line, the bouncy castle had already been deflated and folded up. Not that I was going to let a little thing like that stop me celebrating finishing the race! I held my arms aloft and dipped as I crossed the line as though I was involved in a photo finish!

'And then, unbelievably, [I really don't see how Chris can even think of using such a word at this stage of the story, but he does] despite all my efforts and probably being one of the few runners who had actually completed the race under my own steam, the race director and his driver greeted me with a slow hand clap!'

Shoot them, Mr Mainwaring!

'There was no sign of any other runners or spectators…'

Hardly surprising given they'd all been driven to the finish and probably by that time were enjoying their Sunday roast or whatever the African equivalent is.

'I asked the race director what was my time. He looked at his watch and told me it was about 5 hours 37 minutes, which I was quite surprised by as I'd expected it to be around 4 hours. Maybe my surprise showed on my face because the race director's driver then joined in the conversation and said he thought it was more like 5 hours 10 minutes, as if this was some sort of consolation, and reminded the race director that they had been late starting.'

You may as well have asked the ox, Chris.

'I asked the race director when the previous runner had finished,' he goes on. 'The race director looked into the distance and shuffled his feet, and then told me it was about an hour ago. So I asked if he had to wait for anyone else and his assistant said in a low voice, "No, there is no one else."

'Only then did it dawn on me that they were embarrassed to tell me that I'd come last – and by a long way!'

Yes, but only because you and the ox were the only ones who didn't cheat, Chris!

'At that point, I decided I'd encroached upon their Sunday afternoon long enough, recovered my tracksuit from an ice cream parlour (where I'd left it in the absence of any changing facilities) and, by way of recompense, helped them load the bouncy castle into the back of their car. Then they offered me a lift back to my hotel, which I accepted.'

As opposed to offering him a lift halfway through the race…

'There wasn't even a finisher's medal,' he adds. 'All I got to remember the day by was sunburn on the back of my legs, where I'd forgotten to apply sun block! Oh, and a racing heart that went on far into the night – probably a combination of the sunburn, dehydration and altitude. It was an extraordinary experience.'

And that last comment earns itself the 'understatement of this book' award.

Certainly, this was an experience that Chris could never have foreseen when he ran his first marathon at Scarborough in 1981 at the age of just 19.

'I'd trained specifically for it, and finished in 3 hours 36 minutes 33 seconds,' he recalls, 'although I wasn't at all bothered about the time – I just wanted to finish.'

Having joined a running club at 14, by the time Chris was in his mid-20s he had become quite a serious runner.

'I ran my fastest marathon in 2 hours 48 minutes when I was 27,' he says. 'I'd run 22 marathons by then, but then due to other commitments which meant I couldn't put in the time for training and racing, I stopped running altogether. However, I took it up again seven years later with the intention of completing 100 marathons.

'To be honest,' he goes on, sounding a little dismal, 'since I achieved 100, I've lost a bit of motivation. These days, and certainly for the last five years, I've stopped thinking of myself as a serious runner. I'm not bothered about the numbers and I'm too old to go for times.

'Still,' he adds, sounding a mite more cheerful, 'I do it as much for the social side as anything else now, meeting up with my running friends at the races I go to. I think of it more as a leisure activity and only do about four or five races each year. They tend to be the same ones each time – Berlin, Hamburg, Rotterdam, Amsterdam – I like big cities with flat courses!'

How very sensible.

'And,' he goes on, decidedly more cheery now, 'apart from a little bit of knee trouble over the last few years, I've been very lucky not to have suffered from any serious injuries all the time I've been running. Given that most of my training and racing has been done on the road, that's really something of a miracle!'

SUMMER SHORTS

Unfortunately, one of the difficulties of having started running early in life is that you never better your best times set when you were younger and in your running prime. However, as Chris has discovered, there are many other aspects of running that can motivate and inspire you, such as the social side, the travel and the camaraderie. Not forgetting some rather unusual after-dinner stories gathered along the way…

MILE 7

AN EXPEDITION TO THE NORTH POLE

Running marathons has given Osy Waye a much-needed boost of self-confidence.

OSY WAYE
Born: 1950
115 marathons:
- 1st marathon: 1987 – London
- 100th marathon: 2006 – North Pole
Records:
- Slowest Marathon in 100 Marathon Club (10 hours+).

Osy Waye was determined to run his 100th marathon somewhere special, so he opted for the world's most northerly marathon, the North Pole.

'But isn't it rather snowy there?' I venture the fairly obvious question, 'for running, I mean.' I put this in hastily, lest he think I'm some kind of bimbo journalist who'd be more at home asking him what colour his favourite running shoes are.

Luckily he laughs rather merrily and I feel considerably mollified.

'You could say that,' he agrees. 'In fact, the day I ran it, there was even more snow than usual.'

That seems quite hard to imagine but it is nonetheless true, so Osy assures me.

'We were told beforehand that the first lap or two of the course [the race involved running 17 laps around the Pole] would be hard running on fresh snow,' he explains, 'and therefore we would have to run in snow shoes but that once the snow had been trodden down a bit and compacted, it would become easier and we'd then be able to change into our normal trainers for the remainder of the race.'

It didn't work out that way, though.

'Due to there having been several extra inches of snowfall just before the race, it was impossible for the front runners to keep to a single track as they had to keep stepping aside to avoid the worst of the snow. In turn, this meant that instead of the rest of the field being able to follow them and run in their tracks, forcing the snow to compact, we were all running our own routes, which meant there was constant fresh snow to run through for everyone. Consequently, we had to run the entire race in our snowshoes!'

Being a bit of a beach bum kind of girl, who steers clear of snowy mountains wherever possible, I've never even seen snowshoes, let alone worn them and so I enquire whether they were very heavy.

'No, they weren't heavy,' Osy says, 'but they were strange to wear. I'd bought them early so I could practise wearing them, but we didn't have any snow in London that winter so I was unable to wear them at all to get used to them. That made it hard and I actually ended up walking for most of the way.'

Poor Osy! Still, by way of consolation, he did end up gaining a record: the slowest-ever marathon run by a 100 Marathon Club member with a time in excess of 10 hours!

And then a thought strikes me – trudging through armpit-deep snow at the North Pole for 10 hours surely must have been a pretty chilling experience?

'Fortunately,' he says, 'I was dressed as a polar bear.'

Of course!

'I was the only polar bear at the North Pole,' he tells me with what sounds like a rather wry sense of humour, 'but at least the costume helped keep me warm.'

I ask a bit more about the costume – how much could he see, was it heavy, how did he breathe?

'I could see out of the eyes and maybe the mouth a bit, too but I removed the mesh that covers the eyes so I could see more, then I replaced it after the race,' he adds, sounding a little guilty, as if the owner of said costume might read this book and discover his misdemeanour.

But it turns out I have misidentified his tone: Osy actually owns the costume himself.

'I bought it on eBay,' he tells me. 'It was used by Diet Coke in the days when they used a polar bear as part of their advertising campaign.'

Gosh! I remember that.

'I didn't have any problem with heat or weight,' he continues, returning to my original question, 'but I did have a problem with the head.'

I assume he means the bear's head, and not his own?

'Oh yes,' he assures me, earnestly. 'It was hard to breathe through. I found I was breathing in my own air so I had to keep removing the head and taking in some fresh air.'

I'm so glad we have already clarified this is the bear's head he is referring to.

'It's much worse being a rhinoceros,' he suddenly advises me just as I'm about to launch into my next question, taking me unawares so that for a moment I wonder exactly what my book is meant to be about.

'They are much heavier,' he expands, 'although they are better for breathing because the rhino's head is below the top so you can get in more air. Not that I've actually worn one – I've just looked at it and it appears that way. The polar bear is a heavy costume too, but not a problem for a strong lad like me,' he boasts, 'it's just the breathing that's difficult.'

Ah, yes, right! The difficulties of running in fancy dress… It would appear Osy is something of an expert in this field.

'I've done a fair bit of it,' he agrees, cheerfully. 'I ran as an Egyptian mummy in Luxor and then wore the same costume in London. The mummy costume can be very useful for runners like me,' he goes on chattily.

Oh yes? I lift my head from where it has been bent in concentration over my notebook and raise my eyebrows in a questioning kind of way. Of course Osy can't actually see this, being 100 miles east of me on the end of a telephone line, but still…

'I can be quite cold in the second part near the river,' he explains, 'and it keeps me warm, but it also keeps you cool when it's hot.'

Really?

'Oh yes,' he assures me. 'You don't see many Egyptians in the desert walking or otherwise, wearing shorts and no tops, do you?'

True, but you don't see many of them wandering around dressed as mummies either. However, I take his point and wonder whether there are any other costumes that he is partial to running in.

'Only a clown,' he says.

The things you can buy on eBay!

'Oh no, I only bought the polar bear costume from eBay – I made the clown and the mummy.'

Naturally.

An image suddenly bursts into my head: it is midnight, lights blaze from a cottage window outlining the shadow of a man. He is sitting in an armchair beside a blazing log fire, head bent in concentration as he forces an oversized needle through a mountain of garishly colourful clown-like material that covers his entire lap. On a rug beneath his feet, a black cat sleeps peacefully...

Funny, you know, this is not at all how I saw this book going.

So, I just have to ask – does he practise running in the costumes prior to racing in them?

'I didn't feel I could run round Muswell Hill, where I live, dressed as a polar bear without being attacked by youths,' he concedes, sounding somewhat saddened by this fact, 'but I did wear it at Hornsea Carnival to get a feel for it and at the London one mile and 10K runs for charity,' he adds, rather more cheerfully. 'They were like a dress rehearsal.'

'Actually,' he goes on, as if to impart a great secret, 'I have a funny story along those lines about the polar bear costume...'

Ooh, do go on, Osy! I encourage.

'Well, somehow the *Saturday Telegraph* had heard about the North Pole run being my 100th marathon and wanted to do a feature on me,' he begins. 'So they asked me to meet them at the Mall to have my photograph taken. I was to wear the polar bear costume.'

How exciting!

'I arrived a little early... and was instantly set upon by the police!'

No!

'Yes,' he avers. 'They wrestled me to the ground and then interviewed me. It seemed they thought I was one of those "Fathers for Justice" demonstrators!'

(For those of you not in the know, Fathers for Justice were in the news a lot at that time, mainly for dressing up in costumes and appearing at prominent venues within the city to publicise their cause, which was supporting single fathers.)

'It took me about 20 minutes to convince them of the truth and then they released me!'

Well, thank goodness for that.

'But the worst thing,' says Osy, 'was that the *Telegraph* never even ran the story!'

Sometimes, life can be so unfair.

Aside from dressing up, Osy's main motivation for running marathons is travel.

'When I first started running abroad,' he explains, 'I saw it as an activity holiday. I've always loved travelling but I really didn't like spending all that money just to sit on a beach – it seemed so expensive – but the combination of running and travel make it seem okay. These days I have no children or mortgage, so am free to travel as and when I want to, subject to work. I've run in so many different countries that if the world was square, I'd have run in all four corners of it, plus the top and the bottom!'

He's not kidding. Osy's running has taken him to 32 different countries so far, including less-visited ones such as the Lebanon, Japan and South Korea. It has also brought him membership of the prestigious Grand Slam Club – an organisation whose members have run a marathon on all seven continents, plus the North Pole.

So, where are Osy's favourite places to run?

'I enjoy running in big and spectacular races or interesting ones with some sort of history,' he says, 'such as the Boston Marathon, which is the oldest marathon in the world. The year I ran it, 1996, was the race's 100th year and there were 39,000 runners. Normally the biggest fields are London and New York, but not that year.

'New Zealand was another special one – I ran it in the

Millennium Year, on New Year's Day. It was the first marathon of the Millennium and when we finished, we went back to the hotel and watched London celebrate New Year.

'And running in the Antarctic, that was a different experience. It was so wild! We were watched by penguins and seals. And the North Pole was so quiet.

'Berlin was also special for personal reasons. I am German by birth and was adopted by my English stepfather,' Osy explains. 'We moved to Berlin for a couple of years when I was eight. I mention that because when I went to run my first Berlin marathon in 1987, the day before the race we went on a coach trip over to East Berlin. On the day of the marathon we started with the wall and Brandenburger Tor behind us and I remember thinking there at the start how great it would have been if, for the marathon, a small opening could have been made and we could run both sides: East and West. Never did I expect that two years later there would be no wall there at all and that in 1990, I would actually run both East and West!

'That was like some kind of magic,' he muses, wistfully.

Not quite so magical was the year after he'd run a marathon in Beirut, in 2005.

'The race had to be cancelled,' he recalls, 'because of bombing. I watched the report on TV and saw a crack in the middle of the road, which I'd run along only the year before. That shook me.'

On a lighter note, he turns to Walt Disney – and you can't get much lighter than that.

'I ran the Disney Marathon because of the medal,' he tells me with a chuckle.

Share the joke, Osy.

'The first time I saw it was at the London Expo,' he adds. 'Other medals are just round and boring, but this one had two Disney ears on it and that's what made me decide to run the Disney Marathon.'

Quite, and who wouldn't want to run 26.2 miles with the promise of a big-eared medal at the end of it?

'And then, at the other end of the scale, quite literally,' Osy continues, 'is Texas. Texas is a very small marathon and it was a long way to go, but I'd never been and the marathon gave me a good excuse to go.

'What I didn't realise,' he goes on, starting to chuckle again, 'was that the medal boasts being the largest medal in the world, weighing 20 times more than the average marathon medal! I had to put it in my hand baggage coming home as otherwise I'd have had to pay excess on my baggage allowance!

'I thought I'd avoided all the pitfalls, but when my bag went through the security x-ray, it showed up a large solid mass which they weren't too happy about, so they made me unpack my entire bag so they could examine it.'

Now that could only happen to Osy!

'It was worth it, though,' he says with a sigh, 'I love my medals. I have them displayed on a big framed pinboard secured with Velcro and every time I look at them, they bring back happy memories of the races.'

So, which one was his first-ever marathon medal?

'London,' he recalls, instantly. 'It was watching it on the TV that inspired me to run my first marathon. I'd never done any running before that, other than the ubiquitous school cross-country, which I hated. And was it any wonder?' he asks.

Er, I don't know – you'll have to tell me.

'Once a year we were told to go out and run round the cross-country course with no training or anything. Usually it was cold and wet, and the whole thing was totally horrible.'

Hmm, put like that, even I – a huge fan of anything that would get me out of the classroom and into the great outdoors – must admit that it doesn't sound too appealing.

'But then I ran my first marathon in London, in 1987. It was a mixture of happiness and pain at the same time. My head was full of the noise of the crowds cheering me and everyone else along. It was hard, but every mile closer to the finish it might have got harder but at the same time I felt more and more joy, knowing that I could do it. It took everything I had, but it was all worth it.

'I've always loved travel,' he tells me, as if he's already forgotten that he's taken me on a world running tour, 'and after that first marathon I decided to run abroad, in Berlin and New York. I was running two or three marathons a year then. Then, when I'd done 40 marathons, I heard about the 100 Marathon Club. I knew I would never be fast but I always had stamina and I love to achieve something. I thought this was something I could achieve.

'I also realised that if I carried on running just three marathons a year, I would be over 80 before I reached 100 so I upped it to eight to ten a year, although once I'd made 100, I brought it back down again to seven or eight.'

So, having met his numerical target in 1987 and having run in just about every country in the world, what's Osy's next goal?

'I guess I want to reach 200,' he admits. 'I certainly don't ever think of giving it up – I enjoy it all too much.

'Imagine being someone like poor Liz McColgan,' he muses. 'She runs one marathon, gets injured and can't run any more – or not for a long time. Better doing what I and others do.'

Now that's a novel way of looking at one of Scotland's greatest marathon runners of all time!

'I like the idea of setting my own goals and achieving something through my own endeavours,' he continues. 'It gives me a lot of pleasure. I also think that as runners get older and they have more time, they do more marathons. I see myself doing that. There are some places I haven't been to yet that I still want to see.'

So, what does his wife make of it all?

'She's amazing,' he answers immediately. 'She fully supports me in my marathons' quests and loves spectating, although she's never run herself. Actually,' he adds, almost in a whisper as if to impart some great secret, 'she has a bit of a reputation...'

Really? Excitement causes me to grip my pen tighter.

'For being a great supporter to everyone, not just to me,' he divulges.

Right, of course. My grip loosens.

'She helps out at water stations, marshalling and encouraging. She shouts at everyone, cheering them on,' he continues, admiringly. 'It always amazes me that she likes watching so much – I once watched half an hour of a race I wasn't running in and got so bored, I had to leave.

'Sometimes, though,' he adds, sounding ever so slightly petulant, 'she manages to miss me, even when I'm dressed up in costume.'

Now that seems hard to believe.

'One year,' he goes on, sounding as if he too finds it hard to believe, 'I was dressed as a very bright clown and we'd arranged that when she saw me at the water station where she was, we would arrange where to meet up at the end of the race but she was so busy chatting to someone else that she didn't even notice me! So I took a cup of water and deliberately spilt it over her so she would notice me.'

I can't help but notice a hint of victorious pride in Osy's voice.

'What did she do?' I ask, knowing that if I'd been her I'd have sought some kind of vicious revenge, if not straightaway, then certainly later on.

'Oh, she laughed,' he says airily, adding, 'Luckily she has a good sense of humour.'

Even more luckily, I think to myself, he is married to *her* and not me.

'Actually, I'm dressing up as a clown again in this year's London Marathon, for charity,' Osy informs me, earning himself total redemption. 'I'm raising money for a local children's home in South London – it's a bucket run.'

A *what*?

'A bucket run,' he repeats. 'You know, I carry a bucket and stop to beg people to put money in it.'

Oh, of course.

'I've done bucket runs for bigger charities in the past, but these days I'd rather do it for the smaller ones who don't get the same exposure. Of course they're all good causes and add another dimension to running.

'Normally,' he goes on, 'if I'm not running for charity, I would hide in the middle of the field but when I'm doing it for a cause, I become a celebrity and put on a performance.'

'I actually used to be really shy,' he says suddenly, surprising me. 'Running has given me confidence. The fact that I have achieved something, set my own targets and goals, and achieved what I set out to do – it feels good. People admire me, and that gives me confidence and I feel proud of myself.

'When people tell me they admire me, I tell them they could do it, too but they say they couldn't – they get out of breath just running for a bus. I tell them that I puff and pant for the first two or three miles then the breathing eases and it's fine. If I can do it, most people can do it but they do need to have commitment.

'I don't actually enjoy running,' he adds, surprising me again. 'I enjoy what it brings, such as running alone late at night in the dark – it gives you a chance to catch up with things that there's not enough time otherwise to think about in the day.

'I always train alone, but I'm surprised by how many other people must do too, because the streets of London are always very busy with people running. You only used to find it like that a month or two before the London Marathon, but now it is most of the year.

'Although I like running alone, I would like to belong to a club so I could get involved in social activities but my work as a church caretaker makes it difficult as I have to work most weekends. I'm actually very lazy in training – if I can get away with it, I will. The worst thing is I notice that if I'm not racing as much, I need to train more although now I'm getting older, I have eased off a bit.'

Define easing off.

'Well, I used to run seven or eight marathons a year. Then I got injured, but not because of running,' he hastens to reassure me. 'Bit of a funny story, actually!'

I tilt the pen expectantly towards my notepad.

'I was in Bejing on my way to watch the Olympic Opening Ceremony,' he begins, 'and I tripped up a kerb.'

I resist the urge to laugh or to ask whether he was wearing any kind of fancy dress at the time.

'It really hurt, but I left it for a couple of years and it got worse.' He sounds surprised. I, on the other hand, am not but then I am a woman.

'Turned out I'd chipped a piece of cartilage. Eventually I got it all sorted and it's okay now. I haven't actually suffered any injuries from running and my weight is still 15 stone 5 pounds – exactly the same as it was 25 years ago when I ran my first marathon.'

Despite all his races and the fact that he is now aiming to reach the 200 mark, Osy doesn't think he's obsessed with running marathons.

'I won't worry if I don't make it, but I do like the idea of a new achievement. I see marathon running as fun and an excuse to visit new places. Each country is so different – the way they run the races, from China to Russia – yet there is always common ground with the other runners, no matter where you are. Most people are talking about where they are going to run the following weekend.'

'Ah, sluts,' I say, knowledgeably.

'Yes,' says Osy, 'quite! But that's not for me,' he puts in hurriedly, as if feeling the need to defend his position and protect his reputation. 'It's too much rushing around and too expensive.'

So, does he have any advice to give any aspiring 100 Club members out there?

'Not really,' he says, 'but if you do fancy it, you've got to be a person with staying power, endurance.'

And would he recommend the sport to others?

'Absolutely!'

SUMMER SHORTS

Goal setting is one of the best things about running – each person can set his or her goal and achieve it through their own endeavours. In achieving their own goal they are as successful as the race winner who has achieved his by winning. If an individual's goal is to finish the race, better their previous time or raise a sum for charity, they too have achieved what they set out to do. It is no less an achievement and can increase self-esteem and confidence.

And if you enjoy dressing up, take up marathon running!

MILE 8

76 NOT OUT!

Kay O'Regan is 76 and still running marathons!

Catherine (Kay) O'Regan
Born: 1936
102 marathons:
• 1st marathon: 1985 – London
• 100th marathon: 2010 – Dublin
Records:
• Dublin Marathon course records for Women's 60, 65 & 70
  age groups
• Irish Women's Marathon Champion for age 60, 65, 70 & 75
• Irish Women's Marathon record holder for age 60, 65, 70 & 75
• Oldest Female Member of the 100 Marathon Club/Oldest
  Female in UK to Run Over 100 Marathons.

Catherine O'Regan, known as Kay, holds her son Fintan
entirely responsible for her foray into marathon running, nearly
30 years ago.

'It all started when Fintan was studying for his A-levels,' Kay tells me, speaking with a gentle Southern Irish lilt mixed with a few English colloquialisms from her 41 years living in England, where she worked as a PA for the Home Office Probation Services.

'He would go out for a run most evenings as part of his rugby training. Then one night when it was raining, he said he was going to give it a miss and I told him that he couldn't let a drop of rain stop him. He came straight back at me with, "Right, tomorrow night you join me" – which I did, and that's how it all began.'

Schoolgirl error, if you don't mind me saying so, Kay.

'After that, my husband Joe and I started to go out for small runs and then we got up to half-marathon distance and ran our first half marathon in 1985. Then I guess we got ambitious and decided to enter the London Marathon, not expecting to get in but we both got a place.'

Don't you just hate it when that happens?

'So, in 1986 we both ran our first marathon in London and as I crossed the finishing line I said, "Never, ever again!"'

Oh, if only we could hold on to those moments forever and time would stand still.

'The following year we moved house and I ran just a few halves and 10-milers, etc. Then, in 1988 I lost a sister to cervical cancer aged 36, so that year I decided to apply again for London and got in, but Joe didn't so we both decided to run the Dublin Marathon. We did a sponsorship for the Royal Marsden Hospital in London (where my sister had died in the January) and collected around £2,000. After that, I carried on running between three and seven marathons every year until I had just five left to get to 100.'

She makes it sound so easy.

'I wanted my 100th to be in Dublin, as it's my favourite one,' she says.

Now that wouldn't have anything to do with the fact that she holds the course records for the women's 60, 65 and 70 age categories, as well as winning Gold medals for the Irish Marathon Championships held there for the past few years, would it?

Kay acquiesces.

'I'm hoping to get the 75 age category as well,' she confides, 'it's currently held by a Norwegian.'

No probs, Kay. That Norwegian will be run out of town before she laces her trainers!

'Also, unlike London,' she adds, 'we get a nice plaque, as well as money prizes, and I like the course.'

A good course *and* a nice plaque, eh? A little tempting, maybe. Oh, and prize money? So, how much training has she had to do to get to a position where she actually wins money? Just as a matter of interest…

'A typical week when I'm in full training can be anything up to 40–50 miles a week up to two weeks before a marathon, then I taper down up to about two days before the race.'

Interest waning.

'It doesn't take me long to recover from each race. When I first started running marathons, I would ache after racing but haven't done so for years. I usually feel like I haven't run a marathon.'

Really? How does that work, then?

'Maybe I don't work hard enough to ache,' suggests Kay.

Or perhaps her body's just got so used to running 26.2 miles, it's given up the protest?

'I don't rest after a race,' she continues, 'I just carry on as before, doing shorter training runs for maybe a few days, then I get back to normal.'

Interest fully waned. Hurray! No need to pursue temptation to earn money via physical prowess after all. Besides, I'm sure I'd never have enough time to fit in whatever the requisite amount of training might be in order to reach the money-earning potential of running 26.2 miles.

'It varies according to the amount of time I have and my other activities,' says Kay, 'but I try to run at least four times a week, sometimes five, in the summer evenings.'

So, any other activities?

'I used to do a bit of cycling,' she tells me, 'but not any more since we moved into town, as I feel it's too dangerous with the heavy traffic, and Joe and I do modern and set dancing every week. I also do voluntary work at our local Cancer Support Centre.

'Joe and I are also both very involved in our local running club, Slaney Olympic Running Club. We've been members for the past 12 years and organised the first 10K road race for the Club as up to then they did mostly cross-country with no real road races,' she says, honouring the 100 Marathon Club's stated aims to share knowledge and experience.

'Also, from our experience at our old club in England, Runnymede Runners, where we were members for some 13 years, we started both summer and winter handicap road races, which we built up from a steady number of six or seven runners to eventually about 50 runners today. However, in February this year, after the 10K road race – which was in its sixth year and which had been growing in success and popularity year on year – we finally decided to hand over the organising reigns to some of the younger club members although we'll still help out, if needed.

'We also opted out of the committees so as to give a chance to the youngsters. Both Joe and I have been made life members of our club, as everyone over 70 is given that honour. We have about six at the moment. They're all active runners still, but for my sins I'm the only marathon runner, the others have more sense and opt for the shorter distances!'

No comment, Kay.

'I'm also writing a book…'

Yes, well, she had to find something to do to fill all that spare time, I suppose.

'I started it 10 years ago,' she confesses, 'it's about the changes I've seen in my 70+ years.'

I would imagine there are quite a few and I also imagine that it may well take Kay another 10 years to finish off the book if she keeps as busy as she currently is.

She reluctantly agrees.

'Maybe when I stop running marathons,' she says.

Maybe, though it's clear she has no intention of doing that any time soon.

'It's funny,' she muses, 'I certainly didn't set out with the intention of running so many marathons, I just kept on running.'

Didn't she see *Forest Gump*?

'I'm hoping I can still do so for a few more years,' she continues, 'and hope that as long as I can walk, I can run. When people say to me, am I not afraid I'll get a heart attack while out running, my answer is that when my time comes that's the way I would want to go – out for a run! And I tell my running colleagues from our running club that I don't want flowers on my grave either, just their old trainers will do.'

So, as a lady with much marathon experience under her belt, what sort of advice would she pass on to any aspiring 100 Marathon Club members?

'Listen to your body, as we are all different when it comes to training and racing. Some have more tolerance than others, but do your own thing and don't worry about what others are doing. Be happy with your own training and goals.'

Sound advice.

'It's also important to realise that everyone has bad and good years with running and it's the same with individual races. If I have a bad run in any marathon, I just come back again the next year and have a better one usually; I never let it put me off running.'

But even Kay, with her remarkable running record, tells one funny story that as she puts it, 'put me in my place' – 'I was running the Snowdonia Marathon one year and met a guy on the course, who I'd always wanted to meet. He'd done the Seven Sisters Marathon on a Saturday, Snowdonia on Sunday and Dublin on Monday. After he told me what he was doing that year, I said, "I'd heard about you and always wanted to meet you," which pleased him, of course. He then asked how many marathons I'd run, so, at that time I said with pride, "49", and he said "Snap"! Then he said, "But how many marathons have you run in total?" and I said, "I just told you, 49", so he then said, "Oh, I thought you were talking about this year!"'

So, with all the racing, training and other activities Kay does, I guess she doesn't have time to suffer from injuries?

'Touch wood, as they say! I'm lucky, I guess, as I've had few injuries and have never had to pull out of a race that I've entered yet. I hope it continues that way for the future.'

In that case, is it safe to assume she does a proper warm-up before racing?

'I'm afraid I'm not great at doing warm-ups.'

Oh, Kay!

'I always go out slowly,' she says, as if to appease me, which it does a teeny-tiny bit, 'which is my warm-up, and I do a bit of stretching when I finish a race and training runs.'

Oh okay, Kay, not so bad as I at first thought.

And what about nutrition? Does she follow any special diet or anything?

'I eat what I like and never eat during a race, apart from sucking the odd wine gum. I also only ever drink water during a race as energy drinks and gels make me sick.'

Sounds like a good reason to avoid them.

'After a marathon I'm never very hungry so I eat a light dinner and then go back to normal dinners the next day. I never eat pasta, as I don't like it.'

Fair enough, it's not everyone's plate of potatoes.

I know Fintan is responsible for getting Kay started on the marathon pathway, but is there anyone else who's influenced or inspired her?

'Not really, but I do admire Paula Radcliffe and Sonia O'Sulllivan, who I've met and spoken with, but I can't say they influenced me as I had run many marathons before they came on the scene.'

Nice answer, but I'm still wondering what motivates her to keep on running the distance.

'I don't know, really. I prefer the longer distances, I guess, as I feel I don't have to work as hard as at the shorter distances.'

Ah, the logic of the Irish.

'Whereas Joe,' she continues, as if she's now given the matter serious consideration, 'he ran 26 marathons, then decided to stick with the shorter distances, such as half marathons, 10-milers, etc. Of course, we both loved to travel and usually planned a holiday around a marathon.'

And there you have it – running to travel or travelling to run. One seems inextricably linked to the other, at least as far as members of the 100 Marathon Club are concerned.

Certainly for Kay and Joe running has taken them all over the world, although not everywhere has left Kay with the fondest of marathon memories.

'The humidity in Athens was awful,' she recalls, 'and we had to run in the middle of the road with two lanes of traffic both sides of us. The fumes from the vehicles, as well as the humidity almost choked us. But the worst weather conditions I've ever run in were in Florence. It was very cold, wet, sleety and windy.

Not only that, but apart from the start (which was on a main road), most of the course was run along narrow streets, with twists and turns and cobbled stones.'

But it's Florence, Kay – that's how it is, although I accept you might not necessarily associate the bad weather with the place.

She has slightly fonder memories of Germany, though.

'Joe and I ran the Berlin Marathon for the first time 20 years ago,' says Kay, 'and it felt easy. Then I ran it again in 2010 with a friend. By then it was very crowded, with 42,000 runners, but it was still an easy course apart from being very wet and cold. I found it the easiest marathon I had done in a while.'

She has even run in Australia.

'I ran my PB [Personal Best] of 3 hours 35 minutes in the Melbourne Marathon in 1993, when I was 57,' she tells me, rightfully proud. And that reminds me of something I've scarcely bothered to mention. This woman is 76 years old. As such, she is the oldest female member of the 100 Marathon Club, which means that, potentially, she is the oldest female in the entire world to have run over 100 marathons.

'I don't know the age of the oldest woman to have completed 100 marathons,' concedes Kay. 'I would have thought there may be others older than myself, as usually older women from countries like Norway and Sweden still run good marathon times, especially around the world. I tried to look it up on the Net but was unsuccessful.'

You and me both, Kay!

Regardless of that, she is 76 years old and still running marathons. I'm not putting an exclamation mark because that statement is too remarkable for just one and it's considered bad form in literary circles to use more than one. Oh, sod it – Kay O'Regan is 76 years old and still running marathons!!!

Perhaps more amazing, though is the fact that she's not slowing down – far from it. As recently as June 2011, she knocked a staggering three minutes off her Personal Best! And she clearly has no intention of quitting, although she does talk about cutting down – but only in a very Irish way.

'I don't intend to do as many as I have been doing in the past few years, just the odd one so I may just come down to halves and shorter distances from next year, hopefully. For the record, I have run a marathon back-to-back as they say – that is, two marathons in a week, one on a Sunday and the next one the following Sunday, and twice I have run a better time in the second marathon in a week. Hopefully, I would like to carry on running for a few more years or for as long as I can walk, as to date, I don't have any plans to retire from running. For instance this morning, Thursday, 17 February 2011, a friend and I ran 17 miles.

'I am now in training for my next marathon in Connemara on April 10, then Belfast in May, Cork in June, maybe one in September abroad but not yet booked, Dublin in October and the French Riviera in November – that is one I have not run yet. I also hope to race some halves, 10-milers and a Kilomarathon here in Ireland, in August.'

I'm assuming a 'Kilomarathon' is 26.2 kilometres as opposed to miles?

'That's right,' confirms Kay. 'It's a fairly new distance, which is springing up around Ireland and the UK. Our first one here was last year on a tough hilly course so this year they have changed it to an easier route, we're told. It's held in Moon, County Kildare, so Joe and myself are hopefully running that again in August. All the proceeds go to the children's hospital. We won't run any of the highly priced private races,' she adds, 'just the charity and club races.'

As I've said, no intention of giving up.

And, ahem, does she think she is obsessed with running marathons?

'I don't think so. As I say to people when they ask why I run – I don't really know, it's just something that I do. Some people play bingo, I run!'

What about other people, how do they react when they know she has run over 100 marathons?

'They tell me I'm great, marvellous, an inspiration to others, etc. They say they could not do it, not even run for a bus, so my answer is neither could I do that 27 years ago. You could not just go out and run a marathon or any other race, you have to start at the beginning: walk and jog, and build it up gradually.'

Just as Kay did when she was 50, until 25 years later she'd run 100 and became a member of the 100 Marathon Club.

Oh, and by the way: after 25 years of marathon running, Kay finally got her own back on her son.

'Fintan ran his first marathon with me at Dublin in 2010 in honour of my 100th marathon,' she says, proudly. 'Joe also ran, making a comeback after 10 years, and his 60-year-old niece also ran her debut marathon.'

It's a family affair!

'Fintan was 50,' Kay suddenly adds, as if it's only just occurred to her, 'the same age I was when I ran my first marathon.'

Now that's just perfect. Only 99 to go, Fintan!

SUMMER SHORTS

You're never too old to start or continue running marathons, provided you're in good health. A general check-up with your GP before taking up running is advisable if you are new to sport – whatever your age. It is also advisable to do a warm-up and warm-down, including gentle stretching, before and after running and to build up the miles slowly, starting with a run/walk programme. Advice can be found in most good running magazines, on running websites and from your local running or athletics club or gym.

Revenge is a dish never sweeter than when served on a loved one or close relative!

MILE 9

SO, HOW FAR IS A
WHEELCHAIR MARATHON?

I n 1987 Royal Navy clearance diver, Mike Marten, broke his
neck. Four years later, he completed his first marathon.

MIKE MARTEN
Born: 1958
141 marathons:
• 1st marathon: 1993 – Berlin
• 100th marathon: 2005 – Belfast

The first time I met Mike Marten it was two o'clock in the
morning and he had luminous green plaits and was wearing a
matching shiny-plastic, hippy-style hat. On his lap he carried
a box and inside was a glistening silver trophy with his name
on it following his victory in the Wheelchair Marathon in
Calvia, Mallorca.

And he tells me he's rubbish at marathon racing!

Perhaps I should just clarify at this point that Mike is not
really a cross-dresser and he didn't used to be called Michelle

either, although he was once married to a sailor. The wig and the hat were merely remnants of Running Crazy's after-race party.

Remove the wig and the hippy hat and instead picture, if you will, a better-looking version of Oscar-winning actor Jack Nicholson (less leprechaun, more laddish, less lean lips, more sculpted mouth, and better, much better-behaved eyebrows). Now put him in a wheelchair.

And there you have him, Mike Marten – wheelchair athlete and wit extraordinaire!

Born in 1958, Mike joined the Royal Navy as a clearance diver at just 19 years old. Ten years later, he was sent to the South of France on a big NATO exercise.

'We'd been there for a week and had been working hard,' he says, charismatic Nicholson grin in place, brown eyes twinkling so I'm not entirely sure whether he's serious or not about the hard work. 'It was our first day off, and me and some others decided to go scuba diving in the morning and water skiing in the afternoon.'

Ah, a day of rest then.

'The scuba diving had been great and then we went on to the water skiing…'

But this was water skiing with a difference – there was no boat. Instead, an overhead moving cable followed a course around the water. Attached to it at equal distances apart are ropes and attached to the lower end of each rope a handle. The skier stands on a ramp, his feet attached to his skis. When ready, he gives the nod to the operator. The operator catches the next rope to come round and passes the handle to the skier. There is then a fairly violent jerk as the rope becomes taut and takes the skier round the course.

Now when Mike was originally describing this to me I must confess I had some difficulty in picturing it, so he helpfully sent me some videos from YouTube with the message, 'A picture paints a thousand words.'

Indeed it does. For someone who considers riding her bike in a properly marked cycle lane some ten feet away from the road to be an extreme sport (so do pedestrians sharing the pathway but that's another matter), it was up there with climbing to the top of Mount Everest without oxygen before bungee jumping off the top, without a bungee.

'I'd been round the course once and fallen off a number of times,' says Fearless Mike, 'but decided to have a second go, anyway.'

However, unbeknown to him, a couple of expert water skiers had turned up while he'd been walking back to the start and the speed at which the cable was moving round the course had been increased in line with their ability. Unfortunately, the operator assumed Mike was with the expert skiers and didn't bring the speed back down so when he was passed the handle, there was no smooth transition from the ramp on to his feet, instead he was jerked so violently as the rope tautened that he fell head-first straight into the water, his skis remaining exactly where they were.

'It was like some kind of comedy set-up,' he says.

The force of Mike hitting his head in water that was at that point only thigh-deep could have only one consequence – he broke his neck.

'I was face down in the water and couldn't move, so I had to hold my breath while I waited to be rescued. My friends waded out to me as quickly as they could, but I still gave them a load of abuse for taking so long to reach me!' he tells me, grinning ruefully.

'They knew straightaway that I'd broken my neck, though of course they didn't say anything to me. They didn't need to, I knew anyway. I don't know how I knew, I just did although my friends assumed I didn't.

'Normally, you wouldn't move someone in those circumstances,' he goes on, 'but they had no choice but to turn me over so I could breathe and to get me back on to land. My first thoughts were that

I was paralysed and all the implications of that, and I felt sorry for my wife but within 20 minutes, my brain had buried all of that and all I thought about was how I was going to get better. Within 30 minutes, I was in the ambulance telling my mates to get a camera and take a picture ready for the time when we would look back and laugh!'

Mike and I take a moment to marvel at the brain's ability to shut out what it knows can't be coped with until a time when it can.

'Amazingly, the Navy got my wife and mother down to the South of France within 24 hours of the accident happening.'

He was later taken to Odstock, near Salisbury, as that was the nearest hospital to his home with a spinal unit.

'As luck would have it, the hospital had just acquired a brand new spinal unit,' he recalls, 'and the care there was wonderful.'

He spent the first three months looking at the ceiling with traction on his head. Then about two months into this period, he was having a session of physiotherapy.

'When the nurse finished, she asked me if I was okay and I told her I didn't feel very well. My heart was thumping hard in my chest. She practically ran out of the curtains.

'Next thing I knew, I was waking up and there was this bloke on top of me banging on my chest. He told me later that they'd lost me for a couple of seconds but then I came back. I was so lucky – if it had happened anywhere but in hospital, I would have died and I wouldn't have known anything about it.'

The accident happened on 13 June 1987 and Mike was in hospital for a year. A year later, he left the Navy and a little over a year after that, his wife left him.

'She was a Wren,' he tells me, 'or a sailor as they're now known,' he adds with a wry grin, 'but I can never bring myself to tell people I was once married to a sailor!'

No, but I can!

'We'd been married four years when the accident happened,' he continues. 'After the accident, we moved to a bungalow.'

It's the same bungalow where Mike lives now.

'Poor girl,' he says with feeling and it is not the only time he says this during the interview. 'She'd left the WRNS by then and was working full time, as well as driving to see me on Wednesdays and at weekends at the hospital, and realising she had to keep my spirits up. At the same time she was being told to get the house up and running on her own for when I eventually came home. She was under immense pressure.

'When she said she wanted a divorce, of course I was very upset but it was only relatively so. I think that's because the accident had taken me so low, rock bottom, the divorce was somewhere above that in terms of pain.'

Certainly, one of the hardest things he had to come to terms with was no longer being physically active.

'I'd boxed from the age of 13 to 23, had run to keep fit for that and for the Navy and my job, and had always prided myself on being physically fit. After the accident, my pride was injured and I felt I was weak and pathetic. Ever since the accident, I've worn a metaphorical bullet-proof vest to protect myself.'

And who can blame him?

While he was upset and not happy about the divorce, he is certain it was the right decision for them both: 'We may otherwise have ended up hating each other – as it is, we have remained friends.

'Being left on my own meant I suddenly had to cope with everything myself, but I feel it's made me far more capable than I would otherwise have been if I'd had someone to do everything for me. At first, I had a twilight nurse. She would come in some time between 9 and 11pm, but couldn't say exactly when. I didn't want to be in as early as 9pm, so I made myself do everything for myself and got rid of the nurse.

'It sounds weird, I know,' he continues, 'but it's been the little things that have given me greatest satisfaction, such as tying shoelaces. I know it's nothing for most people, but for me I find immense satisfaction from succeeding in such an achievement. It's the same with the marathons and if I hadn't been on my own, I'd never have done what I have done.'

He likens it to climbing hills.

'If you climb ten hills, you feel pretty darn pleased with yourself. Every day I have to do things that are difficult, a challenge. Each one I do is like climbing one of those hills and I feel a sense of fulfilment, which in turn makes me feel happy. In some ways it's ironic that my disability has enabled me to feel that sense of fulfilment and happiness every single day, which enriches my life whereas other people only get to feel it occasionally.'

2012 will mark Mike's 25th anniversary of being in a wheelchair. By then, he will have spent a longer portion of his life in a chair than out of it.

'I celebrate every five years with a party,' he tells me, 'but next year will be an extra-big one!'

Being the positive type of person that he is, he has used his experience to help others and every three months he goes to Odstock hospital to talk to newly injured paraplegics about sex and relationship issues.

'I tell them what they can expect. I've tried over the years to get them to join in the discussion, ask questions, etc., but this doesn't work as they are too new to the situation – they are in a roomful of strangers and too embarrassed to ask what they really want to know, so I just tell it to them like it is and all I have learned over the years.

'One of the other things I tell them,' he goes on, 'is to get as much help as possible outside of the relationship, then if the other person decides they want to help you themselves, they will offer. This puts no pressure then on the relationship and prevents the other person feeling they have to do it – they have enough to cope with as it is.'

There are two things Mike reckons every person has to deal with when they first go home after becoming a paraplegic: adapting and accepting.

'They both have to happen,' he says, 'but which one leads to the other, I'm still not sure.'

As well as giving talks at Odstock, he also works occasionally with the Appeals Tribunal Service.

'There is a panel of three,' he explains. 'We get the papers for someone who has claimed but been refused Disability Living Allowance. Hopefully the person attends the Tribunal, which allows us to get additional information and then the Tribunal collectively make a decision about the case.'

Apart from climbing at least ten hills a day, giving talks at Odstock and assisting the Appeals Tribunal Service, he also finds time to take part in marathons, not only at home in the UK, but also abroad. When running abroad, he will occasionally travel with an organised group, but 90 per cent of the time he organises himself and travels on his own.

'It's not difficult,' he assures me. 'I use my race chair as my trolley, place my bag on top of it and push it in front of me with a belt attached to the chair so it can't run away from me on a slope! Airlines are happy to take it in the hold and people are generally helpful, if I ask for assistance.

'The only time I encounter any problems is in France. For some reason the taxi drivers there don't want to push down the back seat so I can get the racing chair in. They tell me it isn't possible, even though I know it is, as I've never had a problem anywhere else. Basically, they just don't want to know. The worst one was a driver in Paris – I actually had a stand-up/sit-down row with him!

'Hotels are generally helpful – they'll put me in a disabled room – but sometimes I have problems with the bathroom door being wide enough for me to get my chair through. It's vital for me to get in and out of the bathroom as I need to empty my bag. Occasionally, when that hasn't been possible, I have been known to put the bag inside my rucksack and find a garden somewhere to empty it, without getting arrested – so far!'

I want to say I am shocked, but frankly, sitting there in the perfect English summer sunshine in Mike's back garden, sipping coffee that he has made in his adapted kitchen and brought out to me, I merely consider him practical.

So, how did he get started with the marathon lark?

Mike laughs.

'A girlfriend told me there was no way I could complete the Portsmouth Half Marathon, which meant I had to do it.'

Of course it did. And of course, he *did*.

'I did it in an ordinary wheelchair and completed it in 6 hours. I was last – the person second to last finished 3 hours ahead of me,' he tells me, with a candid grin.

But he wasn't put off having another go. Oh no, he's made of far sterner stuff.

'I did it again a year later – this time in 5 hours 30 minutes. Some other runners saw me and decided to raise some money to help me buy a racing wheelchair. They donated £750 and the Portsmouth Round Table donated the same amount. I took part in the Portsmouth Half for a third consecutive year but this time did it in my new racing wheelchair and completed it in 1 hour 25 minutes.'

Just shows what the right equipment can do!

'From there,' he continues, 'the next step was naturally to try a full marathon, which I did in Berlin, in 1993.'

After that, competing in marathons became pretty much a way of life for Mike. So much so, he wasn't even sure when he completed his 100th.

'I think it was probably in 2007 – I had actually completed 121 marathons at that stage and had happily skipped right through the 100-mark without even knowing it,' he says, offering up a grin that is not only infectious but so Jack Nicholson it's hard to believe he isn't related in some way.

'I'm not,' he assures me, 'but if I had a pound for every person who thinks I am, I'd be a wealthy man!'

Maybe one day the real Jack Nicholson will be offered the starring role in a movie about, oh, say a guy in a wheelchair, who takes part in marathons and Mike will be able to play his body double when it comes to whipping the wheelchair up hills and round difficult bends!

So, I take it there must be a knack to using a racing chair on courses designed with probably no real consideration for wheelchair users?

'Definitely,' he affirms. 'For example, if there's a very steep hill to go up, the only way to get up it sometimes is to turn the chair round and go up backwards!'

But he's never had any actual training in using his racing chair, instead learning through his own experiences and talking to others.

'I'd always found braking hard could be a problem, then another wheelchair racer told me to use my gloved hands on the back wheels to slow the chair down. Since then, I haven't had any problems.'

With regard to punctures, Mike says he's been pretty lucky.

'I've only had about six or seven punctures, although I did once have two going round the same roundabout! I had a puncture repair outfit for the first one and some guys at the side of the road helped me repair it, tipping the chair on its side and fixing it for me. Off I went, only to find another puncture a few feet further on – only now, of course, I had nothing to fix it with! So these same guys went off and came back with some Sellotape and managed to get it going again somehow, but it made the rest of the race much harder than it needed to be.

'These days,' he adds with a grin, 'I take the easy way out. I carry a repair outfit and a spare inner tube, and get a taxi to take the punctured tyre to the nearest cycle repair shop and bring it back and pay whatever the fare is!'

To date, Mike has completed 141 marathons, averaging eight or nine each year.

'I didn't set out with the intention of doing so many,' he explains, taking a sip of coffee. 'Then in 1998 I lost a very good friend,' he adds slowly, the memory clearly still etched in his mind and heart. 'His funeral was one of the darkest days of my life. I decided I wanted to complete a marathon a month to celebrate being alive and in each of the races I wore a T-shirt commemorating my lost friend.' He pauses, his furrowed brow clears and then he smiles again. 'Then I guess I got the bug!'

Having got the bug, I wonder whether over the years, he's developed any kind of pre-race routine?

'No, not really,' he says, after thinking about this for a moment. 'I'm often too nervous to eat breakfast because I'm worried about finding someone to help me into my racing chair. Then I'm a little worried about getting to the start line. However, as soon as I'm at the start line, I'm completely relaxed and can often be seen munching a Snickers bar...' he pauses, 'or two!'

Having travelled pretty much all over the world in pursuit of marathons, does he have a favourite?

'Luxor in Egypt,' he says immediately, a smile lighting up his face. 'It starts over on the West Bank in the Valley of the Kings, at the foot of the Hatshepsuit Temple. The weather is gorgeous. The roads are wide and quiet, and the course has some undulations and also some long flat bits; the gangs of children love to run along with you.'

Gangs of children seem to be a common theme when it

comes to Mike and marathons – the same thing happened in Calvia, when he was joined by about 20 local children, who ran the last 200 metres with him to the finishing line. His smile widens when I remind him of this.

'Oh yes,' he says, 'that was really special. I couldn't believe it when all these kids came running over and started running alongside me – it was wonderful.'

And what was his least favourite race?

'Nashville, Tennessee used to be pretty darned hilly. Five or six years ago they re-branded it, proclaiming proudly they had creatively removed five miles of hills. As far as I'm concerned, that just leaves another 20 miles to get rid of!

'Then there's Orange County in California. That has an 11-mile continuous incline – I'll do that just the once, I think.'

Is there an easiest marathon?

'If there is,' he proclaims, without a moment's hesitation, 'it's one I haven't done yet!'

I wonder if the weather has much of an effect on his ability to race well and if he has special wet and dry tyres as they do in Formula One.

'No, just one set does the lot,' he says, with a kindly chuckle as if he thinks the question is funny in some way (personally, I don't get it), 'although they do have pressure tyres set at around 110 PSI – pounds per square inch – for the likes of me, and 150-170 PSI for elite racers.'

Er… Okay.

'The average car has around 34/35 PSI,' he adds helpfully, noting no doubt the glazed look of a non mechanically-minded female before him.

'As for weather generally,' he continues, 'anyone who has completed a number of marathons will have come across cold, hot and wet conditions. I've been pulled out twice due to hypothermia, once in Seville and once in Denver.

'It wasn't just me who was pulled out,' he adds, as if feeling the need to defend himself. 'Those two times are the only times I've cried after not completing the marathon. I don't know why I cried, I think it must have been because of the hypothermia rather than because I didn't finish, as I've not finished in about 20 races for various reasons and never cried then.

'I felt I had let myself down in those two races and when I was swept up by the sweeper bus [a bus that picks up competitors who won't finish in the maximum time allowed for the race], another guy in a wheelchair was in there and when he saw me later, he said, "I remember you, you're the guy who cried!"

'That made me furious! I saw it as reference to what I considered a huge weakness on my part, but which realistically, I can only put down to the hypothermia eliciting some kind of emotional response in me.

'Another time I did the Dublin Marathon when it was so cold the *Dublin Times* described it as "The Marathon of Suffering" and I also completed the Phoenix, Arizona Marathon, which took place on its coldest morning for 22 years.

'I also did the Chicago a couple of years back, when it was so hot that after two hours the organisers decided to stop anyone not at the halfway point. Police were in position, shutting off the course and directing all runners to a shortcut to the finish. Fortunately [yes, Mike really did say that], I had already passed that point and was allowed to finish. One runner died, 40 were hospitalised and just under 400 were treated for heatstroke at the end of the race.'

Dear Lord!

'If I get too hot when I'm racing,' he explains, 'I try to get people to pour water over me at the water stations but sometimes, especially in non-English speaking countries, it's difficult to make them understand exactly what I want, as they just assume I want a drink. So then I have to mime at them and when they eventually get it, they all run at me and start pouring bottles of water all over my head and I end up getting drenched!

'They mean well though,' he adds – generously, in my opinion. 'But the worst weather occurred in a huge wheelchair-only marathon in Switzerland, around Lake Sempach. Just prior to the start a huge thunder and lightening storm erupted. The torrential rain was pouring down the steep hillside, bringing small trees, bushes and debris onto the road, and also causing streams of water to pour across the course. Great fun – not!'

It occurs to me at this point that anyone contemplating entering an overseas race would do well to check the entry list first and if Mike's name is on it, find somewhere else to run.

So, does he think he is obsessed with running marathons?

'No. They are a hugely positive part of my life but they are not an obsession,' he insists.

And what do other people think?

'They are often very complimentary but sometimes they're not sure whether to believe me or not and then they ask questions like, "So how long is a wheelchair marathon?" – as if they expect me to say, "Oh, a wheelchair marathon is two miles long."'

How about injuries?

'I've been very lucky with injuries, I rarely suffer from them.'

Is that because he does a warm-up and warm-down?

'Sure,' he agrees. 'I start slowly – that is my warm-up; I continue slowly – that is my warm-down.'

Okay, funny guy, do you ache after racing, then?

'Only when I breathe!'

Good! How about full recovery – how long before you're ready to start training again?

'I usually give myself a full week unless it's the winter, in which case it could be a month or two. Actually, I pretty much skip training outside in my racing chair for the entire winter. Guess I'm just a soft, lousy, warm-weather trainer!'

I can't tell whether he's joking or not, but regardless of this it is clear that when he does train, his regime is well thought-out.

'I do a lot of light-dumbbell workouts at home. Light weight, high reps. I have very limited function in my hands so I designed a strap that holds the dumbbells in place.

'Some time after the accident, I had an operation on my left arm so I could bend and grip with my fingers,' he tells me, and then proceeds to demonstrate by giving me a Chinese burn – no, not really! He just gently grips my wrist. His hand gives a normal pressured grip, which he says he couldn't do before.

'They offered me the same op on the other arm,' he goes on, 'but I declined. I felt it was better for me to have one hand that I can grip with, and one hand with straight fingers which I can't bend, but can slip easily into a pocket or scoop stuff up off the floor. I feel that together they make a good pair with differing abilities.'

It seems a bit daft asking a man like Mike if he has any funny stories – it's a bit like asking the Queen whether she's travelled much.

He shakes his head. This time I know he's kidding.

'How long's the book?' he asks.

Undoubtedly not long enough.

'Just give me one,' I suggest.

He thinks for a moment.

'Okay,' he starts, 'here's one for you...'

I sit back in anticipation.

'I was racing in Portugal when a runner fell on top of me and broke my racing chair in half. Him and his mate dragged me and the two halves of my chair to the side of the road and then carried on running.'

I gasp. I mean, that's like a driver knocking someone down in their car, getting out and placing them on the side of the road so they don't get run over again and then driving off! However, I don't have time to dwell on this as Mike is continuing with his story.

'A policeman on his motorbike arrived a short while later. He spoke no English, I spoke no Portuguese. He indicated I should stand up. I tried to explain I couldn't because I had a broken neck. He spoke into his radio. Before I could blink an eyelid, an ambulance was racing with blue-lights and two-tones towards me. They put me on a stretcher and raced with me back to the first aid tent, where I was stripped naked so they could inspect my body for unseen injuries.'

I am horrified. I mean, why would they do that?

'They thought I meant I'd broken my neck in the race,' Mike explains. 'That's why they reacted so quickly. Of course I couldn't speak the language so couldn't explain what I really meant!'

I strongly suspect the race organisers gave their race insurance policy just as much careful scrutiny as the medics gave Mike.

'I have never been so embarrassed in all my bloody life!' he tells me.

I can well imagine. Mike is clearly a proud man, with the emphasis firmly on both those words. So, what motivates him to keep on doing marathons and does he have an ultimate goal?

He puts his head on one side and considers the question, then gives me that now-familiar, charismatic smile.

'I guess 200 is a nice round number.'

I nod in ready agreement and hesitate to suggest the same could be said of 300, 400, 500…

How about lucky charms? Does he carry any with him when he's racing?

He shakes his head. 'No lucky charms,' he tells me. 'But seeing as I have completed all these races and have hardly ever beaten another wheelchair racer, I'm on the lookout for a large wooden spoon to strap to my chair. I'm rubbish,' he tells me for a second time, without a trace of false modesty.

But whether he's rubbish or not (and take it from me, he isn't), Mike doesn't care, because for him the marathon is not about winning trophies or medals and it's not about totting up the numbers either. His motivation comes from something entirely different, something that perhaps only someone who has had an experience like his can properly understand and appreciate; someone who, having had such an experience, is still without a shadow of a doubt much the man he has always been.

'I get quite a lot of self-respect each time I complete a marathon,' he says. 'There are nearly always tough parts in the race that require you to dig deep. It is always a boost to discover the determination is still there.'

For a man who has to climb hills, if not mountains, every day of his life to want to seek other means to continually test his own mettle pretty much sums up the man that is Mike Marten – wooden spoon and tissues included.

SUMMER SHORTS

Sport is a great equaliser, offering the same challenge to able and disabled athletes alike. It therefore offers the same rewards – the same feelings of achievement and satisfaction that come only through one's own endeavours. A marathon is a test of not just physical but mental strength. As such, it offers the greatest satisfaction of all.

If you're in a marathon and need tissues, look for a man in a wheelchair.

MILE 10

LONG GRASS AND DIRTY CARS

Dave Moles finds guiding a blind runner round a marathon particularly rewarding.

DAVE MOLES
Born: 1953
376 marathons:
• 1st marathon: 1981 – Canvey Island
• 100th marathon: 2003 – Abingdon

When I ask 58-year-old Dave Moles, banker-turned-postie (following voluntary redundancy in 2005), what made him start running marathons, he replies: 'I saw the first London Marathon on the television and thought I wouldn't mind having a go at that.' Now I begin to suspect there is something seriously wrong with me.

I mean, almost half the people featured in this book have given me the same answer to that question, so why, apart from that one time from the safety of a hospital bed, have I never watched the London Marathon and wanted to be a part of it?

Maybe it's simply because I don't like crowds. I remember once going to watch the Christmas lights being turned on in Oxford Street when I stood near the back of an ever-deepening throng, close to a major department store. Suddenly they started to move as one, like a giant tidal wave, pushing me backwards towards the store's plate-glass window. Next to me a mother with a baby started shouting: she, too was being forced back towards the window and had begun to fear the strength of that crowd would push her and her baby through the glass. It was a very scary moment, which luckily passed without damage, but did nothing to dispel my dislike of crowds.

Yes, that must be it. There is nothing wrong with me. Phew!

And so, Dave… Now Dave is the sort of man who isn't afraid to 'fess up when asked whether he thinks he might be obsessed with running marathons.

'No doubt about it! I get in a terrible state if I'm stuck at home on a Sunday without a marathon – I start doing daft things, like cleaning the car or mowing the lawn.'

Heaven forbid!

And what about other people – how do they react when they know he has run over 100 marathons?

'For some reason their first question always seems to be, "Have you ever run New York?", followed by questions about the state of my knees.'

And has he? Run New York, I mean.

'Yes, I got New York ticked off in 2010.'

Probably felt obliged to do it.

And how *are* his knees?

'Touch wood, the knees are fine!'

Good, I'm very pleased to hear it. Shame about the handful of splinters, though.

It would seem Dave isn't the only member of his family who is none too keen on staying home on a weekend, though. His wife Janet, while not a runner herself, loves going to marathons, he tells me.

'Janet enjoys meeting up with the many friends we have made on the circuit and loves travelling to all the venues, especially new places we have never been to before. She has always said she will not let me retire.'

Now I happen to know this is true: it is not just a husband out of tune with his wife, believing what he wants to believe because it suits him. Not that I'm saying that's what husbands do, I'm just *saying*, that's all. How do I know this to be true? (The bit about Janet, not about the husbands, that is.) Because I met Janet when I was in Malta. Admittedly it was at the back of a wine bar and there may have been a teeny-tiny bit of imbibing going on, but from her sparkling blue eyes, lightly flushed cheeks and overall happy, smiling demeanour, there was no doubt in my mind that here was a lady who was happy with her lot and wouldn't have wanted to be anywhere else.

'I really do enjoy it,' she tells me, 'we've made so many friends through the marathon running.'

And then Dave removes the gun from her head... Just kidding!

I also happen to know that the rest of the 100 Marathon Club are happy and appreciative to have Janet along with them on their trips, because she is a constant source of support not only to her husband, but also to the rest of them, looking after kit while they run, offering solace and cheer as necessary and generally being there to encourage them in their endeavours.

As fellow 100 Club member, Gina Little, said to me in Malta, 'It would be nice if you gave her a mention in the book because people like her make such a difference and it's really good to have them along.'

Of course Janet is not the only non-running spouse to offer support in this way. I also met Julie Wing and her husband Steve in Malta. In this case it is Julie who is the runner, while Steve offers the support.

As for Dave and Janet's kids, though, according to him: 'They just don't get it! Steve is 30 now and Louise is 26, and both of them are more into the arts and have no interest in active sport.'

Ah well, there's plenty of time yet, Dave. Indeed, I would suggest that the majority of serial marathon runners take up the sport in their 40s – I rather suspect it's become part of the mid-life crisis ritual. Waking up every morning, joints stiffer than the previous day and coming face-to-face with your mother or father in the mirror usually does the trick.

Not, of course, that this is true for Dave. He was a mere puppy of 28 when he ran his first marathon in Canvey Island, in 1981.

So, was it then that he decided to go for 100+?

'Not at all! In the beginning I was quite happy just running one marathon a year.'

How very sensible. So, what went wrong?

'A member of my local running club was trying to run 100 marathons and every week I would run with him on club nights and he would tell me about the adventures he had had the previous weekend.'

Enid Blyton's *Famous Five* stories leap unbidden into my mind and present Dave and his merry marathon gang deviating off the racecourse to solve the mystery of the disappearing goat or to catch the marathon medallion thief, rounding off their boyish adventure with ham rolls and lashings of ginger beer.

'This started to get me interested,' says Dave, oblivious, probably fortunately, to the images in my head of him wearing schoolboy grey, flannel shorts and an off-white, short-sleeved cotton shirt, 'and was about the same time as my kids left home to go to university, so I had more time on my hands. The rest is history.'

Indeed it is, Dave.

So, having established earlier that London was responsible for his initial interest in the sport and an irresponsible fellow club runner lured him with tales of adventure and derring-do, I wonder what it is that has turned him into someone who has run nearly 400 marathons and is still motivated enough to carry on running – apart from his wife refusing to let him stop, that is.

'I don't really know,' he says by way of an answer. 'I just get a buzz from completing them, going to places I would never have gone to otherwise, trying to complete challenges – for example, trying to complete every marathon in the UK and then keeping it going every time a new one comes along, or trying to run marathons in as many different counties as possible.'

Interestingly, Dave's progression has been quite erratic. He ran his first marathon in 1981 at Canvey Island and did only 13 more over the ensuing 18 years. But then, between 1999 and 2003, the numbers suddenly surged and he ran 75 marathons in just four years to reach his century in Abingdon which he ran alongside fellow 100 Club member John Dawson. Since then the number has continued to surge, having reached 376 by the time I met him in Malta, in February 2011.

'I can't really explain the surge in numbers,' says Dave. 'I was slowly getting more into it, then all of a sudden, bang, and I was hooked – I hated going a weekend without one. Ideally I would run one every week, but sometimes you just can't find one, or there are family commitments or sickness, etc., which prevent you running. These days I average around 40+ a year.'

Presumably, given the number of marathons run and the length of time Dave has been running them, he must have his pre-race routine all worked out?

'Unfortunately, as the logistics of every race are different, it's impossible to have a routine,' he tells me. 'I might be camping in a field, staying in a hotel, travelling on race day or through the night; it might be an early start, a late start or a night start...'

Okay, I get it! They are all different.

What about lucky charms or superstitions then?

'I don't have any lucky charms,' he says, 'although I always have a small jar of Vaseline with me.

'As for superstitions, I would never wear a race T-shirt or buy a race souvenir until after I had finished the marathon. Likewise, I am often asked during a race what number it is today. I will never tell them what number it is, just how many I have completed already. Never count your chickens.'

A cautious man, then... And so does this adventurous-cautious man have any marathons he would care to recommend or advise avoiding?

'Snowdonia is my favourite marathon,' he answers straightaway. 'The scenery is stunning! There are some candidates I would recommend are best avoided, but I wouldn't like to name them. It seems a bit ungrateful when someone has put on an event for you to give them the title of Least Favourite Marathon.'

Fair comment for it's no mean feat putting together any sort of race. It takes months to organise, excessive energy to carry it through and arithmetical agility to sort out all the results afterwards.

'The most unusual marathon I've ever run in has got to be the Greenwich Foot Tunnel. Run in a tiny foot tunnel under the Thames in the middle of the night, with only white wall tiles to look at for 26.2miles. That was weird!'

Now the Famous Five would love that!

'My worst memory is of getting caught in sandstorms at Fleetwood during the Blackpool Marathon. It really stung the exposed skin, and turned my eyes red and sore and they were full of sand.'

'Not so keen on that one,' says Anne (she was the wimpy one of the Famous Five, by the way – in case you're under 40 and/or have never read an Enid Blyton book in your life).

'My vote for the hardest road marathon, I think, goes to Great Langdale in the Lake District. They advertise it as the World's Toughest Marathon. I don't know about that, but it's the toughest I've done. The easiest is London, because it's as flat as a pancake,' continues Dave.

Ooh, I love pancakes! They come second only to marshmallows. Preferably with lemon juice and brown sugar, although I did once have some with stewed apple and warmed caramel sauce that were pretty tip-top. Actually, they may have been crêpes. Whatever, they were definitely yummy.

So, Dave, diet. Anything special you'd recommend (apart from ham rolls and ginger beer, that is)?

'Ideally, I like cereal and toast a couple of hours before a race. Afterwards, sometimes I'm absolutely ravenous and eat anything I can lay my hands on, other times I have no appetite and can't face anything to eat for a couple of hours.'

And how about clothes, any favourites for running in?

'I always wear Union Jack shorts when running abroad.'

So, a patriot – how very lovely!

Now, let's talk about the more serious stuff. How about training?

'I don't train.'

Oh, okay then. Warming up/down?

'What's that?'

Er, right!

Do you ache after racing?

'Not from the racing as long as I move about, but I can suffer if I have a really long drive home straight after the marathon.'

Well, you see, Dave, it's like this: if you were to do a wee bit of the warming-down stuff (aka stretching) after the race, you might find the drive home doesn't have quite such an ill effect. Just a suggestion…

I hardly dare mention injuries, but then again…

'Touch wood, I've never had a running injury.'

Thousands of splinters, though.

But, wait! A man who does no training, no warming up or warming down and has never suffered an injury? Bring him in for scientific examination immediately. No wonder he doesn't bother with good luck charms.

There is one thing in particular I want to talk about with Dave, however, and that is the guiding he does with fellow 100 Club member Blind Paul (Watts).

'I have seen other blind runners who run with a hand on the shoulder of the guide and others who use a rope,' says Dave, 'but Paul prefers to be guided using a rubber dog pull.'

'Guiding varies – it can be fairly easy on a low-key event on country lanes with not many runners. In contrast, if you have a large city marathon with thousands of runners, it can be a bit of a nightmare. Not only do you have to run your own race, but you also have to concentrate 100 per cent on your guiding as you have to dodge and weave around other runners, watch out for bollards, lamp-posts, waste bins, uneven paving stones, stepping on and off kerbs, and so on. Despite this, it can be very rewarding taking a disabled runner round: the support you get from the crowds is extra-special. I remember the ovation we got at the long run in at Musselburgh Race Course for the finish of the Edinburgh Marathon, it really was quite moving.'

I am beginning to think that maybe Dave's good fortune comes from the place where good deeds are rewarded.

So does this extremely fortunate, adventurous/cautious, patriotic man have one piece of advice he might give to aspiring 100 Marathon Club members?

'Do something sensible instead, like taking up golf, tennis or swimming!'

Thanks, Dave.

What about the man himself then, does he do any other sport apart from running?

'I play table tennis two or three times a week in local leagues and also badminton.'

Which makes the man with the long grass and dirty car sound far less obsessive than he claims to be, nay, almost well-balanced.

Oh well, you can't win 'em all!

SUMMER SHORTS

As Dave and Janet have discovered, running marathons is a great way to avoid those boring weekend chores and if you're finding the motivation to keep on running a problem, seek out a blind runner and offer to be his guide. That way, you'll both be winners – you'll be helping someone out while at the same time helping yourself. Perfect. Well, they do say there's no such thing as a selfless act.

Buy shares in Vaseline!

MILE 11

RUNNING IN THE DARK

If you find it difficult to imagine running over 100 marathons, try to imagine running them in the dark. For that is what Paul Watts does every time he lines up at the start of a race or steps out of his door to go on a training run.

PAUL WATTS

Born: 1964

220 marathons:

- 1st marathon: 1989 – London
- 100th marathon: 1999 – The Potteries Marathon, Stoke

Records:

- Only Blind Person to Have Completed the 3-in-3 (Seven Sisters, Snowdon, Dublin)
- Only Blind Person to Have Completed 2 Bridges, Scotland (35 miles)
- Only Blind Person to Have Completed Coventry Way 40-Mile Cross-Country (101 stiles).

From the moment I got in touch with the 100 Marathon Club and started talking to its members, whether on the phone, in person or by email, there was one name that kept cropping up and each time it was mentioned the message was the same – 'You must speak to Blind Paul.'

So I did. (I am nothing, if not obedient.)

'Blind Paul', as he is known to everyone in the 100 Club is 47-year-old Paul Watts. And yes, he is blind.

Paul became blind at the age of six. Having been born fully sighted, it took his mother just three months to realise something was wrong. Unfortunately, it took the doctors rather longer and it was two years before they discovered Paul had water on the brain. They duly inserted a valve, sometimes known as a 'shunt' or 'stent', into his brain to pump the fluid from the brain into the body, where it would then be expelled in the way of other fluids. Two years later it collapsed and Paul had to go through the whole process again. Another two years passed and it collapsed a second time. This time, Paul's mother was told there was nothing wrong and he was sent home.

Accordingly, Paul started school as a sighted person. Four terms in, he was constantly complaining of feeling dizzy and said his legs kept going like jelly. Again, his mother took him to the doctor and again she was told there was nothing wrong with him.

On the 3 January 1971, at the age of six, Paul turned to his mother and said, 'Mummy, I feel sick.' He got up and collapsed at the bedroom door. Later, that same day, he went blind.

Even as I write this, the simplicity of those words and the stark bleakness of the outcome have the power to really upset me so when Paul tells me that he knows because of his doctors he is blind, I anticipate his next words will be full of rage and bile.

But that isn't the case.

'I am not bitter,' he tells me, 'because I know it could have been worse. My condition could have given me things apart from blindness – I could have been brain damaged, had spina bifida or even have died. It strikes me that blindness is probably the lesser of them all and I am thankful that's all I have to deal with.'

He's thankful?

'If I hadn't been blind,' he goes on, as if to answer my unspoken question, 'and didn't want to prove it wasn't an issue, I wouldn't have done half the things I've done or had the life I've had.'

Such as running marathons…

'Exactly,' he agrees. 'If I hadn't been blind, I wouldn't have been knocked down by a car at ten to nine on 9 December 1982.'

Eh? What question did I ask?

'And if I hadn't been knocked down by a car, I wouldn't have broken my leg and ended up spending five-and-a-half weeks in traction in hospital in Hereford and six weeks in plaster.'

Er, okay, so now we have a blind man with a broken leg and a phenomenal memory for times, dates and places, but I still don't see how this led to him running marathons.

'If I hadn't been in hospital with a broken leg,' he elaborates, 'I wouldn't have watched the London Marathon on the telly and I wouldn't have promised the nurses that I was going to run one to show how good their treatment of me had been and bring them back a medal!'

Ah ha! Now I get it.

'Which reminds me,' says Paul thoughtfully, as if talking to himself, 'I never did take them that medal – I must put that right.

'People wrote some disgusting things on my plaster cast,' he says, chortling away gleefully, 'and the nurses wrote the worst! Unfortunately, I didn't keep the cast, although I did keep the bolt that was put through my knee to keep it in traction.'

I'm beginning to detect rather a large sense of humour in our Paul.

'I get it from my mother,' he readily admits. 'She finds everything funny. When I was in hospital it was Christmas time and there was this advert on the telly for Harvey's Bristol Cream Sherry. It was on all the time and it showed this guy in plaster, going round and round in traction. My mum laughed every time she saw it because it reminded her of me!'

And that, he tells me, was despite the recent loss of her husband and grandmother.

It would seem a sense of humour is not all that Paul has inherited from his mother; there's also the small matter of a grittily tough resilience, too – a resilience severely tested when Paul went away to boarding school at the tender age of seven.

'It was a special school for the blind,' he tells me. 'I hated that first term – I missed my parents and my family. But then I settled in and really enjoyed it. The only bad thing was not having friends near home in the holidays.'

It was while he was at that school that Paul first discovered his love of sport, representing them in cricket, football and running.

'I started running because we were given a choice of two hours' prep after school or one hour's prep and an hour of something else. I chose running. I'd do five or six miles around the school grounds. The course was familiar and I knew it totally, so it was completely safe.

'Every year we'd have a sports match between local schools for the blind and partially-sighted. I won Gold in the 60 Metres, the 100 Metres and the Shot Put,' he boasts, 'so, in fact you are talking to a Triple Gold medallist!'

I doff my invisible cloth cap and sweep a respectful bow before such greatness. Not easy sitting in an armchair, phone tucked beneath chin, pen clenched between fingers, notebook on lap.

Paul left school in 1981 and continued his education at a college for the blind in his hometown of Hereford, where he took a course in Business Studies, including Shorthand and Typing. This led to a job with Barclays Bank, where he worked for 20 years until he was made redundant in 2006 whereupon, in his words: 'They sent my job to India!'

Since then, he has returned to the college and gained an NVQ in Fitness Instruction, as well as a B-Tech Level 3 in Braille. Unfortunately, neither of these has yet led to further employment, though. However, it was while at college that first time in the autumn of 1983 that he heard a group was to be taken to train for a half or full marathon in Hereford on 8 April 1984.

'I applied to be included, but they told me I was not up to running a full marathon but I'd be okay for the half.'

He duly completed the half and thoroughly enjoyed it, but then, on finishing his course, he left college and the training scheme. Luckily, though he'd met some guys from a running club in Edmonton, who invited him to join them – which he did.

'Some of the members thought I'd be good to run with, if they fancied a slower run, but they don't think that anymore,' he tells me with a hint of steely laughter in his voice. However, it wasn't until 1989 that he finally got the chance to fulfil the dream of running a marathon, seven years after his promise to those hospital nurses.

'I got one of the two club places for the London Marathon,' he recalls, sounding as excited as if he's only just heard. 'One of the members of the club said he would help me train for the race. We were to start off with 15 to 20 miles a week, build it up to over 60 miles and hit an average of 45 miles.'

Privately, Paul thought this sounded horrendous but went with it. And he was glad that he did: the training got him round the London Marathon in a very respectable time of 3 hours 58 minutes and 40 seconds.

'The only thing that hurt afterwards was my back,' he informs me, with a surprisingly gleeful laugh. 'I had a sign on my back to warn other people that I was a blind runner,' he goes on to explain, 'so everyone kept coming up behind me and slapping me on the back, wishing me a good run and offering other well-meaning and encouraging remarks. It took three weeks before my back felt better!'

Almost as soon as he'd finished, people started asking him if he'd do another one. He responded by running two more that same year.

'I loved it,' he says simply.

By now Paul had started regularly bumping into members from the 100 Marathon Club at various races.

'They immediately offered to help me get to and from races and run as my guide,' he says. 'A lot of them will put themselves out for me. Roger Biggs, the chairman, has often run with me but if he doesn't, he always makes sure that someone can do it by putting a notice on the Club's website whenever I'm racing. He's also organised things at the last minute to make sure I have someone to run with me at races.

'My running club are also very good at guiding me on training runs,' he adds. 'I use a triangular piece of rubber, like a dog's chewy toy, to attach me to my guide. It's bright yellow so it can be seen in the dark and I always wear a bright yellow hat and top and a yellow Sam Brown [a fluorescent strap that goes diagonally across the shoulder and around the waist], especially in winter.

'If I'm running in a race with a guide, I must cross the finish line ahead of the guide,' he continues, 'otherwise it's construed that the sighted runner has pulled the blind runner round the race, giving him an advantage over other runners.'

Yes, of course — because being blind is clearly a massive advantage when it comes to running a marathon! Actually, it saddens me to say that I was once coaching a junior blind athlete who ran with a guide in a low-key, inter-club cross-country race. The mother of another runner beaten by the blind athlete put in a complaint in which she claimed the blind athlete must have been pulled round the course by her guide! I still find it hard to imagine anyone could seriously believe that.

'I do have a small amount of vision,' Paul admits, 'it's like looking through the spyglass in a hotel door. I can also differentiate between dark and light shades so if I'm out running, for example, I can see the darkness of a lamp-post or a tree, although I couldn't tell you which one it was but I can avoid it.

'Well, most of the time,' he adds, laughing in jolly fashion. 'I did run into one last year in a race, which put me out of the run!'

This reminds me of the St John's Ambulance man who, when asked if he'd had to deal with many casualties at one of the first-ever women-only road races, replied, 'Only one, and that was a man running on the other side of the street who was so distracted by all the women, he ran smack-bang into a lamp-post and knocked himself out!'

Tee-hee!

So, have Paul's other senses developed more to compensate for the loss of his sight?

'That's what a lot of sighted people seem to think,' he says, 'but I don't necessarily subscribe to that theory. I think, rather than the other senses being better because of blindness, you just use them more. Close your eyes,' he suddenly commands.

Naturally, I obey.

Immediately I find myself concentrating much harder on listening for any sounds, a bit like when you wake up in the middle of the night in the pitch-black thinking you've heard something and you strain to listen for any further burglar-like sounds. In the same way that if you then decide to investigate downstairs without turning on the light, you feel your way, sniffing the air for any unusual scents like a rabbit's twitching nose checking for the faintest foxy whiff.

All of which makes me think Paul may well have a point.

So, apart from the occasional argument with the odd lamppost or tree, does he suffer much from injuries?

'I'm very lucky in that respect,' he says, 'I've hardly ever had any problems. I'm lucky with my health too, although I am mildly epileptic but that doesn't cause me any problems when I'm running. In fact, it's a few years since I've had any problems at all in that regard.

'I guess the only thing running gives me problems with is eating,' he adds. 'When I've run a hard race I can't eat any big meals for several days afterwards and in the past this has caused me to lose a lot of weight.

'I remember when I finished my first marathon,' he continues, 'I went home and my mum remarked that I wasn't looking too good. That was because I'd lost 18 pounds through training, then I lost another 4 pounds on the actual run itself, but I felt brilliant, jubilant, elated!'

And apparently, by way of celebration he accidentally swallowed a Thesaurus, but unfortunately that didn't put on any weight either.

'Since then, though I've put the weight back on in the form of muscle by working out in the gym three times a week. I can leg press twice my own bodyweight,' he boasts.

As if that isn't enough boasting for one interview, he goes on to regale me with the following, purportedly true, story.

'It was 2008,' he begins, 'and I was in the lift at the College for the Blind when a blind woman accidentally caught my leg with her hand. Turned out she was a remedial therapist and masseur.'

A likely story!

'She told me my quadriceps were very well defined,' Paul continues to brag. 'And then she asked me to show her my tri/biceps. So I did!

'You would be the perfect case study for my course,' she then apparently told him.

What a great chat-up line! I must remember this next time I see an attractive guy in a lift, or anywhere for that matter.

'You have muscles like a soldier!'

This girl is good.

'She was so keen to make me her case study, she offered me a free massage when I came back from the marathon!' he finishes with a flourish.

I bet she did!

Aside from using the gym to build up rock-hard muscles that apparently make perfect case studies for budding therapists, Paul also runs three times a week with his club and races an average of 10 to 15 times a year, although he did once run as many as 28.

So, does he have any advice for aspiring 100 Club members?

'Take it at your own pace. If you feel you must do a lot in a year, do it but if not, don't kill yourself – do your own thing.'

And does he have any favourite races?

'St Albans in 1989, because that was the first time I got to run with the 100 Marathon Club guys; the 3-in-3 (three marathons in three days – Seven Sisters, Snowdon, Dublin) in 2006, because it was the last time the event was held and I will therefore always be the only blind person ever to have completed it. Also, because fellow 100 Club member John Dawson, who has since lost his own sight in one eye due to a tumour, ran the Dublin race with me and let go of the lead near the end and called me in [a method of directing blind runners by calling out instructions to move left or right], so I was able to cross the finish line on my own. That is always a special experience for me.

'Then there's the Potteries Race in Stoke, where I ran my 50th, 80th and 100th marathons. The 50th meant I could become a 100 Club "wannabe" member; the 80th was started by one of my heroes, Sir Stanley Matthews, who was celebrating his 80th birthday and found out I was running my 80th marathon, so came over and said to me, "Good luck, enjoy it!", and at the 100th, fellow 100 Club member Peter Sargeant and his wife Lesley supplied all the food and drink for the after-race party and a large group from the Club turned out to run with me, taking it in turns to guide me before Sid Wheeler ran ahead of me and called me in to the finish, so I was able to cross that finish line on my own, too.

'Also, my 35th birthday run when Sid took me round the Two Bridges 35-mile race in Scotland and everyone who'd finished ahead of me was on the finish line and clapped as I crossed it, as I was the first blind person ever to have done it; the Coventry Way 40-mile Cross-Country race, which involved climbing 101 stiles – I'm the only blind person ever to have run that one, too; and the 100 Club's own event in London in 2008, when they replicated the Olympic Marathon of 1908 to celebrate its centenary, running the exact same course as had been run in the Games.'

Phew!

'Then there was Cornwall,' he continues, clearly on a roll. 'It was the worst weather I've ever run in. I was running up a steep hill into gale-force winds and snow was being driven straight into my face. I dropped out at 14 miles and was put in an ambulance and driven back to the start line.

'They gave me two hot coffees and a hot pasty, and after I'd been in the warm a bit longer, they took my temperature (which was 35°C/95°F, which was almost hypothermia). I hadn't realised I was that bad, although I do remember I couldn't stop shivering. I have done the race again since then and completed it, but thankfully, never in such bad weather.'

Silly question perhaps, but are there any races he hasn't yet done that he would like to complete in the future?

'Iceland, the Grand Union Canal Run (GUCR), the Coast-to-Coast, the 2 Oceans, Comrades in South Africa – you win a jacket for completing it, but if you don't finish it or do it within the allocated time limit, you get nothing. You can carry on and finish and you can say you've done it, but you get no memento.'

You go away with nothing. The uninspiring tones of *Weakest Link* presenter Anne Robinson spring uninvited (obviously) into my head. I ignore this unwelcome interruption and turn my attention back to Paul.

'My ultimate goal is to run 250 marathons by the time I'm 50. I'd also like to do a cycle ride on the back of a tandem around the coast of mainland Britain,' he tells me, his enthusiasm apparently knowing no bounds.

It transpires that Paul has in fact already done a few tandem rides: one from London to Brighton, one from London to Cambridge and another from Lincoln to Skegness, so this may not be quite so crazy as it first sounds.

I also happen to know – not from Paul, but from a fellow 100 Club member – that Paul is also a bit of a football fanatic and is in the process of going to all 92 of the Football League grounds, which he does entirely alone. So far he has visited over 80.

So, it has to be asked – does he think he is crazy – in respect of marathon running, I mean?

'I think I probably am,' he concedes, with that now-familiar chuckle.

Craziness aside, I wonder what else keeps him motivated.

'Meeting people and meeting challenges,' he replies straightaway. 'Plus the camaraderie of the 100 Marathon Club guys and gals. If not for the blindness and the 100 Marathon Club, I wouldn't have got to do half the things I've done today – I am grateful.'

A few months after this chapter was written, I once more caught up with Paul. He was barely able to contain his excitement and I could hardly blame him: he'd been nominated to carry the Olympic Torch on 24 May 2012 by the Hereford Association for the Blind. But that wasn't all: he'd just been invited by another runner at his club to join him on a 145-mile run next year – the Grand Union Canal Race [GUCR], which has to be completed within 45 hours.

'It's something I've wanted to do for some time. Now I have no excuse!'

And that to me pretty much sums up Paul Watts. A man for whom being blind is not an excuse not to do things, but rather the inspiration to do more.

SUMMER SHORTS

It seems to me that running marathons allows everyone, whether they are blind or not, to do something that gives them a real sense of pride and achievement. I could hear it in Paul's voice – and that was without even closing my eyes.

And if you get caught checking out a guy's pecs, pretend you're a remedial therapist looking for a case study.

MILE 12

FAGS, FRY-UPS AND FITNESS

A heart attack and two bouts of cancer couldn't stop John Dawson from becoming the oldest man in the world to complete 10 marathons in 10 days at the age of 73.

JOHN DAWSON
Born: 1937
383 marathons:
- 1st marathon: 1993 – New York
- 100th marathon: 2003 – Abingdon
Records:
- Oldest Man in the World (73) to Complete 10 Marathons in 10 Days.

If you'd known John Dawson 20 years ago, you'd know a slightly overweight man who drank, smoked heavily and loved nothing better than greasy fry-ups and convenience foods. But then, at 52, he had a heart attack and his life changed profoundly.

'Out went the junk food and cigarettes, in came the healthy

alternatives,' says John, who was then the owner of an engineering factory. And, after a rather unusual start, in came the running, too.

'When I first came out of hospital, I was advised to walk but eventually got fed up with it,' he explains. 'Then, one evening, my children wanted a video. The shop is about 300 metres away and slightly downhill, and for some inexplicable reason I ran there. I liked it and within a couple of days I was in the local park, running 100 metres and puffing badly, then walking 100 metres and then repeating the process. I gradually built it up and when I first ran right round the edge of the park – one-and-a half miles – I thought I had won the Olympics!'

With the love and support of his wife Corazon and their daughters, Tanya and Emma, John continued to run his way back to good health.

'I carried on running and eventually bought the *Runners World* magazine and saw an advert for the New York Marathon. It was several months away but I knew that it would make me focus – and it did. Being New York, it also gave me a sense of adventure.

'The marathon itself was the first time that I ever ran with anyone else – I had nightmares about 30,000 runners all being in front with me being all alone, about two miles behind!'

Nightmare on Fifth Avenue!

Of course that didn't happen. Instead, John returned home much enthused.

'Not long after returning from New York, I joined Lichfield Running Club. At that stage, I had no thought of running 100 marathons,' he tells me, 'it just builds up. You become addicted.'

To what exactly?

'The challenge, camaraderie, a sense of self-worth and of course a lot of satisfaction; also the overall health implications.'

By 2003 this addiction had taken him all the way to that magical 100 marker and he became a proud member of the 100 Marathon Club.

Now, if the mathematical part of my brain is working this means it took John 10 years to get from 0–100, averaging a reasonably sensible 10 marathons a year.

'Not exactly,' he corrects me. 'Five years ago, I ran 52 in a year and another year I did 47, and I've run 365 since the start of the Millennium.'

And there was I thinking I'd found a guy with perspective.

'It was a challenge,' he says, as if by way of defence, 'and the year went well in terms of injuries and illness. These days I run a marathon nearly every week.'

Now look, John, you're really not helping the cause…

'I just think it's easier to run one nearly every week,' he explains, 'you keep yourself on a fitness plateau, which is then easier to manage than building up to one or two per year. Illness and injury permitting,' he adds, as if this might make it better.

Which it does, kind of, because it makes me think that perhaps, when you've been faced with serious health issues, you tend not to put off until tomorrow…

Certainly, John has had more than his fair share of ill-health. Just over 20 years after his heart attack, he lost an eye to cancer.

'It was 2010,' he tells me. 'I should have been running in the Brathay 10-in-10 in Windermere but instead I was in hospital having my eye operated on. One of the nicest things that happened though was that the operation was actually on the same day as the 10-in-10 and they sent me a card signed by everyone who was taking part in the race. That was really special.'

Having lost the sight of one eye didn't stop him from running, though. In May 2011, exactly one year after the operation, he travelled to Windermere to attempt the awesome 10-in-10 Challenge a second time (the first successful attempt being in 2007). Again, he successfully completed it, but this time he broke a World Record to become the oldest man ever to complete 10 marathons in 10 days, at the age of 73. Not only that, but it was also the 295th marathon he had completed as an OAP.

'I am proud of what I have achieved and hopefully it will inspire other, more mature people to get out and run, or just to become more active,' he is quoted as saying on the Brathay Trust's website, following his success. (The Brathay Trust is a charity that helps vulnerable young people and monies raised through the race go to it.)

And so he should be – proud, that is. Not least because, unbelievably, the cruel hand of ill health was about to strike him a third blow – this time, bowel cancer. Indeed, I have his input into this book at a time when he has only just come out of hospital, again having undergone yet another operation. But John isn't the sort of person to sit around bemoaning his fate.

'I am lucky that with both the eye and bowel cancers I found out about them through having check-ups,' he says. 'I would like to make more people aware that regular health check-ups can be essential and save a nasty problem from getting an awful lot worse.'

But, other than taking note of John's advice, let us not dwell on his ill health, instead moving on to the far jollier topic of his injuries – should he have any, that is.

'I do suffer from time to time,' he admits. 'The last one I had was the worst. It was a metatarsal stress fracture and put me out of running from September 2010 to March 2011.'

That's a long time. I guess it must have taken some training to get back to form, especially given the 10-in-10 was in May 2011?

'I just did my usual training, which is about 45 miles a week, including the marathon,' he says. 'During the week I train a guy with Down's Syndrome, who has now done eight marathons with me.'

Isn't that just typical? You get a guy who's suffered heart disease and cancer, and he's out there helping someone else!

In that case, is it safe for me to assume as a coach, he practises what he undoubtedly preaches and does a proper warm-up/warm-down?

'Well, I always like to arrive early at races, which gives me time to do a five- to ten-minute running warm-up,' he offers.

I'll take that as a 'no' then, shall I?

'I recover quite quickly,' he goes on, as if to justify himself, 'I usually feel a bit stiff after a race, but I'm fine again the next morning.'

However, if John's pre-race physical preparation is a bit hit-and-miss, his pre-race diet is the opposite.

'I always eat pasta the night before and porridge on race day, as well as carbo/electrolyte [a sports drink that rehydrates and delays the onset of fatigue] before the race and Isotonic drinks and gels during the run. I'm not usually hungry after a race, but I always eat a McDonald's ice cream, if possible!'

Not completely off the junk foods then, John? Sorry, Mr McDonald, I'm sure your ice cream is very healthy, really – I'm merely pertaining to the fat content of ice cream in general.

Apart from the inspiration of a McDonald's ice cream after completing a marathon, is there anybody or anything else that inspires him?

'Paula Radcliffe,' he answers immediately. 'She has achieved so much for UK athletics, marathons in particular. And of course my peers in the 100 Club.'

Naturally. Although it's not just his peers that inspire John, it's also the 100 Marathon Club kit.

'I always run in my 100 Club kit,' he tells me, 'and twin-skin socks' (double-layered socks, which help prevent blistering).

John, his vest and socks have been to some memorable places together, including Connemara in Ireland, which he cites as his favourite marathon, 'because of the scenery.'

'I couldn't possibly name a least favourite,' he adds, 'they are all good, except maybe the Bologna Marathon in Italy. It was on New Year's Eve,' he goes on to explain, 'and the weather was the worst I've ever had to run in, with temperatures being several degrees below freezing.'

Oh, come now, John! I'm sure it can't have been that bad, not once you'd done your warm-up.

'The most unusual marathon I've ever done,' he continues, clearly having decided the best strategy is to pretend he hasn't heard me, 'has to be the Greenwich Foot Tunnel Marathon organised by the 100 Club to celebrate the Tunnel's centenary. We started the race at 2am to avoid public use!'

That's what makes it unusual? Not the running back and forth 58 times along a 1,217-foot tunnel underneath the River Thames?

'Marathons on a running track are particularly hard,' he adds, with some feeling.

Tell me about it! Not that I've ever done one but I once ran 3,000 metres (seven-and-a-half laps) on a track and was so bored I started reciting the phonetic alphabet to myself just to pass the time. To complete 105 laps would mean reciting the phonetic alphabet forwards, backwards, upside-down, inside-out, back-to-front in Chinese, Japanese and Timbuktu-nese. No thank you!

So, apart from advising aspiring 100 Marathon Club members to avoid track marathons, does he have any other words of wisdom for them?

'Keep at it, but try to avoid injury.'

Wise man.

And what about those virgins out there?

'Make sure your body is balanced and that you get good advice when buying shoes – and don't wear them once they are worn out.'

Very wise man.

And does he consider himself to be obsessed by marathon running?

'Definitely!' He makes this acknowledgement with a gleeful chuckle.

And, finally, how do others react to him once they know he's run over 100 marathons?

'Most are completely amazed — I think the word is "gobsmacked."'

And so they should be.

SUMMER SHORTS

If you don't want to spend a fortune on trainers, buy them in last season's colours. With the recent surge in popularity in barefoot running, manufacturers of training shoes have finally admitted that many past technological changes have been unnecessary or minimal and offer no real advantage to the wearer. Therefore all you are paying extra for is colour trend.

However, if you have a reputation for high fashion and wouldn't be seen dead (or alive) in last year's anything, find a muddy field and take your new trainers for a spin. Mud-caked trainers not only disguise the year of birth but also suggest you are a running pro.

MILE 13

HALFWAY THERE!

If, like Peter Dennett and Liz Tunna, you can't wait until you've run 100 marathons to become part of the 'Crazy Gang', all you have to do is finish 50 and sign up as a 'wannabe'.

PETER DENNETT

Born: 1967
81 marathons:
- 1st marathon: 1998 – London
- 100th marathon: TBC (hopefully, 2012)

'I am a wannabe, a wannabe I am!' so sings 44-year-old Peter Dennett when I meet him in Malta. Actually he doesn't, I just made that up because I think it makes rather a nice little ditty and I can hear a fitting tune in my head. Sadly, I can't write music, so you'll have to make up your own tune. Sorry!

Now, where were we? Oh yes, Peter Dennett, 44-year-old wannabe, a keen bean who couldn't wait until he'd completed 100 marathons to join the 100 Marathon Club, and is currently on 81 with a plan to reach 100 some time in 2012.

'A woman from work told me about the Club,' he says, shifting blame straightaway. 'Her husband's a member.'

Peter doesn't have a wife himself, which is no doubt why he picked on his friend's partner although he apparently does have a girlfriend, whom he says plays the part of marathon widow very convincingly.

Go, girl!

'She once ran a 10K in Dresden at the same time as I ran a marathon there and afterwards she said "Never again" and has stuck to it.' Peter can't keep the surprise out of his voice. 'Most people tell me I'm mad,' he adds, with an air of quiet acceptance, 'although people in some sporting circles such as triathletes tend to be a bit more admiring of my actions.'

That will be because he's one of them: a triathlete. Indeed, 5 of his 81 marathons were actually achieved during Ironman competitions.

'Initially I started running to raise money for charity,' the five foot eleven inch dark-haired, brown-eyed Peter tells me, 'specifically the local cardiac unit, in memory of my late father. The numbers have only ballooned relatively recently as I started to consider doing so many for the sheer challenge. However, the number isn't that important, my main goal is to run a marathon in every European country. So far I've done 37. I'm determined to do them all within reason – availability, time and budget.'

That's quite some target given Peter tells me he thinks there are 50 countries in Europe, at least theoretically.

'It depends on a number of factors,' he expands. 'For instance, whether you consider Kosovo separate from Serbia and whether you include Vatican City. Otherwise I think it's 48. Also the "Council of Europe" only has 46 members – Belarus and Kazakhstan aren't members – and the EU currently has only 27 members, of which I've done 26. Bulgaria is the only EU member I've not done yet. Of course very small countries like

San Marion and Andorra holding a marathon looks unlikely –
they haven't so far, though Liechtenstein and Monaco have.'

I feel quite Euro-elucidated. Thanks for that, Peter.

'I've also started to consider running in every German state
because German marathons are so well organised, if not the best.

'At the moment, I'm running around 15 marathons a year,
although some months, such as April and October, are busier than
others due to more races being available in the UK and Europe.
I've only run in Europe except for Morocco and Istanbul, if you
include the Asian element.'

Peter may not yet have reached his century but he is already
enough well versed in the vagaries of running marathons to have
developed a tried-and-tested pre-race routine.

'I stop running a few days before a race and change my diet
from mainly protein based to carb-based foods, like pasta and
rice. Generally I avoid eating anything new on race day. I'll have
a light breakfast of cereals, porridge or bananas. I never eat
during a race (my stomach can't take food when I'm running),
so I consume energy gels not bars, along with whatever is given
out on the racecourse although I only drink water and isotonic
drinks. After the race I'll have isotonic drinks and protein-rich
food – and of course, beer!'

Of course…

'Prior to the race itself experience has taught me to ensure I
have used plenty of talcum powder, Vaseline and plasters where
needed in preparation and I always lay out my kit the night before
so I don't have to worry about it first thing in the morning, which
is when most marathons occur.

'I always generally wear the same watch too, just because I
know how the stopwatch works in it and it's comfortable.'

Wow, this man is organised! His attention to detail doesn't end
there, though.

'When I'm racing I prefer to wear the triathlon-style spandex shorts,' he tells me [why am I seeing Borat?], 'rather than the traditional running shorts. They help to minimise chafing.'

If you say so, Peter.

As for his top half, Peter dons, 'A light and cool running vest and mid-length running socks as opposed to those short ones that just come above the edge of the shoe. If it's sunny, I'll wear sunglasses, too.'

Ooh, I can picture him on the catwalk right now.

With such a methodical approach to everything, it occurs to me that maybe running 100 marathons is actually all part of some cunning plan.

Peter shakes his dark head emphatically. 'I certainly didn't plan to run so many marathons – they just gradually built up from doing one or two a year to around 15. Then I realised that the goal of 100 was achievable, if not challenging, and running marathons around Europe was a good way to also explore parts that I may not have made a point of visiting for sightseeing alone.'

Okay, so if it was his work colleague's fault that he first got to hear of the 100 Club, does he have anyone else to blame for influencing/inspiring him to carry on – apart from his 'unexciting' job as an IT bank worker, for which he apologises and which he thinks might be responsible for his marathon activities?

'I'm not sure about influencing me but in terms of admiration I do recognise the efforts of certain members of the 100 Club, such as Steve Edwards for running so many, so quickly; Brian Mills for simply running so many and both Roger Biggs and Gina Little for putting in times not much different from my own, yet they are quite a few years my senior.

'Outside the Club, Haile Gebrselassie for setting so many World Records at the distance, Paula Radcliffe for showing that a woman can run nearly as fast as a man, António Pinto (who, in

London 2000 missed out by a few seconds on setting a new course record, thus missing out on the associated prize money because he slowed down in the final metres to wave to the crowds in appreciation of their support) and Bella Bayliss née Comerford, who is the UK's most successful long distance triathlete – essentially the Paula Radcliffe of the triathlon world, yet is very down-to-earth – I spoke to her at the UK Ironman in 2008.'

Just a few, then…

What about a favourite marathon?

'I ran my fastest in London in 2004, with a personal best of 3 hours 24 seconds exactly, but my best race technically with respect to being the closest to achieving the "perfect race" – trying to achieve a negative split [running the second half of the race faster than the first] – had to be Vienna in 2007, when my second half was only three and a half minutes slower than the first half.

'The most emotional marathon I've ever run was London in 1998. That was my first and also had the backdrop of recently losing my father. The most well organised was definitely Berlin in 2001, which coincidentally also included free full-strength beer at the finish. Florence had the best scenery…

'Most satisfying with respect to achievement was the Ironman UK in 2007 – that was the first time I'd run a marathon straight after a 2.4 mile swim and 112-mile cycle. It was also my quickest Ironman to date on what is internationally recognised as one of the toughest Ironman courses in the world and as the official Ironman motto says: "Swim 2.4 miles! Bike 112 miles! Run 26.2 miles! Brag for the rest of your life!"'

Thanks for such a full and frank disclosure, Peter (I mean answer!).

'London in 2005 wasn't so good, though,' Peter continues, regardless. 'I collided on the course with a spectator who came out in front of me. The spectator came off worst, falling to the ground whilst I continued.'

So putting the literal into 'hit and run'.

'But my rhythm and focus wasn't there for the rest of the race. That was the first time I went over 4 hours. Istanbul in 2005 was pretty awful, too, with low crowd support and very humid weather, which ended in a heavy thunderstorm 2K from the finish.

'Undoubtedly the most unusual marathon was Monaco in 2003. We ran along parts of the F1 course, as well as the French Riviera and Italy; Liechtenstein in 2010 was pretty tough as it was uphill and off-road for most of the course and the heavy rain and fog didn't help much either! Athens wasn't very enjoyable either. It may be the "classic route" but as most of it is on a motorway, it's not the most scenic or interesting of runs. Plus, it's mostly uphill. It was only the fact that I didn't want to do a "Paula" that kept me going!'

Thank you for sharing that with us, Peter.

While he takes a breath, I take the opportunity to break away from his race catalogue and inquire after his luck with injuries.

'I sprained my right ankle in an off-road 10K in 2010 and in 2003 I had tendonitis in both ankles, which led me to take up multi-discipline sports like triathlons and thus include some non-impact training.'

Rather excitingly, I have finally found someone who actually does a warm-up before he starts running and a warm-down afterwards as well.

'It's only a short one,' he warns, clearly alarmed by my enthusiasm. 'I do it on the starting line, mainly to pass the time as I hate waiting.'

I refuse to be disappointed.

'After the race I just keep walking to avoid stiffness brought on by the lactic acid build-up. It usually takes a couple of days to fully recover from a race. If I race on Sunday, I'll go for a swim on Tuesday to loosen up and then a light run on Wednesday. I normally do three or four days of running unless I'm in a week between marathons, then I just do one or two recovery runs and three or four lunchtime swims, subject to work commitments. In summer I replace the runs with evening bike rides, which may include a time trial.'

Now seems an appropriate time to ask whether he thinks he's obsessed with running marathons.

'No,' he says straightaway, 'there are people who run far more than I do!'

Oh well, that's okay then.

'I also do other sports, such as triathlons, duathlons, cycle time trails, alpine skiing, Telemark skiing [also known as 'free heel skiing', whereby the boot is connected to the ski at the toes only], snowboarding and shorter distance running. I've actually done over 100 10K races. Running is the only sport that isn't seasonal, though.

'I also enjoy writing about my marathon weekends, not just the race but the organisation and the visited place in general, and submit these to the 100 Marathon Club's website as well as my local triathlon club. I started doing them to inspire others to write and share their experiences but more lately it's because people have told me that they found them interesting and inspirational in helping them aspire to some sporting goal, even if it's not always a marathon.'

No wonder his girlfriend is so practised in the art of being a marathon widow!

And if he could offer one piece of advice to aspiring 100 Club members, what would it be?

'Don't give up!'

Sorry, Peter's girlfriend, but at least you know where you stand.

LIZ TUNNA

Born: 1986

84 marathons:

- 1st marathon: 2009 – Windermere
- 100th marathon: TBC (hopefully October 2011)

I haven't actually met 25-year-old Liz Tunna but I am nonetheless extremely grateful to her for stepping in at the last minute to be my female wannabe owing to the departure of my original sample due to a combination of work overload and shyness (hers, not mine obviously – on both counts). At least that's her story. I have a feeling it may have more to do with my response at being told that at the Niagara Marathon, the competitors are taken out to the start by bus and then have to run back to the finish.

Personally, I think, 'You silly, silly people' is a perfectly acceptable response. However, let's not digress on what might have been, apart from pausing for just one moment to thank her for putting me in touch with Liz and to concentrate instead on her story.

Now Liz tells me she is a student studying for a Masters in Exercise and Nutrition Science, so no work overload problems there, then. (Only kidding, Liz – and all students, everywhere.)

But this is not her first degree: Liz already has one in English and Drama.

'I just find the whole nutritional side to exercise really interesting and helpful,' she adds, with a jolly laugh.

What's funny about that, you may well ask, as did I.

'I initially got into running to lose weight and lost about 4½ stone,' Liz explains.

Ah ha, *now* I get it.

'When I first set out to lose weight I made a conscious effort to eat more healthily and cut out junk food,' she expands (actually she doesn't – quite the opposite).

'Although, as soon as I started to exercise – which I never did before the weight loss – I found that I started to lose it quite easily. I was never big growing up; I just seemed to put it all on around the ages of 15–18. I also started to eat breakfast, which I never used to do when I was bigger. I wanted to do something fun with the weight loss and always thought of running a marathon.'

Really? She didn't think of learning to ski with a handsome Italian instructor or salsa dance with a sexy Latin American, then? Must just be me! But pause a moment to consider – with her new, svelte five foot nine-inch figure, burnished brunette locks and intriguing hazel eyes, just think of the possibilities. Naturally I'd be writing a slim paperback with a rose on its spine.

Fortunately, Liz has not gone off into the realms of my fantasy, but remains firmly planted within the book I am really writing.

'I started off running shorter distances,' she informs me. 'The first event I entered was the Great North Run in 2008. At the beginning of 2009 I completed two 10K events and then I did a few more half marathons.

'I entered my first marathon on a bit of an impulse and wasn't sure if I was ready or not, but I'd never have known if I hadn't tried. How bad could it be? It turns out that I really enjoyed it and I wanted to see what else was possible.

'I did that first marathon at Windermere and was inspired by the runners doing the 10 marathons in 10 days challenge,' she says. 'The hills didn't seem as bad as I had imagined and the scenery and atmosphere were amazing. I was so excited, running to that finishing line, and as I did, it started to pour down with rain.'

But even that didn't put her off and these days she runs a marathon almost weekly.

So, what sort of training does she do?

'I do a lot of cross-training at the gym. I love spinning; I do weights and a little speed work on the treadmill and bikes. All of my training is done alone and I don't have a coach, although I do belong to Ellesmere Port Running Club. However, I don't go running with them often because they leave me for dust!'

And what about injuries and health?

'I get the occasional cold and manky feet,' she concedes.

No! I don't care how many readers want to know about Liz's 'manky' feet, I refuse to go there other than to report she is a regular user of Vaseline and Sudocrem, which she reckons is, 'really good on sore feet!'

'I've never suffered badly with injury though, touch wood,' she adds.

Returning just for a moment to the subject of diet, but in relation to running and given her studies, does Liz follow any particular nutritional regime?

'Nothing specific,' she admits, 'but I do try to eat as healthily as possible and drink lots of water. During a race I mainly drink water and take electrolyte capsules as the thought of taking on energy drink and gels sometimes makes me feel ill. However, I do often crave fizzy coke. Furthermore, I have learnt through ultras to take on "real" food, so I am now more inclined to eat a banana or a biscuit, or something along those lines, during a marathon.'

So, apart from a desire to lose weight, what would she say was her motivation for running so many marathons and does she have any heroes or heroines who have inspired her?

'I love the adventure,' she says immediately. 'Longer distances suit me and I love that feeling of accomplishment and the adrenalin. I also really enjoy a good off-road ultra and I have completed over 30. The longest I've gone so far is 85 miles, but I have goals to run much further.

'The only trouble with running ultras is that my time for the marathon has got a lot slower,' she adds. 'When I first started, my times were quite respectable and consistently around the four-hour mark, with a personal best of 4 hours and 06 seconds at Loch Ness.

'As for heroes, I have met so many amazing people through taking part in events who have inspired me. Their tales of adventure and accomplishments make me smile and drive me on. Well-known figures that have inspired me are people such as adventurer Sir Ranulph Fiennes (I think his achievements never fail to inspire any person) and ultra-runner Dean Karnazes, who never fails to amuse and interest me – such stories make me want to get out there and run.'

And of the 80+ marathons she has run so far, does she have any favourites or least favourites?

'Scenery nearly always makes or breaks a marathon route for me. For this reason, Loch Ness, Snowdonia and Brathay Windermere marathons rank amongst my favourites. They are beautiful and hilly, but so interesting. I love Nottingham and the atmosphere at the Robin Hood Marathon is excellent, but I don't like the rowing lake stretch in the second half too much. Furthermore, I wasn't so keen on the Llanelli Great Welsh Marathon since the course mainly consists of loops and out-and-back sections along small pathways. Also, upon reaching mile 20, you have to run three miles out, passing the finishing line and three miles back to finally finish. It was pretty soul-destroying, definitely not my favourite.'

And what about other sports or hobbies?

'I don't participate in any other sport, other than going to the gym and currently, I don't have any major hobbies.'

So, does she consider herself to be obsessed with running marathons?

'I thought about this point a while ago and pondered whether it was obsession or simply that I really enjoy running and embrace it as a major part of my life. I'm perhaps a little bit obsessed, but only in the same way that some people are obsessed with sitting around and watching TV a lot. In this instance, running is a positive "obsession."'

Now that's an analogy I particularly like.

And what about other people, what do they think of her achievements?

'When other people find out what I do, I think some of them don't always believe me because I can come across as a bit ditsy sometimes and don't always look like a marathon runner.'

Why, because she's not always wearing Lycra and trainers? And as for 'ditsy', of course someone who's working on her second degree is bound to be a bit 'silly or foolish' – the *Oxford English Dictionary* definition of the word.

'Some people question the amount,' she goes on, 'They say, "You mean, *full* marathons?" Some people are excited and intrigued. Some will caution me and tell me that one day my knees will give up and everything will fall apart with doing so many – these are mostly non-runner types.'

Well, that pretty much covers everything there. Let's move on to any amusing or heart-warming stories she may have to tell.

'The final day of this year's Brathay 10 Marathons in 10 Days Challenge was hugely heart-warming. The day started with David "Foxy" Bayley [a fellow 100 Club member] bringing a few tears to all our eyes with his reference to David Bowie's popular song about everyone being a hero for a day in his speech before our final marathon. Getting over that finishing line on the final day was so full of raw emotion from everyone involved and the icing on the cake was that we were all there at the finishing line to see the legendary John Dawson [another 100 Club member] complete the 10-in-10 and claim his World Record as the oldest person to do so. We all just hugged and cried, and cheered.

'Funny things that have happened include stepping into sinking mud up on the Yorkshire Moors and getting my shoe sucked off my foot. I managed to get it back, but I was so tired by this point that I literally laughed out loud. Getting chased by cows is quite funny when I think back – I certainly ran very fast, but it was pretty scary at the time.'

Stop cow-ering and moo-ve it!

'Sometimes,' Liz continues, somehow managing to ignore my clever quip, 'I can't help but think how surreal and amazing all this running lark is. Nowhere else do you come across so many lovely, friendly people – I guess they're all hyped up on endorphins!

'There are so many beautiful marathons out there and I aim to discover a lot more of them. Ultimately, I would love to run somewhere exotic or in a beautiful part of the world over a vast distance.'

And I have no doubt in the fullness of time she will do just that, but for now, she must content herself with her more immediate goal – that of completing her 100th marathon at the end of October 2011. Of course, what she doesn't mention is that in so doing she will also take the record from fellow 100 Club member Naomi Prasad and become the youngest woman in the UK – and possibly the world – to have run 100 marathons, something she says was in no way part of her plan when she first began.

'When I first started, I simply wanted to experience what running a marathon would be like – I was just really curious. I enjoyed it so much that my mindset changed pretty quickly and I then wanted to see what I was capable of beyond running just one marathon. I didn't realise straightaway that running marathons wasn't necessarily something that a lot of women my age did. A little while later, once I had completed a few more events, I came to realise that I was on the younger side. I also started to meet more and more people who were aspiring to be in the 100 Marathon Club, or had already achieved this. It was something that I had thought I may one day achieve, but meeting these inspiring people made it all so real and achievable. Of course, realising I might be one of the youngest women to achieve this was exciting, but it wasn't and isn't my main goal; I simply want to experience as many amazing runs as possible and make the most of doing something I really enjoy doing. Everything else is just a bonus.'

Catching up with Liz a few months later, I'm delighted to learn that she duly completed her 100th marathon in October 2011, in Chester, at the tender age of 24 years and 351 days. That makes her the youngest female in the 100 club (and potentially in the world) to have run 100 marathons over road and trail by some four years. Happy though Liz was to have achieved her goal, she told me she also felt a sense of sadness that her quest was now over. However, she's not a girl to wallow in misery or rest on her laurels, and she has set herself a new challenge – to run the Thames Path Ultra-Marathon (100 miles) and the Grand Union Canal Run (145 miles). All I can say to that is 'Good luck, Liz'!

SUMMER SHORTS

As Peter discovered, it's a good idea to mix in a bit of alternate sport to avoid becoming injured from the jarring caused by constant running on a hard surface. Swimming is a particularly good choice as it replicates the same cardio-vascular effects as running, while the water supports your bodyweight.

And as Liz found, the best way to lose weight is to combine diet with exercise – and eat breakfast.

Buy shares in Vaseline!

MILE 14

GIVE ME YOUR MONEY, OR GET OUT OF MY TOILET!

Ever since Gina Little's husband, Hen, died at the unfairly young age of 55, marathon running and the 100 Marathon Club have been her salvation.

GINA LITTLE
Born: 1945
400 marathons:
• 1st marathon: 1983 – London
• 100th marathon: 1999 – South Coastal (previously Thanet)
Records:
• UK Fastest Veteran Lady (age 65–70)
• Most Marathons Run by a Lady in the UK & Ireland.

It's embarrassing when meeting someone for the first time to want to call them a liar but honestly that's how I felt when I first set eyes on Gina Little in Malta.

Gina, in perfect harmony with her surname, is petite and pretty with the shiny blonde hair of a 'Because I'm worth it' model, except hers is all-natural and there is no way she looks like a woman of 65. Even as I write her age, I can visualise her smiling, unlined face, her lively, sparkling blue eyes and that shimmering blonde hair that add up to a healthy 45-year-old, not a woman in her sixties.

But short of insisting she allows me a look at her passport and birth certificate I have to believe she is telling the truth and therefore I'm forced to stop doubting her and simply admire how well she looks.

Not only does she look well, she also runs well. For Gina has completed the most marathons of any female in the UK and Ireland, with 400 under her belt at the time of writing – and still counting. She is also the fastest lady in the UK for her age group (65–70) and has an all-time Personal Best of 3 hours 26 minutes, which she did appropriately enough in her beloved hometown of London in 1993, the site of her very first marathon 10 years earlier.

'I love it,' she says, as if I might not realise this. 'I loved the whole running thing, right from the beginning.'

For Gina, the beginning was back in 1983, when she was 39 years old.

'The London Marathon course passes the end of my road,' she explains. 'It was the second year they did London and I saw the runners and thought, "I *will* do that next year."'

'I'd always been involved in sport, but not running. At that time I played badminton for a local club and after my first week of marathon training I turned up at the club feeling somewhat stiff. I noticed another woman seemed to be suffering similarly,' says Gina, with a girlish giggle. 'We got talking and it turned out she'd just started running as well and was feeling the same as I was. So we decided to start running together.

'We did a few marathons, but then I started doing more running and leaving her behind, so eventually we stopped running together.'

Ah-ha, so beneath the angelic good looks lies a sharp, competitive spirit!

Competitive spirit notwithstanding, marathon running is about so much more for Gina, especially since losing her adored husband Henry (known to Gina as 'Hen'), in 2000, after 36 years of happy marriage.

'Hen ran one marathon with me but suffered a heart attack a couple of months later,' she says, 'though not because of the marathon,' she adds, her blue eyes darkening sadly as she recalls the man she so obviously dearly loved. 'He didn't run any more after that, but he always supported me', she continues, a faltering smile hovering about her lips. 'I'd like to think he would be very proud of me for carrying on.'

I look at this woman, petite and pretty with sadness in her eyes, and want to reassure her that there's no doubt but that he would be proud of his lovely wife, who has bravely soldiered on alone – well, apart from the support of the 100 Marathon Club, that is.

'After losing Hen, running became my saviour,' she says, 'and I really threw myself into it. It gave me a direction, something to focus on.'

And Gina shows no sign of slackening off, running an incredible 41 races each year for the past two years. She is not content to run just marathon distance either.

'The furthest I have ever run in one go is 88 miles, which I did in Berlin with a group suffering from Down's Syndrome. We actually ran the race with them so it wasn't a quick time, but it was still very much a challenge,' she recalls.

I can imagine. Well, actually, I can't – I just know 88 miles would take me almost all the way to London from my home in Dorset and there's no way I'd think of getting there without using some form of transport.

Her next furthest run was a mere 80-miler.

Slacking, Gina, slacking!

'It was in 1986 and was run off-road along the South Downs Way,' she tells me. 'There were four of us in a team.'

Ah, a relay. Tick-tock, tick-tock, mathematical genius at work... So, 20 miles each then?

'No, *80* miles each!' she laughs.

Silly me... and what a waste of mathematical genius brainpower.

The race incorporated the eighth World Trail Running Championships and Gina's ill-concealed competitive streak was fully ignited by the high standard of the other competitors. She romped (if that's possible after 80 miles of off-road running), home to win her age group category (50–54), finishing in fifth place in the ladies' race and 112th overall from a field of 1,000 participating runners in the remarkable time of 15 hours 56 minutes.

How long? I'm rarely awake for that long in one go, never mind running non-stop.

By way of comparison and to really appreciate just how fast Gina was running, it took 27 hours for the last of the competitors to cross the finishing line, a maximum-allowed time set by the race organisers, after which all checkpoints are closed and anybody still running must either pull out or carry on running on their own, but will not officially be counted as finishers.

Twenty-seven hours? I'm *never* awake that long in one go!

'We were running in the dark for some of the time,' says Gina, as if she feels the mere fact of running non-stop for over 15 hours might not be impressive enough. 'We had to follow directional instructions and wear head torches. I was wearing shorts and a T-shirt, but then had to also put on a fluorescent jacket when it got dark so I could be seen by Hen, who was there supporting me.'

Good old Hen!

And then it occurs to me to ask about food and drink. I mean, if by some peculiar, utterly unlikely stroke of ill-fate I should find myself on the move for over 15 hours, I think I'd need a little snackette or two to help me along the way. A Hawaiian pizza might be quite nice, all that juicy pineapple and melted cheese, or perhaps a plate of steaming fish and chips. In fact, it might be the ideal time to eat them – when all the greedy gulls have gone to bed.

'Oh yes, there were refuelling stations,' Gina chimes in, interrupting my glutinous gull-less ruminations. 'They had sandwiches and biscuits, and I remember having soup, mashed potato, rice pudding and fruit as well.'

Okay, Gina, that's carrying competitiveness a little too far. I mean, I was happy to settle for pizza or fish and chips; you're going for a full four-course banquet there! How on earth could you carry on running after that lot? I mean, and there's no nice way of putting this, weren't you sick?

Gina laughs gaily – absolutely the best description of her light, tinkling laugh that is so in tune with her whole persona: think Tinker Bell.

'Oh no!' she says, still chuckling, 'I didn't eat it all at once – there were lots of checkpoints with various foods at each one.'

Oh, right, okay then – that does seem a little more reasonable.

'Then at 56 miles we had breakfast in a barn sitting on bales of hay!'

Fry up?

She tinkles, bell-like again, and shakes her fairy head. 'Just cornflakes,' she reassures me.

'It was a great day,' she adds, smiling and looking more as though she is fondly recalling a family gathering rather than an 80-mile slog up hill and down dale, 'despite the cold showers at the finish and having to go upstairs for breakfast, which is pretty much the last thing you want to do after running for that long.'

I'm suitably reassured. There is a part of me that wouldn't have been at all surprised if she hadn't actually considered the stairs an excellent way to warm down after a race like that.

'There were sleeping bodies all over the place, you had to step over them!' she adds cheerily.

Now wait a minute... How did she know they were asleep and not dead? I mean, did anyone think to check? And then I remind myself that the race was in 1996 and by now people would probably have noticed any dead bodies still lying around and I really don't need to concern myself over this.

Instead I turn my attention to my next potentially rather silly question, given the number of marathons and ultra-marathons Gina runs in a year. Does she train much between races?

'Not really,' she admits. 'I prefer training with others, and belong to Plumstead Runners and will fit in with whatever session they're doing, but if I do run on my own I'll go round my local park and generally do about a 50-minute run on a Tuesday and just over an hour on a Wednesday. Oh, and I do yoga three times a week and circuits once or twice a week.'

Not much at all then.

And what about injuries?

'I've been lucky with injuries,' she responds initially, before adding, 'apart from plantar fasciitis [inflammation of the sole of the foot]. I had it before for two years and it cleared up, but this time I've had to have a cortisone injection – I'm hoping it's going to keep it at bay.'

Which almost answers my next question. Does she ever think of stopping running?

'I haven't made a conscious decision when or if to stop, but I do wonder sometimes what it is that will force it to happen. I accept that something will make me stop one day.'

So, what is it that keeps her motivated?

'With a lot of the races, we [the 100 Club] tend to go away

for the weekend. The travelling and socialising is definitely a big part of the attraction for me, especially since I've been on my own.'

What about favourite marathons?

'That's easy!' she says. 'Number one would be London – for the locality, memories of my first one and the atmosphere. Second would be Berlin – I've done it 22 times. When you run Berlin 10 times, you get a number for life. If I never run another Berlin, that number will never be used by anybody else. Those numbers are a special colour: green. You also get given a T-shirt with all the names on it of everyone who has done it 10 or more times.

'Berlin – the place – is also special because it's twinned with Greenwich, where I live, and every year we do a swap. One year the people from Berlin come over here and run the "Grizzly Down" – a tough, fun, off-road 18–20 miler over hilly, muddy, boggy, stony terrain in Seaton.'

Fun? Seriously, Gina – somebody give that girl a dictionary!

'And the next year,' she continues, ignoring what she no doubt considers my rude and unnecessary interruption, 'the people from Greenwich run in the Berlin Marathon. We've been doing it since 1990, when we were first twinned with Berlin. Over the years we've all become good friends.

'One of the most picturesque places I've ever run is in the Outer Hebrides on the Isle of Harris. We ran a marathon on Saturday and then another one on Sunday or Monday on another island. The scenery was breathtaking.'

The *scenery* was breathtaking? Personally, I'd blame the running.

'Another scenic run is Beachy Head,' she continues, 'but I'd choose that also for the camaraderie, the bands and the volunteer support. Also, the checkpoint food! At the end you have a swim, then you're given jacket potato, beans and sausage, followed by rice pudding. The perfect way to end a run!'

My sixth sense, which if I do say so myself, is pretty sharp, is twitching like Peter Rabbit's nose.

'You like your food, don't you, Gina?'

She laughs, the laugh of one who knows there's no point in denying the charge.

'My friends always tease me about the amount I eat – loads of everything!' she tells me unashamedly.

Not that you'd know this from her figure, but then I guess the running counter-balances the amount she eats.

'I've always been petite,' she continues, 'it hasn't happened because of running. In fact, I'm heavier now because I'm more muscular.'

Hmm… I want to admire her bulging biceps and curvaceous calves but from where I'm standing, she just looks tastefully trim. I'm suddenly aware of my own less-than-tastefully trim torso and decide to turn back to the subject before Gina notices.

Having covered a few of her favourite runs, what about her least favourite?

'Davos in Switzerland,' she answers without hesitating. 'It's all off-road, up the mountainside and jumping over waterfalls – I didn't enjoy that at all.'

Really? Why ever not?

'One of the most bizarre series of races I've ever run was in Northern Ireland at the invitation of another 100 Club runner, Peter Ferris. We ran a marathon in all six counties of Northern Ireland in six days, starting in Belfast on the Monday and finishing in Londonderry on the Saturday. Because the local priest was running with us, the races had to be run between the Monday and the Saturday as he couldn't run on a Sunday!

'I prefer to go to as many different places as possible to race,' she continues, 'rather than repeating the same races. As I no longer work, I can stay for longer than a weekend, but generally it's just a weekend as most of the 100 Club are only there for that time as they have to get back to work on a Monday.

'Marathon running has taken me to some really fabulous places, such as Hawaii, Cuba and much of North America. I was running in Marakesh recently,' she goes on, smiling, 'and came across Martin Bush [fellow 100 Club member] with his camera, taking photos of a camel. I took the camera from him so I could take a picture of him with the camel, then I carried on running and left him to it!'

However, there is one race in particular that sticks in Gina's mind, but not for the best of reasons.

'It was in Russia, St Petersburg,' she begins. 'Partway through the race I desperately needed to find a loo. Eventually, I came across two Portaloos together. I yanked open the door of one and had just got inside and closed the door when a woman outside started screaming in Russian and trying to pull the door back open. I was on the other side trying to keep it shut, also screaming, but in English.'

Ooh, how exciting!

'Eventually the woman managed to force open the door, dragged me out of the loo and demanded money for the use of "her" Portaloo! Of course this was mid-marathon and I was only wearing my race gear and had absolutely no money on me at all.'

Maybe more scary than anything else…

'Luckily, Roger Biggs [100 Club chairman] was nearby and saw what was happening but he didn't have any money on him either. Eventually some other runners came by and we managed to gather together enough to satisfy the woman and I was able to do what I needed to before joining in the race again.

'It seems funny now but at the time it was really quite frightening, especially because I couldn't understand a word the woman was saying and she was screaming and tugging at me. That was only about five or six years ago and we'd paid £70 for our race entry fee and couldn't believe we had to actually pay to use the Portaloos!'

Imagine that happening in London…

Gina also remembers the first time she ran in South Africa.

'It was the Comrades Marathon,' she informs me.

What she doesn't tell me but I happen to know is that the Comrades Marathon is considered to be one of the toughest ultra marathon races in the world – all 56 miles of it!

'I actually won some money, about £120, but I didn't know I'd won it until I got home and received an email telling me. Because of the exchange rate, the race organisers didn't want the cost of exchanging the money into sterling pounds.'

Cheapskates!

'So they asked if I was likely to run there again the following year,' continues Gina. 'I had already decided I wanted to do it again [no accounting for taste], so they said they would pay me the money then – which they did, in South African rands – but that was okay because I needed some spending money, anyway.'

You are just too accommodating, Gina.

I imagine aside from winning the occasional £120, this competitive Tinker Bell probably has a fair selection of trophies and medals, too?

'I have loads of trophies all over the house,' she confirms, 'two glass-fronted cabinets full in the kitchen, some in the lounge, the hallway and even the bathroom! My medals are hanging on a door handle since the two boards Hen made for me to display them on have long been full.

'Actually, I asked my son what he would do with my medals when I was gone and he said he would put them in a shoebox. I told him to throw them in a skip! They don't mean anything to anyone else.'

However, one trophy she probably wouldn't want to see in a

skip is the one she won in London in 2010 for winning her age group category.

'That was special,' she agrees, 'to win a trophy in a race with 36,000 competitors and in the place where my marathon running began, nearly 20 years ago.'

For a moment Gina returns to the early days of her running when she used to work in Social Services.

'I started off working with children and ended up with the elderly – one extreme to the other, although similar in many ways!' she says with a laugh.

Indeed. Cantankerous, disrespectful, yet oh-so-charming when they want something!

'In those days, I ran most of my races for charity, raising money through my work colleagues. Once I'd retired I stopped as it was impossible to keep asking the same few family and friends to dip into their pockets every time I ran a race.'

These days Gina runs for the love of running, as she always has, the opportunities it offers her to see the world, make new friends and spend time with those with whom she's become established friends within the 100 Marathon Club. She certainly doesn't think it's an obsession either.

'It's a hobby, that's all,' she insists, 'I enjoy it – social, travel and sport. What's not to enjoy?'

And she has a point – lots of trips to exotic places with a bunch of friends – I must admit I'm sort of beginning to see the attraction myself. If only it wasn't for that darned marathon in the middle of it!

SUMMER SHORTS

Running is a simple sport that consists of putting one foot in front of the other and moving forward. Sometimes when people suffer a loss or pass through difficult times often that is all they are capable of, and all they need do to find their way back into the light and towards recovery.

When in Russia, carry cash!

MILE 15

IT'S COOL BEING
NO. 1 IN THE WORLD

Adam Holland was 18 years old when he ran his first marathon. By 23 he'd become the youngest man in the world to have run 100 of them.

ADAM HOLLAND
Born: 1987
111 marathons:
- 1st marathon: 2005 – Abington
- 100th marathon: 2010 – The Eden Project, Cornwall
Records:
- Youngest Person in UK/world to Have Run 100 Marathons (age 23)
- Fastest Cumulative Time and Fastest Average Marathon Time in the World for 10 Marathons in 10 Days
- Member of World Record 12-Man Team for Greatest Distance Run on a Treadmill in 48 hours (539.86 miles).

Say you are 18 years old and on your way to run a half marathon with a friend, and that friend tells you he's hoping to run 100 marathons before he turns 60 and would you like to run one with him? What would you say?

'Err, no thanks, I think I'm busy that day...'

'Err, no thanks, I'd rather stick to halves...'

'Err, no thanks, I'm only 18 and want to make it to 19...'

Or do you say, 'Of course I'll run one with you,' at the same time as an idea pops into your head that maybe you could become the youngest person in the world to complete 100 marathons? And so thinking, you get home, log on to the internet and check the stats with the *Guinness World Records* to discover the record is held by a guy called Steve Edwards, who ran his 100th marathon at the age of 28?

Personally, I'd go for the, 'I'm sorry, I'm washing my hair/cutting my toenails/waxing my legs and plucking out my nose hairs every Saturday and/or Sunday for the next 10 years. Please don't ask me again. Ever.'

However, Adam Holland (or 'Tango' as he was nicknamed, thanks to an orange pair of trousers worn once during a college wall-climbing exercise), bless him, was an innocent 18-year-old when asked the question and so he wasn't armed to defend himself against such a vicious attack on his sanity.

'Of course I said yes,' he tells me in his delightful clotted-cream Devonshire burr, 'and the idea popped into my head about being the youngest person in the world to run 100 marathons.'

And he can't even blame his parents...

'My mum has never been into sport,' he explains and I can hear his mother in the background, calling out in fervent agreement: 'I can't even run down the street!'

'My dad did manage a local football team until recently and did lots of sport at college – he even once ran the Plymouth Marathon, though I've no idea what time he did,' adds Adam, typically son-like. 'He's built more for rugby than running!'

So, I ask Adam about siblings.

'My brother Nathan, who's 16 now, is a football freak,' he tells me, 'and Jason, who's 11, did karate until recently. Then there's my sister Kayleigh – she's got two kids so she doesn't have time for much else. I did have another sister, Poppy,' he says, his voice level, 'but she had Edmond Syndrome and a hole in her heart, and died when she was five days old.

'But then along came Angel,' he continues, his voice brightening now and I can tell from the tone that he clearly adores his little sister. 'She's three now and she's definitely going to be into sport – she runs everywhere and she loves looking at my medals. Once I was running in a Santa suit and she ran with me on my warm-up!'

No pushy parents or competitive siblings forcing him to take up these challenges, then – just Adam himself.

Perhaps then, with so much self-motivation, it is no surprise that Adam succeeded in his quest to run 100 marathons in 2010 at the tender age of 23.

Now, whether you're a mathematical genius like Einstein or can simply do basic arithmetic like me, you will have worked out that it took just five years for Adam to reach the dizzy heights of completing his 100 marathons.

'Although I ran my first one at 18, I didn't seriously start the challenge until I was 21, so did most of them in two years,' he admits. And he gives me the actual numbers as: 2005 (1 marathon), 2006 (2), 2007 (3), 2008 (25), 2009 (39) and 2010 (32).

My legs ache at the mere thought. And if I was talking to Adam in person, my neck would ache, too for from the photo I've seen of him, Adam looks about six foot tall (he tells me he's actually five foot eleven), with gangly, though muscularly well-defined arms and legs plus a shock of dark hair atop his young head and a moustache in the usual place. When I question him further, however, he tells me he doesn't do any gym work or weight training at all.

'The trouble is,' Adam continues, 'it's very expensive, running that many marathons in a year. I have to work to get the money to go to the races but would like not to have to work all the time so I could train harder and more often.'

He does receive kit, energy drinks and gels from Votwo, a company involved with maximising human performance based at Silverstone, who work with the Formula One Porsche team. They also organise and sponsor coastal marathons around the country and as Adam was the only person to have run all four of their races, when he asked if he could join their team, they had no hesitation in signing him up so he now represents them at team events.

He also gets some support from his local 'Pasty House' and 'Val's Around a Pound' shop, who dedicate one of their windows to his pursuits and sell badges engraved with his personal 100 marathon logo.

'The logo was actually designed by Jade Hughes, a student at Tavistock College,' Adam tells me. 'I set up a competition to see who could come up with the best logo and Jade won. Any proceeds raised from the badges go to my chosen charities,' he continues, 'the Plymouth NHS, where Poppy was born, and the Brathay Trust, who do a lot of work with vulnerable young people and organise the 10-in-10 at Windermere.'

And talking of the 10-in-10, in working towards his 100 Adam also took another record from fellow 100 Club member Steve Edwards, that of the world's fastest accumulated time for running 10 marathons in 10 consecutive days at the Brathay event, knocking a staggering three hours off Steve's record.

'It was a fantastic experience,' says Adam, who raised money for his travel costs and entry fee by running bingo sessions in his hometown, as well as raising a considerable sum for the Brathay

Trust. 'It was out of this world, something completely different,' he continues. 'It takes you away from everything else – work, home, everything – you become totally focussed on what you are doing and the camaraderie between everyone is just amazing. It's an experience you never forget.'

Well, no, probably not. I've never forgotten having a tooth removed by gas when I was four years old and being pushed home in the by-then outgrown pushchair by my mum, a handful of tissues stuffed in my mouth to stem the flow of blood.

But just in case Adam should prove himself wrong and the experience didn't remain forever forged in his memory, he decided to repeat it the following year, smashing his previous record by a further two-and-a-half hours and simultaneously bringing down the record for the fastest average time for all 10 marathons.

'My slowest time was 3 hours 13 minutes on the second day and the fastest was 2 hours 56 minutes on the last day, which averaged out at 3 hours 02 minutes for all 10,' he reveals.

It's hard to imagine how anyone can get up every day for 10 days and run 26.2 miles, let alone trying to imagine how they might get up on the 10th day, having just run an accumulative total of around 235 miles in the previous nine days, run another 26.2 miles, taking their total mileage up to a whopping 262, while managing to run faster than they've run on any of the previous days. But that is precisely what Adam did.

Another marathon he will certainly never forget, but for very different reasons is his 100th, which he ran at the Eden Project Marathon of 2010: in 2 hours 57 minutes.

'It was such an amazing atmosphere,' he recalls. 'Everyone was cheering for me. And then after the race, we all went into the Eden Dome and ate huge slabs of cake that had been baked in Tavistock especially for the occasion!'

Now there's a World Record I might be tempted to have a

bash at – the person to eat the most slabs of cake after watching a marathon!

Adam goes on to tell me the cake was an iced sponge (not chocolate, which is actually his favourite – please note), with his personal logo representing his 100 marathons on the top.

Still on the subject of World Records, though – not cake, I asked how it felt being hailed as a World Record holder.

'It's cool,' he answers, in total accord with his generation.

However cool it might be, Adam hasn't been content to use his talents merely to collect British and World Records (or to eat huge slabs of cake) for he is one of those increasingly rare breeds who willingly give up their time to help others, combining his paid job as a primary school meal-time assistant with encouraging children to be active.

'I make sure all the children have got their meals and cut up their food for them if they need me to, then I take them outside to play after they've finished eating. They know what I've done and like to race me!'

And that job is only part-time. Adam also works full-time at a newsagent's, sorting out the morning paper rounds and making sure everything is in order.

'If a child doesn't turn up to do a round, I'll do it,' he tells me.

As if two jobs wasn't enough and bear in mind those jobs mean Adam is working from half past six in the morning until five o'clock in the afternoon (no wonder he wants sponsorship), he also leads a running group for children in the evening.

'I take them cross-country running round the park,' he explains. 'I had this idea that as part of the Tavistock Half Marathon the children could run a mile a week for 12 weeks leading up to the race and then run 1.1 miles on race day, so that overall they would cover the same distance as the race and would get a medal the same as the people who were racing. The children loved it!

'I started that up in 2010 to get them involved, as not everyone gets the chance to do it through their school. They don't have to run the whole thing, they can walk if they want to,' he adds, as if afraid I might consider him to be galloping along behind the kids, cracking a large whip.

It turned out the scheme was so successful that after the first race had taken place, some of the parents asked Adam if he would carry on with it throughout the year. Of course he said yes!

'It was actually featured on the BBC *Breakfast* programme,' Adam tells me. 'Mike Bushell came to Tavistock and interviewed me.'

So, was he nervous about being interviewed?

'Not really. I've been on television a few times,' he says, casually, as if it's an everyday occurrence. 'I also take a running group for children aged 6 to 15, known as the Tavistock Meadow Running Group.'

It seems pertinent that Adam should be involved in coaching children as that is when he himself got started in running.

'I was about 13 and a friend of mine joined Tavistock Athletic Club, so I followed him into it. I did the 1500 metres, 5,000 metres and Cross-Country. I also did Triple Jump because nobody else wanted to do it – I jumped about 12 metres!'

I'm impressed. Twelve metres is pretty good for a young triple jumper.

'I just kept getting better and beating more and more people, including my friend,' he continues, 'it was just the way it worked out and was very good motivation.'

For Adam, yes – for his friend, not so much, I suspect!

'I had a coach but I stopped when I was about 18 because lots of people in the club were getting injured and it put me off. Then I started with the road running and went on to do the marathon with my friend. I really enjoyed the experience of that first one because I wasn't doing it for a time at all, it was just about completing it and I didn't push myself to the limit. That said, I do remember it was a very different experience to anything I'd done before and I struggled to get round it, probably because I hadn't done any specific training for it, although I was doing a lot of shorter races.

'I ate Jelly Babies while I was running along,' he adds, laughing.

Now you're talking my language! I may even be tempted to give it a go myself. Then again, you can eat Jelly Babies without running anywhere, can't you?

'I've also eaten Jaffa Cakes, Mars Bars and bananas on the run. And when I was doing the 10-in-10, the masseur gave me an ice cream and I ate it. Since then, I've been known to seek out mobile ice-cream vans during other runs, too!'

Do not try this at home – well, okay, you *can* try it at home but do not, under any circumstances, do this out on a run. You will be sick. All I can think is that Adam must have an amazing metabolic rate to be able to digest those sorts of food on the go without throwing up. These days, he takes his preparation and training a little more seriously, although he says he still eats on the run, especially on the longer ones.

Longer ones?

'I run ultras, like the South Downs, which is a 35-mile race and the Dartmoor Discovery, which is 32. I actually can't believe people run a marathon without running at least 26 miles in training or a race first.'

He's also cut down on the numbers of marathons he does, instead concentrating on getting his times down.

'I have a coach now, so I'm doing properly structured training these days. When I was going for the numbers, I didn't do any training,' he explains. As a result he has brought his times down to 2 hours 45 minutes for the Marathon and a highly respectable 1 hour 14 minutes for the Half.

He also tells me that despite the amount of running he does, he doesn't suffer from injuries – apart from once. 'It wasn't from running,' he hastens to assure me, 'it was from playing hockey and it's all fine now.'

Turns out that as well as training and running marathons, as well as working full time, as well as coaching the children, somehow Adam still finds the time (and energy) to play the occasional game of hockey, oh and football, and also darts. Not forgetting of course one of his favourite hobbies – dancing to rock and roll music, which he does once a week!

It may be a little inappropriate to ask someone as young as Adam what keeps him motivated but his accomplishments belie his years, so I ask him anyway.

'I enjoy exploring different parts of the country,' he says. 'My favourite races are by the sea.'

Ah, yes, the sea – a man after my own heart. The shushing of waves, the tang of salt, the flock of gulls trying to steal your fish and chips and ice-cream cone (though I suspect Adam would either have eaten his before they got a chance or outrun them). How I love the seaside!

I wonder what he wants to do next in terms of specific goals or whether he's just hanging around waiting to be invited by someone else to, oh, I don't know, maybe run non-stop from the North to the South Pole or from Venus to Mars – but no, now I'm just being silly. There's no way he would be able to carry enough Jelly Babies, Jaffa Cakes, Mars Bars and bananas to do that, is there? I stop trying to think up new challenges and ask the man himself.

'I'd love to run for the GB Team at the Olympic Games but failing that, I'd like to get my marathon time down to under 2 hours 20 minutes and get my average time down in the 10-in-10 to sub-3 hours. I'd also like to do the Country Music Marathon in Nashville.'

Here's an idea, Adam – how about dancing your way around

the Nashville Marathon and in the process adding another new World Record to your name? Adam has now brought his total to 116 marathons – including a new PB of 2 hours 41 minutes – and joking aside, there can be no doubt that if Adam applies himself to achieving all or any of his goals in the same way as he did attaining his 100 marathons, I don't see how this innovative, imaginative, inspirational and impressive young man can possibly fail.

SUMMER SHORTS

Jelly Babies – buy them!

And no, I've not mistaken this page for my shopping list. Many marathon runners use Jelly Babies as a short-term energy fix. They are easy to digest and full of energy-giving sugar. Oh, and real fruit juice too, according to their manufacturer. But, as with any foods or drinks that you intend to consume during the race, practise eating them on training runs first to make sure they suit your body. Regurgitating Jelly Babies halfway through a marathon is not so cool!

MILE 16

THE STREAKER

Ron Hill is not a member of the 100 Marathon Club but no book about those who have run over 100 marathons would be complete without at least a mention of the man, who for many of those Club members, is their hero and inspiration.

DR RON HILL, MBE
Born: 1938
115 marathons at sub-2 hours 50 minutes:
• 1st marathon: 1961 – Liverpool
• 100th marathon: 1985 – Athens
Records/Achievements (marathon only):
• Most Marathons Run in Sub-2.50
• Longest Unbroken Running Streak
• Holder of Bahrain Marathon Course Record
• Former Marathon World Record Holder
• Former Commonwealth & European Marathon Champion
• Former Boston Marathon Course Record Holder.

There can't be many people who can claim to have run halfway to the moon – metaphorically speaking, of course. In fact, I rather suspect there is only one: the great, the legendary master of marathons, Ron Hill.

And I'm about to speak to him.

I must confess to feeling a little apprehensive about this. I mean, this is one of the world's greatest runners of all time, a former World Record holder, who remains a hero and inspiration to runners all over the world; a man whose name appears on at least one piece of every runner's kit, including my own – not because he has his name tag sewn into every piece of clothing he owns and is a careless sap, who leaves it lying around just asking to be nicked, but because, with a Ph.D. in Textile Chemistry, he developed his own sports clothing label and chain of stores.

I am just debating whether the etiquette of speaking to an internationally renowned World Record holder demands that I address him as Mr Hill or just plain Ron, when the great man himself speaks and all my anxieties fly out the window. For it turns out that Ron is a down-to-earth, softly spoken, grittily northern, real-life Alf Tupper (and if you don't know who Alf Tupper is, you will by the time you have read this chapter), who not only prefers to be addressed by his Christian name but can't speak to me right now because, 'I've just mixed a fresh load of grout.'

Grout? For a moment I wonder whether this is the real Ron Hill or if I've mis-dialled and by some strange quirk of fate I've found another man called Ron Hill, who happens to like grouting. I decide to give him the benefit of the doubt and arrange to call back the following day.

More relaxed, I ask if he finished tiling and listen to a ripple of laughter.

'No,' he admits, 'I ran out of grout, so I had to buy some more. I'm going to finish it off later today.'

Still, a practical man, yes?

'Not really,' he answers with blunt candour. 'I put the tiles on a few years ago, now they're falling off. I think the house is okay but May – my wife – always sees something that needs doing. It's what women do, isn't it?'

'Yes, I suppose so,' I say, doubtfully, glancing around my own modest abode and wondering whether I ought to be more concerned about the faded paintwork in the conservatory, even though I had decided it gave it more of a weathered, beach-hut look, to which I'm rather partial.

'I'd rather be working in the garden,' Ron continues.

Now that fits more with the image I have of an outdoorsy sort of man, who is as famous for his running streak as he is his international performances, having run every single day for the past 47 years, and continuing. However, Ron – in what is fast becoming clear is his usual forthright manner – is quick to correct me on the subject of his outdoorsy-ness.

'I don't mind being indoors,' he says.

As if to prove his point he tells me he's actually written two autobiographies, while sitting indoors at any one of his five desks.

Two autobiographies? *Five* desks?

'They started off as one book,' he explains, 'but the publishers told me it was too long and they wanted it halved at least because I'd put in so much detail. I got out the red pen but felt it was all necessary – diet, training, times, etc. – so I ended up publishing it myself, but in two volumes.'

I'm impressed, especially when he goes on to inform me that the two volumes, entitled *Long Hard Road: Nearly to the Top, Part 1* and *Long Hard Road: To the Peak and Beyond, Part 2*, now sell for something like £70 and £50 on eBay!

And the desks?

'I love desks,' he says, I'd like to say 'sheepishly' but that would be a lie because he actually sounds rather proud of the fact. 'I wrote bits of the book at different desks depending on which room I happened to be in when I thought of something I wanted to write.

'Actually, I saw another desk the other day and wanted to buy it, but May put her foot down. She says I have enough.' He says this almost disbelievingly. 'It's one of the other things she's always going on about,' he adds, but the potential irascibility of his words is eradicated by the gentle way he speaks her name and it's evident that Ron Hill is extremely fond of his 'demon' wife.

They met in a dance hall in Accrington when he was just 16 and May 17-and-a-half.

'She was a cradle snatcher!' he tells me, with what for him is a hearty laugh, yet somehow more of a caressing chuckle. Presumably, after all these years then, she's unconcerned by his running?

'My running has never caused friction between us,' he says immediately, 'because I've run since I've known her and for a long time she ran with me on my morning run.'

It turns out that May has actually done more than accompany Ron on his morning runs, she has also completed the London Marathon herself – at the age of 51.

'She was given an official finishing time of 4 hours 22 minutes,' says Ron, 'but because there were no chips then and it took 11 minutes for her to cross the start line, this was actually 4 hours 11 minutes.' He sounds rightfully proud of his wife's sterling effort.

'She's also taken part in the River Kai Half Marathon and several other races abroad,' he adds, and I can almost see him puffing out his chest. 'She still runs a little, especially when we're on holiday, and she walks every day.

'She understands the health value of running,' he adds. 'In 2004 she had a breast cancer scare and the surgeon messed up the operation so she had to be put on medication, which put weight on and she struggled to keep on exercising.'

However, it's not just May who uses running as a tool for good health in the Hill family. Apparently their sons, Steven and Graham, now in their forties, run for health although Graham used to run competitively.

'He was a good runner at one time,' says Ron. 'He won the Leeds Marathon in 2 hours 23 minutes when he was younger but then he had a knee injury and said that was it. He wouldn't go and seek medical advice.'

It would seem that Ron Hill continues to inspire not only members of the general public to run, but also those closer to home.

What of the man himself? Who or what was the inspiration that initially got him running?

'Alf Tupper!' he tells me, unbounded enthusiasm ringing in his voice.

Alf *who*? I ask, casting my mind back to previous athletic superstars but not recalling one who went by any such name.

'Alf Tupper,' Ron repeats. 'He was a character in *The Rover*, a boys' magazine,' he informs me after a moment's hesitation. 'It couldn't be called a comic, it had too much written information in it for that,' he adds, almost as though he feels he must defend his boyhood reading choice.

No wonder I hadn't heard of Alf Tupper.

'I first started reading about Alf when I was 11 and at Accrington Grammar School,' Ron continues.

'I felt an instant resonance with Alf, or "The Tough of the Track", as he was known to regular readers!' he says. 'Like me, he was from a Northern town and a poor family, and we both lived in a two-up, two-down house with a toilet in the back yard.

'Alf would be running around in the pouring rain in vest and shorts,' continues Ron. 'He had no advantages but he went on to win races despite his problems and despite always getting into trouble with running officials. I saw Alf as this guy who was doing something entirely on his own and succeeding through his efforts alone and despite problems. I admired that, and wanted to be like that.'

Bizarrely, the resonance the young Ron felt with the fictional Alf increased as Ron's running career progressed, culminating in 1970 with him winning the Commonwealth Games in Edinburgh, just as Alf Tupper had done in one of his stories!

Back at school and under the influence of Alf, Ron says he was the only kid who looked forward to cross-country, finishing ninth or tenth in his first-ever race, confirming there was some natural ability present despite the fact that neither of his parents were runners, although his father was a keen footballer. As a result he joined Clayton-le-Moors Athletic Club, near Accrington and was with them until 1960, when he transferred to Bolton United Harriers.

'Bolton was a bigger club and I could get into big-time road races with them,' he explains. 'Later, in 1976, I did go back to Clayton-le-Moors and I'm now a life member even though when I left them, I called them a lot of goats!'

Goats?

'Older, slower runners,' he says, without a hint of remorse at his younger self's rudeness.

'I was very slow to improve,' he says of himself, with enough honesty and self-deprecation to make me appreciate his previous comment is meant more as a truthful observation rather than an outright, disrespectful insult.

'Then I went to Manchester University in 1957,' he continues, 'and found out more about training and started running twice a day. Giving up was something that never entered my mind. Every time when the big games came around and I failed, I knew there was something there and I had to find a way to bring it out on the important occasion.'

In the fullness of time his perseverance paid off and in 1964 he ran 2 hours 14 minutes 12 seconds, breaking the previous World Record, but still having to be content to finish second to Basil Heatley, a future Olympic Silver medallist, who was given the new World Record of 2 hours 13 minutes 55 seconds.

'We both broke the old World Record,' says Ron, 'but I was very annoyed because at 20 miles, an official allowed me to turn on to a wrong road. It may not have made a difference to the end result – Basil was a class runner – but it was very frustrating.'

I can't help thinking it was just the sort of thing that would have happened to Alf Tupper. As is what happened to the real-life Ron in the Commonwealth Games Marathon of 1970.

'I won the race in a new World Record of 2 hours 9 minutes 28 seconds,' he reveals, 'but at the same time Derek Clayton from Australia claimed to have run 2 hours 8 minutes 34 seconds in Belgium. However, all marathon courses that have a World Record set on them have to be measured again immediately afterwards for ratification purposes and when the course Derek Clayton had run on was measured, it was found to be short.'

So, all ended well then?

'No,' says Ron. 'For whatever reason, the IAAF [International Amateur Athletic Federation] still held that the World Record belonged to Derek Clayton.'

Now that's just unfair.

Ron clearly thinks so too, saying he still claims his run to have been a World Record, as does the Association of Road Racing Statisticians (among others), who formally recognise him in the progression of marathon world bests.

Whatever anyone might think about the record, Ron cites the race as one of his career highlights. Naturally, in a career that has spanned over 60 years, there are quite a few of those. Winning the English Cross-Country Championships in 1966 is one such highlight.

'My first love is cross-country running,' explains Ron. 'Ten years before I won the title, I'd finished something like 265th in the youth race and had watched Gordon Pirie win the senior race – I never thought that would be me.'

Another highlight was in 1969, when he won the European Championships.

'I'd been to several major games and not won, so when I passed the leader of the race with one kilometre to go and crossed the line in first place in the 1896 Olympic Stadium in Athens, it was very special.'

As was winning the Boston Marathon in 1970.

'I was the first Briton to win the race and took three-and-a-half minutes off the course record. I won a medal and a bowl of beef stew!'

Beef stew?

Actually, I do remember winning a bottle of orange cordial and a book about Princess Anne at a couple of cross-country races when I was younger – 'twas a different world, back then.

But let's not digress – let's return to Ron's beef stew before it goes cold.

'The Road Running Club had raised money to send me to Boston and the race director had billeted me with a local family, who fed me beef stew!' he explains.

Ah, so not a prize then. That makes more sense. I mean, a vat of beef stew wouldn't keep nearly so well as a bottle of orange squash and would probably be quite difficult to tuck inside your suitcase.

Talking of Boston, Ron tells me he was actually invited back there in 2010 to mark the 40th anniversary of his victory, but was unable to go due to the ash cloud from an Icelandic volcano that disrupted air travel over Europe in April and May 2010. Instead he and May travelled there a year later, seizing the opportunity to visit Rhode Island to take part in a 5K and a 10K race while there.

And why not?

'We've done a lot of travelling this year [2011] – I enjoy running abroad,' he goes on to say, much in accord with the 100 Marathon Club members.

For Ron, though, travelling is an enjoyment developed early on in his career that stems back to university days.

'The opportunity to run really increased my chances to travel,' he explains. 'When I was selected for Manchester University the first time, I was running at Durham so got travel expenses and it was the first time I'd stayed in a hotel.'

Since then of course he has travelled to rather more exotic places. Not that I'm suggesting for one moment that Durham doesn't have its fair share of exotica – it certainly has a rather lovely cathedral.

'My love of travel grew from there,' he continues. 'Running has taken me to the big games in Budapest, Tokyo and Mexico, all round Europe and a lot of the world and is responsible for instilling a huge love for travel in me. The most unusual place I've been to run is Moldova, between Ukraine and Romania. I'd picked up a leaflet advertising the race at a half marathon in Kiev.'

As you do.

'The race was an 11.4K from Chisinau to Caloveni. To get to the start we had to go by minibus in the middle of the night across Romanian countries and we had two punctures!

'I stayed in a tiny apartment in Chisinau. My hosts, Victor and Tamara, were both veteran runners and moved out while I was there as the place wasn't big enough for the three of us. They had little money but Tamara put on a huge spread at our first meal and the food seemed to last for almost the whole of my stay; that sort of kindness is not often seen today.

'The nicest place I've ever been to run was Cambodia, where I did a series of 5K, 10K and half marathon races. All the races started in front of a great palace at dawn – it was beautiful.'

He has also run in Bahrain – where he still holds the marathon course record – and China, where he took part in the Coast of China Marathon, near Hong Kong.

'It was a really hot day,' he recalls. 'Not far from the finish a very big butterfly flew over and I remember thinking that if it hit me, I would fall over – I was so weak!'

Despite that, he won the race 11 minutes ahead of the second-place runner and says he didn't see a single person for the entire time once he started running.

As well as sharing the 100 Marathon Club's love of travel, Ron also enjoys setting himself new challenges.

'I completely understand that concept,' he says. 'I think it's important to have something to aim for. Once I stopped running internationally, I set myself the challenge of getting to 100 marathons.'

A challenge he duly completed in 1985 in Athens, where he finished 25th in 2 hours 43 minutes 56 seconds.

Ron has actually completed a total of 115 'officially run' marathons, by which he means that he crossed the finishing line in every one of those 115 races in under 2 hours 50 minutes. That's a truly remarkable achievement and without doubt a World Record – one I would imagine is likely to remain for some time to come.

'I have actually done more than 115 marathons although I've no idea of the exact number,' he tells me. 'A lot of them were what I call "phantom marathons" – ones where I've been invited to run with someone else or for charity or something, so the time wasn't the important factor. In those ones I would just run up to the finish but never cross the line, unless it was going to be under 2:50.'

So, once he'd achieved his 100 marathons what came next on his agenda?

'My next target was by the age of 60 to have raced in 60 different foreign countries, which I did, so then I set a new challenge of running 100 different countries by the time I was 70, which gave me 10 years to run 40 new countries.'

You won't need me to tell you that Ron duly achieved this, too.

Even when it came to giving up marathons, he turned this into a specific challenge.

'In 1988, I ran my 111th marathon in 2 hours 51 minutes in London and it hurt. I questioned whether I should continue running marathons, but did London again in 1989 (in 2 hours 42 minutes) and felt fine. Then I did Boston in 1990, on the 20th anniversary since I'd won it, in 2 hours 45 minutes, and again felt okay. Then I was back in London again in 1991 and finished in 2 hours 51 minutes. That really hurt and I questioned why I was doing it – I wasn't enjoying it and I was doing a slow time. I really didn't want to do it again. But by then I'd done 114, which didn't seem a good number to stop on, but 115 was a multiple of five so that seemed okay.'

I don't like to admit this but I know exactly what he means.

'So I decided I wanted to do the 100th Boston Marathon and make that my last one but it wasn't for another five years in 1996, so I waited until then. I finished in 3 hours 12 minutes – my slowest-ever time – but next day I didn't feel too bad. But I told myself to shut up and that was the last marathon I did.'

Of course there's one challenge for which Ron is famous across the world – his continuous running streak. And I don't mean running *naked* through the streets, just running every day, fully clothed.

'I began the streak on 21 December 1964,' he recalls, 'and have maintained it ever since, although since taking a holiday in Greece a couple of years ago when I had a heavy cold and came back from my run feeling really tired, I've been trying hard to cut back the mileage from 30 miles a week down to 20.

'The last time I cut it down was when I went from training twice a day – four miles in the morning, nine miles at lunchtime, plus one run on a Sunday – to once a day. I wondered when was a good time to make that change and eventually decided it was appropriate to stop after 26.2 years, being, of course, the distance I'd raced at.'

Great minds and all that – not Ron and me, Ron and my son Jack, whose idea it was to divide this book into 26.2 chapters. Ron has also recorded every mile he's run since he first started keeping a training log in September 1956.

'So far I've logged 155,000 miles,' he tells me.

That's a long way.

'It's the equivalent of seven times around the world or halfway to the moon,' he gleefully informs me.

Okay then, a very long way.

'My actual target is 250,000 kilometres,' he adds.

Whether or not he makes it remains to be seen but one thing is certain: Ron has no intention of stopping.

'I think running is a healthy thing to do and I don't want to stop doing it – I still find it a challenge.'

So much so that even when he had an operation on a bunion, he still went out for a run.

'I wore a modified shoe and used walking sticks to take the pressure off the plaster cast when the toe was operated on, and ran a mile a day for six weeks.'

Er, didn't that hurt?

'Only a bit, unless I concentrated on the pain – after three days I got used to my toe being in plaster.'

Ah – good old resistance training! (A method of training using something to impede freedom of movement, forcing the runner to work harder so when the object is removed, the effort of running is much easier and performance is heightened.) Makes a change from a rubber tyre and piece of elastic, I suppose.

'The nearest I came to missing a run was when I was in a head-on car crash.'

Poor excuse, Ron.

'It wasn't my fault,' he says, as if I was maybe questioning that fact, 'the other driver came round a blind bend at Woodhead Pass. They took me to hospital and told me my sternum was broken in two, and I remember thinking that maybe this was the end of my streak.'

Maybe?

'I wanted to go home but they put those pulse things on the ends of my fingers and my heart showed some damage so they said I would have to spend the night in hospital. But then my heart settled down and they told me I could go home.

'I waited until May went out to do some shopping and then walked to a level stretch of road and ran for half a mile out and back. I kept that up for a week without May realising and built back up.'

At the risk of repeating myself – didn't it hurt?

'Well, I could feel the bones moving about because there was nothing to stabilise them. And I guess there was possibly some pain.'

Possibly? I'm going to take that as a 'yes'. If not, I shall spread the rumour that Ron Hill is actually a robot. Or maybe it's just that he comes from the old school and is, like his paper partner, one of the 'Toughs' of this world.

Certainly, in running terms he says things were different back then.

'In those days if you wanted to win a race you had to be a front-runner. It was a matter of going out as hard as you thought you could and keeping going. There were no negative splits [running the second half of a race faster than the first] then, nobody had even heard of them.

'I think the standards at the top end of the sport in this country today have dropped because there are so many diversions for people's time and the impossibility of winning anything really great in major games because of the Ethiopians and Kenyans. They have such an innate advantage living at altitude compared to people living at sea level. But I would counter that by saying that in my day there were four things athletes wanted: (1) was to break a World Record, (2) was to be in the Olympics, (3) was to be in the Commonwealth Games and (4) was to be in the European Games.

'These days I can't believe, when athletes are selected to run in international events and get their GB or England vests, that they actually turn down the opportunity. That just would not have happened in my day – we would have given anything to get an England or British vest. Surely it's worth being the best in Britain?

'I also think that having been born in 1938 and going through the war years on a restricted diet was an advantage. The food may have been rationed and restricted, but it was much better than the processed foods of today from a health point of view.'

Indeed, like the rest of his family, and apart from the personal challenges he sets for himself, it is largely the health benefits that keep Ron running today.

'I believe so much in the health benefits of running for anyone who runs, whether as a professional international athlete or a fun runner taking part in a big city marathon.'

Talking of which, I wonder what are his thoughts on those big city marathons?

'I don't really know what they're like from the point of view of the average runner,' he admits, 'as I always started at the front with the elite group of about 20. It's like a separate race – there is the race at the front for people who are really racing for a time and then behind them are thousands of other people who have a different motivation.

'Take the Manchester 10k,' he goes on. 'They have 38,000 runners, who each pay £30 to enter and the entries are closed within a few days. But those people aren't so much going to a race as a "happening" – they want to be part of it, part of a huge crowd, all gathering together, sharing an experience. And it's healthy for people, it really doesn't matter why.

'As for those people who do things like running 40 marathons in 40 days or a marathon every day for a year, whilst I would never decry their efforts,' says Ron, 'I would say that anyone who runs marathons seriously does that sort of thing every day in training: the marathon itself is a race.'

It's an interesting observation and in his forthright, down-to-earth way Ron Hill may be stating the obvious but in so doing he makes what some might consider a salient point.

SUMMER SHORTS

Whether you're a World Record holder like Ron, a 'slut' like the 100 Marathon Club guys and gals, or still a marathon virgin, setting yourself challenges along the way is a great technique to stay motivated and gives you a real sense of achievement and self-worth when you attain your goal.

It's also a good way of using the creative part of your brain in coming up with new and original challenges, such as how many jelly babies can you eat during one marathon or how many people can you tell the same joke to during 26.2 miles?

MILE 17

AUTOMAN

S id Wheeler is the only man ever to have beaten 1960
Olympic 1500-metre Gold medallist, Herb Elliott. He has
also beaten three other Olympic & World Gold medallists.

SID WHEELER
Born: 1937
181 marathons:
• 1st marathon: 1983 – Guildford
• 100th marathon: 1996 – Boston
Honours:
• International Cross Country Runner.

Most people turn up at cross-country races in a car or a coach
but not Sid Wheeler – oh no! When Sid was selected to run for
England in a Home Countries and Ireland cross-country match,
he turned up in an aeroplane: a Boeing 737, to be precise!

Not because he is a show-off – he isn't. Nor because he is a pilot – he isn't. But because his ex-RAF-turned-commercial pilot son Andy thought that flying his dad to his first-ever international cross-country match, or at least to the nearby airport at Belfast would make a rather suitable, not to mention original 70th birthday gift for his father.

'It was a complete surprise,' Sid (a retired sales manager, now aged 74) tells me, his friendly voice bubbling over with undisguised delight at what is clearly a very special memory. 'Andy had always promised to take me flying one day,' he adds, nostalgia thickening his voice.

Of course it wasn't just the flight that was special.

'I had to wait until I was 70 before I got my international vest,' Sid says, and I can hear the smile in his voice. 'There were only four picked for each age group and I was the reserve.'

In other words, he might have had to wait until he was 70 but the sense of achievement was no less for the waiting. Just to confirm his status as an international athlete, Sid managed to once more gain selection the following year for the same event, this time as a counting member of the team.

Sid's rise from social runner to international superstardom began when he was 46.

'I was inspired by watching the first London Marathon,' he explains. 'I was fed up with the way football and other sports were going, with hooliganism on and off the pitch and non-sportsmanlike behaviour, so when I saw the two leaders link arms to cross the line together at that first race, I decided this was a sport that I would like to be involved in.'

But it was to be another four years before he managed to get a place in the London Marathon, although in between he started training with a group of work colleagues who would run round Richmond Park in their lunch break and tested out his racing legs with a few 10Ks and half marathons.

'Then I ran my first marathon in 1983, in Guildford where I

was then living. As soon as I'd run that first marathon I realised I preferred, and was far better suited to the longer distance runs,' he says.

Since then he has run 181 marathons, including several ultras, travelling all over the country and abroad to build up his numbers. His next goal is to run 200 marathons by the time he's 75.

'I think it's important for people to have goals, not only in running terms but in life,' he continues. 'Though I do wonder how people get to do 100 these days. When I did 48 in one year, I was retired and it was very expensive having to run overseas to find enough races.

'The 100 Club do try and help by putting on some of their own races, such as the Greenwich Foot Tunnel run, which we did in 2002 to mark 100 years of the existence of the tunnel. Also the replication of the marathon run at the 1908 London Olympics, when we followed the exact same course as they'd run 100 years earlier.'

Despite all his overseas races, Sid cites one of his favourites as homely Abingdon. 'Because that's where I ran my Personal Best of 2 hours 58 minutes when I was 54,' he tells me, still clearly delighted by his time, as indeed he should be. 'I thought I'd win my age group category but someone beat me by 10 minutes!'

Now that's hard to believe. Two hours 58 minutes is a very respectable time at any age, never mind 54.

Another favourite of Sid's is Boston.

'I ran my 100th in 1996, which was the 100th year of the Boston Marathon,' he tells me. 'I ran it with two other 100 Club members, who were also running their 100th, which makes us the only three in the 100 Club who belong to the exclusive 100/100 Club.

'I'd only realised a year before that it would be the 100th Boston Marathon and decided that was where I wanted to run my 100th,' he continues, 'but I'd only run 52 marathons up till then, so I then ran 48 in that one year to reach my target. It meant I travelled about a lot, including going to some places and back, and running the marathon all in one day.'

Now would seem like an appropriate time to ask the question (it's all about timing) – does he think he's obsessed with running marathons?

He laughs good-naturedly.

'Not really,' he says, 'because I have many other interests, not all running, although even my running is mixed as I do cross-country, fell running and ultras, as well as trail and road.'

As if to illustrate this fact, he goes on to tell me that when he was 60, he ran 60 miles on his 60th birthday for charity.

'I organised the route and raised the money, and it was splashed all over the local papers but unfortunately my wife, Jo, was not at all happy with me advertising my age as that meant everyone would know roughly how old she was, too,' he says, chuckling merrily.

He really thinks that's funny? Oh, Sidney, you have such a lot to learn about women!

'So, the following year I didn't tell anyone and ran 61 miles on the same route on the day of my birthday. The day before the run, Jo asked me why I'd got all these buns in [currant buns are apparently Sid's staple pre-marathon food], so I told her it was because I was going to run 61 miles the next day. "You didn't tell me!" she accused, so I told her that all she had to do was to take the dogs round the course, and give me some drinks along the way and nobody would be any the wiser.'

Only a man! Naturally, being a wife who probably got married at a time when they had to promise to 'obey' their husbands and despite having no personal interest in running, having come from an artistic and creative gene pool rather than a sporty one, the lovely and devoted Jo did as she was bid (and carried on doing so) as Sid continued to run the equivalent number of miles to his age every year until he was 70.

As well as being a member of the 100 Marathon Club, Sid also belongs to his local running club, Chepstow Harriers. He joined in 1989 and became its chairman in 1992, when he concentrated all his efforts on increasing female membership of the club, which at the time was virtually non-existent. And he did a good job: the Club now boasts a 40 per cent female membership and its social side is soaring!

In accordance with the 100 Club's ethos to put something back into the sport of marathon running, Sid also organises races for the Harriers as well as helping to coach other runners, but his particular skill lies in pacing people to help them achieve their own marathon times.

'It's something I happen to be good at,' he says, honestly rather than boastfully. 'I take marathoners out for training runs at a specified pace. I will ask them how fast they want to run – say, an 18-mile training run, what minute miles – and then I tell them to sit behind me and I'll take them through almost to the second at the time they want. Often they tell me that I'm going too slowly and I assure them I'm not.

'I tell them to imagine they are on children's reigns and I will pull them back if they go too fast. Many of them want to set off too quickly.'

'Er…' interjects Coach Summer, 'any chance that those setting off too quickly are male?'

Sid agrees this is generally the case.

Okay, I *knew* it! I don't wish to appear sexist, but I've seen this so many times. Macho man blasts off as if he's in a 26.2-metre sprint before blowing up when he suddenly remembers actually it's a 26.2-mile marathon. Wary woman, on the other hand, jogs sedately away from the starting line as if she's afraid anything faster will render her unable to make the finish – Venus and Mars, so to speak.

That said, there are exceptions and Sid is clearly one of them.

'I've never used a Garmin and rarely use a stopwatch,' he tells me. 'I don't need to. I have a natural instinct for pace – how far, how fast. So much so,' he adds, 'that they've nicknamed me Automan!'

As well as his robotic ability to judge pace, Sid has also run about 50 marathons as guide to the 100 Club's 'Blind Paul'.

'Paul became blind due to water on the brain at the age of 8 or 10,' Sid informs me. 'He can't see his feet but he can see the sky.'

Does that mean if he stands on his head, he can see his feet, then?

Sid thinks not and laughs, as does Paul when I later suggest this to him myself. And I add this in here in case you think I'm cruel and heartless to be making jokes at a blind man's expense.

'Some people wouldn't run with Paul,' Sid continues, 'maybe because they're not sure how to talk to him or manage his blindness so I helped Paul move to Hereford Club as they tend to be more helpful there.' It's clear that there is no criticism intended in Sid's statement, it's just said as a matter of fact.

'I can't run with Paul anymore,' Sid explains, 'he's got too fast for me and I would slow him down. I always told him that would happen, but he didn't believe me!'

Undoubtedly the keyhole surgery Sid recently had on his knee, which caused him to take almost a year out of running, won't have helped.

'I had problems through running – particularly downhill, in fell running and cross country in particular. Now I've been told to avoid downhill and off-road running as much as possible. But that's okay,' he says, cheerfully, 'I prefer road runs anyway.'

Because of the knee injury Sid has been forced to cut his

training sessions down to three days, more or less halving training mileage from 40 miles a week to 20.

Despite that, he tells me he still has goals that he wants to achieve: 'I want to do a full Ironman.'

He says this as if he's telling me he wants to take a stroll round the local park and I'm relieved that I haven't just taken a sip of the water that always sits on my right-hand side whenever I'm conducting a telephone interview and which would surely have ejected itself noisily from my nose in response to his blithe statement.

'I've done a half,' he goes on, 'but I want to do a full one once my knee is better – maybe later this year, but if not then next year. I'd like to be the oldest man to do one.'

Which he assures me but doesn't entirely surprise me, he would be at 74.

'One of the problems with the Ironman for older people,' Sid tells me seriously, 'is that they have cut-off times for the different disciplines.'

Don't ask me why but somehow I thought it was going to be something like incontinence.

'One man I know,' he continues, fortunately unable to read my mind down the telephone line (although when he reads this book he won't have to and I crave forgiveness for what I'm sure is an incorrect assumption based purely on TV and magazine adverts), 'couldn't enter a race because he knew he couldn't meet the swim time and the entry fee is too expensive to waste.'

Not one to be deterred, plucky Sid decided to set up his own Ironman course near his home.

'I live in the middle of nowhere,' he explains. 'I've arranged for the use of a hotel swimming pool (which is just a few yards away), the bike ride will start from my house and then we will embark on the run along the River Wye, which follows the old railway line and is therefore fairly flat all the way.'

Perfect! Do you know this reminds me of when I was a kid and wanted to organise a village fête in my parents' back garden? Okay, so we didn't actually live in a village and the garden was the size of a seventeenth-century lady's handkerchief, but I'd seen one on the telly and loved the romanticism of the whole thing. Tombolas, apple bobbing, hoopla, wet sponge throwing… they were all on my list. Unfortunately, Mum and Dad didn't share my enthusiasm and even mentioned something about racketeering or profiteering, something like that. Even when I offered to send half the money to charity, they remained stubbornly unimpressed. I'm only telling you this so you understand why I feel so well qualified to empathise with Sid's pioneering spirit and imaginative innovation.

'I'm going to let the guy who couldn't enter the race use my course to test himself out and get a time with me supporting him,' he adds.

Oh, but that's marvellous – kind and thoughtful. See, parents, *see*!

'Of course it will be unofficial but at least he'll have a chance to complete the gruelling event and know that he is able to do it so then he can enter the proper Ironman competition, if he can do the times.

'It's the same in the London Marathon,' he goes on. 'At age 70 for men and 65 for women, the cut-off time is five hours for a "Good for Age" category entry. However, beyond those ages the cut-off time doesn't change, making it more or less impossible for older runners to get in on a "Good for Age" basis, which I think is a real shame.'

That does seem a pity, especially when there's the likes of Sid still raring to go but denied the chance not only of entering the race but also of achieving one of his goals: to run his 25th consecutive London Marathon.

'Since I had to take the year off with my knee problem, for

the first time I'm unable to get in with a "Good for Age time,'" he adds. 'And with getting older, I don't know whether I'll ever make the 25 now.'

Whatever remains of Sid's future running career, however, he still has some truly golden memories to reflect on. Like, beating not one, two, three but four Olympic and World Gold medallists.

'I'm the only man,' he boasts, 'who has beaten the 1960, 1500-metre Olympic Gold medallist Herb Elliott. It was during a fun run in Hyde Park organised by the *Sunday Times* and they'd invited Herb Elliott. I carried a camera with me so I could take a photograph when Herb passed me, but I had to run so hard trying to beat him and was so exhausted, I couldn't even manage to press the button!

'Luckily, though,' he continues, 'a friend managed to get one of me overtaking Herb!'

Even better!

Unbelievably, in that same race Sid took his second international scalp in beating the slightly lesser known Ron Delaney: 1500-metre Olympic Gold medallist (1956).

His third conquest came in the London Marathon when he beat the world and European 400-metre Gold medallist, Roger Black.

'To be fair,' says Sid with a chuckle, 'he did have to start the race before he could start running it!'

His final victory also occurred in the London Marathon when he beat Olympic walker and early member of the 100 Club, Don Thompson, who brought back Britain's only Gold medal of the 1952 Games: the 50K Walk. ⟶ *1960.*

It's impossible not to wonder what a man who has beaten four Olympic and World Gold medallists and achieved international selection, with a reputation for natural pace judgement, a Personal Best of 2 hours 56 minutes at the age of 54 and a 'Good for Age' time qualifying him for automatic entry

*The only gold medal winner
in 1952 was a horse!*

into the London Marathon for the past 24 years might have achieved, had he started running at an earlier age.

Of course this is something we will never know but I will make so bold as to suggest that it might well have been something rather special.

SUMMER SHORTS

Sid's instinct for pace judgement may well be natural but it can also be learned to a greater or lesser extent. One way to do this is to find a running track or a level field and run one lap at a comfortable speed, timing yourself with a stopwatch. Now work out your halfway time by dividing it in two. Rest for a few minutes (keep warm by putting on a tracksuit and/or walk around slowly). Set the alarm on your watch to go off at the halfway time then run a further lap at what feels like a similar pace to the first. Speed up or slow down as necessary to ensure you are at the halfway point when the alarm goes off.

Repeat once a week and within about six weeks you should reach the halfway point at the right time nearly every time. Think about how you feel while running. With enough practice, you should be able to run a whole lap in your target time without setting the halfway alarm – it's all about learning to listen to your body and reading the signs.

If that doesn't work, find a man called Sid.

MILE 18

TO LOVE, HONOUR AND RUN MARATHONS WITH...

For two couples, running marathons has brought them closer and strengthened their marriage.

COUPLE ONE:

Dave Major	Linda Major
Born: 1964	Born: 1965
453 marathons:	300 marathons:
• 1st marathon: 1996 – London	• 1st marathon: 2001 – New York
• 100th marathon: 2004 – Ireland	• 100th marathon: 2006 – Munich

Records:
• UK/Potential World Record for Number of Marathons Run by a Married Couple

No doubt running marathons virtually every weekend could potentially put a strain on any relationship, not only because one partner is away all the time but because of the financial implications, too. Certainly, the 100 Marathon Club has had its share of marital casualties, but it also has two married couples who reckon their passion for marathons actually enhances their relationship. How can that be, I hear you ask. Well, to put it simply: they run them together.

Couple number one – Dave and Linda Major – have been doing just that since 2001, when Linda ran her first marathon in New York with Dave. Together, they have completed a combined total of over 700 marathons (Dave 453, Linda 300 as of June 2011), which is certainly a UK record and potentially a World Record. Indeed, the couple are currently complying with the stringent rules of the *Guinness World Records* in supplying confirmation of the number of marathons they have run together since being married (none of the marathons run before then can count) to see whether their joint total can better the current record of around 400. Currently, Dave and Linda reckon they have 630 qualifying marathons, so it seems likely the record will be theirs.

Interestingly, neither of them started out as likely contenders for such a title: Linda was born with a hole in her heart and Dave has suffered from asthma since the age of two. However, in 1994, Dave – then an overweight smoker, who had associated health problems – was told he had only five years left to live if he didn't change his lifestyle dramatically. He took the warning seriously.

'Giving up smoking and going on a diet was the easier part of the deal,' he observes. 'The hardest thing was not knowing what I was going to do socially for the rest of my life. I took up running to help me lose weight. The first time I went out, I could only manage 100 yards before I had to turn back.'

However, he persisted and in 1996, ran his first marathon in London. He ran his 100th eight years later in Ireland. Now he plans to run his 500th in Brighton, in April 2012.

'I get annoyed when people say they can't run – very few

people are unfortunate enough to be physically incapable of running. Running gave me my life back and has prolonged it, too,' Dave insists.

And as for worrying about his social life...

'Running has created my social life. My friends are runners or husbands and wives of runners. We have our holidays with other runners and have a common bond with each other, even if we haven't seen each other for weeks or months. It's a very positive experience to talk to runners from all over the world. We have made many friends in many countries.'

However, when Dave first met Linda in 1999 she was a complete non-runner. 'Linda knew that I ran and was very supportive. After a few years she decided she wanted to run a race, so she entered the New York City Marathon in 2001.'

At this point, Linda takes up the story.

'It was supposed to be a one-off,' she laughs, 'but then I realised that racing every couple of weeks was actually easier than going out on 20-mile training runs all the time!'

I'll have to take her word for that.

Linda ran her second marathon in 2003 and by 2006 had notched up a 100th marathon in Munich, Germany.

'It was wonderful,' she says. 'The race finished in the 1972 Olympic Stadium. There were 20 friends from the 100 Club running the marathon, as well as Dave and we all danced across the finish line together doing the Conga!'

It was meeting and talking to other people from the 100 Marathon Club that got Dave and Linda into running more marathons in the first place.

'They shared with us their knowledge, which we now share with other people,' says Dave. 'It is one big extended family, who all have the same love of running marathons and travelling.'

Dave and Linda reckon that running together has not only given them a shared interest as a couple, but has also widened their social circle and given them shared aims in life to complete together.

'We feel it has created a stronger bond between us,' continues Dave, 'we spend a lot more time together than most other couples. When we are training, we discuss things that other couples would do at home.'

So, I have to ask, do they run together in a race? The romantic in me pictures this sweet, devoted couple running along together, holding hands.

'No,' Dave says without hesitation, shattering my idyll with one cruel blow. 'We run separately in most races as we want to compete within our own age groups, peers and club.'

Oh, right… After all this is a book about running marathons and not Mills & Boon.

Both cite their favourite race as the Comrades Ultra Marathon in South Africa, presumably because this is 90 kilometres' worth of time spent together.

'I tend to like the big city marathons with Samba bands or rock and roll music,' says Dave. 'The bigger the crowd support, the better for me!'

'Whereas I'm happy with pretty much any type of race,' adds Linda, 'although I'm not good in the heat or when the race has lots of traffic.'

Together they have run not just marathons but also ultra-marathons, triple-marathons and even 12-hour track races.

'The worst thing for both of us is not finishing,' Dave admits.

Not only do they both feel the same about not finishing, they also share the same views about a lot of things when it comes to running.

'We both believe that the first marathon is a learning process about you and your mental and physical state,' says spokesman Dave. 'We believe in listening to our bodies and believe that if we were to run our hardest every time we raced, we would risk injury.

'And we hardly ever get injured,' he adds, as if by way of confirmation.

Now I have to say at this point I'm a little afraid of putting that bit in as it feels rather like quoting someone's famous last words. However, I'm not overly-superstitious but I would just like it to go on record that if, after this book is published, either Dave or Linda (heaven forbid, both of them) is forced to retire from running due to injury, it's not my fault. Injury lawyers, please take note.

Now we've got that sorted, let's return to Dave and Linda, whose togetherness spills over into nearly every aspect of their lives.

'We both left school at 16,' says Dave, 'we're both divorced [though not from each other, obviously], we have both worked all our lives and we both believe in working to live, not living to work.

'We also both have very understanding employers who allow us to take time off, providing we make it up, if we have long distances to travel to races.'

And that's not all. Despite their respective first marathons being five years apart, both ran similar times of around 4 hours 30 minutes.

Spooky!

Indeed, so together are Dave and Linda that they are known in the running world as 'The Running Majors' and if one attends a race without the other, people will ask if everything is okay.

Now ain't that sweet? Eat your heart out, Mills & Boon!

COUPLE 2

Dave Ross	Mel Ross
Born: 1967	Born: 1974
216 marathons:	156 marathons:
• 1st marathon: 1999 – Durban, SA	• 1st marathon: 2003 – London

- 100th marathon: 2008 – Cork
- 100th marathon: 2009 – Moray

Records (current and previous):
- Mel – Previous UK/World Record for Youngest Female to Have Run 100 Marathons
- Dave – World Records for Fastest Marathon Run as a Cartoon Character (Fred Flintstone) and Fastest Comic Book Character (Dennis the Menace)

Enough of romance, let's get back to running, I hear you say. And so we shall. Just as soon as we move on to Marathon Married Couple No. 2, 'The Running Rosses' (not really, I made that up) – another Dave and his wife, Mel.

Now just before I launch into the next bit, I feel I must add that as I write, Dave and Mel are in the Western States, where they're about to run a 100-miler in Squaw Valley.

'I'm as nervous as a rattlesnake but also very excited,' Dave told me 'We've never run this far before in one sitting, so it's a complete leap of faith for me and Mel!'

I had to put that in, not just because it's an awesome thing that this couple are doing, but because I love the rattlesnake analogy, plus I told Dave I'd get it in and credit him with the authorship. Job done!

So, where were we? Ah yes, Mel and Dave. What say we ring the changes and start with the lady first this time?

Born in 1974, Mel Ross ran her first marathon in 2003 (London) and her 100th in 2009 (Moray).

'I would have got there quicker,' she assures me, 'but I had to have some time off for an operation to strip a varicose vein out of one of my legs.'

Ooh, err… I don't much like the sound of that.

'It's a genetic thing,' she assures me, 'nothing to do with the running.'

Oh well, that's okay then.

Unlike Linda, Mel was a runner before she met her Dave.

'I started running, having watched the London Marathon on TV, joined the local running club and entered the London Marathon through a charity the following year.

'I met a lovely older man called Robbie Wilson at the club – he'd just completed his 200th marathon. I was so amazed as to how anyone could do this. He encouraged me and we entered lots of marathons together. Then a few others started running marathons and then there was a group of us, who encouraged each other. We kept finding marathons that we wanted to run and it escalated from there.'

Mel tells me that Robbie is now 76 and still running marathons. Well done!

As for Dave, he was born in 1967, ran his first marathon in Durban, South Africa in 1999 and his 100th was in Cork (2008) – wearing a kilt!

'I got the running bug after doing my first marathon as I never believed I could cover the distance though having done it, the running became a self-fulfilling prophecy thereafter and the better I did, the more I reaped the rewards.

'That said, I didn't set out to run so many marathons,' he says, seeming to want to reassure me. 'After I'd done 50, the numbers increased as I really wanted to become a fully fledged member of the 100 Club as you get your Club kit and a commemorative medal when you achieve this milestone, which are spectacular.'

For Dave running is not just a physical experience, it is also highly spiritual.

'My pre-race routine usually starts with a silent prayer, thanking the Lord above for the ability to be able to do what I do and I pray for those less fortunate and ask God for help if I'm experiencing a problem. It's a very spiritual connection for me when I run and I feel blessed to be able to run so many marathons.

'Running for me became a form of expression, a spiritual connection and a definite outlet from the constraint associated with everyday life – working nine to five whilst stuck in an office environment every day.'

Mel too says she finds it spiritual to be at one with nature and enjoys the freedom offered by running.

Perhaps it was only a matter of time or perhaps just fate (okay, we're back to the romance again) that through their shared love of marathon running, Mel and Dave were bound to find each other one day.

'We first met in 2005, at the Windmill Marathon in Rottingdean, Sussex,' Dave tells me, 'although at that time we just chatted briefly. It was only after meeting at subsequent marathons that the romance really got off the ground.'

Then in 2009, the two travelled to Davos in Switzerland to run a marathon. The day before the race, however, Dave suggested they should take a jolly jaunt atop neighbouring mountain Jacobshorn.

'We reached the top and Dave disappeared for a bit,' recalls Mel. 'He mentioned something about having a dodgy stomach but then he returned, dressed in his kilt and sporran!'

'I'd taken it with me in a backpack to the top of the mountain so she wouldn't guess anything was afoot,' Dave tells me.

Yes, well, I would agree going commando in a skirt to the top of a blowy mountain might arouse suspicion.

'And then he proposed,' says Mel, beaming from ear to ear.

I get the feeling that the surprised delight of that proposal still hasn't worn off for Mel and meeting the two of them in Malta, I have to say they do appear to be a couple still very much in love. Certainly, when asked independently and out of the company of the other, which was their favourite marathon both immediately named Davos! Interestingly (and this applies to both), after Davos comes the Running Majors' favourite: the Comrades Ultra Marathon in South Africa.

Not only do they agree on their favourite marathons, they have many other interests in common… Not surprisingly, their love of running among them.

Mel says: 'I just love running! I feel good being out there, doing what I enjoy.'

'I love the freedom and the simplicity of running,' says Dave. 'It can be done anywhere in the world and you don't need much equipment, just a bit of willpower. The freedom from the frustrations that this world has to throw at us makes it so worthwhile – it's pure liberation, an outlet valve!'

Then there's their shared love of rash vests.

Yes, *rash* vests!

'Dave introduced them to me as he wears them,' explains Mel. 'They're designed for surfers to wear under their wetsuits but are great for running as the seams are on the outside, so no chafing.'

Also, their love of their grandparents…

'I always think of my late Granda when I run,' says Mel, 'We were very close and would walk hours together.'

'My lucky charm is my St Christopher,' says Dave. 'My Gran gave me this before she died in 1987 – I always kiss it before I run and I never take it off.'

Both enjoy a pre-race breakfast of porridge and bananas.

Okay, enough said apart from their mutual enthusiasm for the 100 Marathon Club and its members.

'Join as a wannabe,' recommends Mel, 'You will meet lots of lovely people who will inspire you, and you will get to know about more marathons and be able to enter exclusive races, too.'

'I became a member of the 100 Club after competing in the Prague Marathon in 2006,' adds Dave. 'There were a number of 100 Club members who had gone there to race and it felt great to be part of such a "band of brothers" and I signed up as a wannabe.'

'I met my husband through running marathons,' says Mel. 'He totally understands why I have to run so much because he is the same. We have the perfect marriage: no kids (by choice) and deciding the next country to go and run a marathon in! My husband is my inspiration. He is an amazing runner – he runs every day without fail. He always makes me feel good if I have had a bad run and makes me realise how lucky we are to just do what we do, regardless of time.'

'My wife Melanie was the youngest lady to be recognised by the *Guinness World Records* as having completed 100 marathons, which she did at the age of 34 years 279 days,' Dave tells me proudly. 'We are very supportive of one another's running and tend to book races, both in the UK and abroad, that we can do together.'

The only time they sometimes argue Dave confides in me (and so I will share this with you all!) is when they train together.

'We go out training together but I'm a wee bit faster,' he says quietly, as if he doesn't really like to admit this, 'and so we end up running mainly at our own pace, which sometimes results in quibbles!'

Aside from that, there's only one real difference that jumps out at me between these two and that's particularly interesting, given the nature of this book.

I ask each of them whether they think they are obsessed with running marathons.

Mel: 'No, I just enjoy it! I'm not sure what I would do at weekends, if I didn't run.'

Dave: 'Yes, I am obsessed with running marathons as I thrive on the challenge and freedom it offers.'

Obsessed or passionate, it would seem even those who participate can't agree.

SUMMER SHORTS

Marital togetherness and freedom seem unlikely bed companions yet it would appear running can (and does) offer both simultaneously to Mr & Mrs Marathon.

If a man offers to take you up a mountain, always check out his rucksack for a skirt first — unless you're prepared to say 'yes'.

MILE 19

THE MAN IN THE IRON MASK

Despite two serious back injuries and a bout of pneumonia, 74-year-old Kio Vejdani has no intention of hanging up his running shoes for a long time yet.

KIO VEJDANI

Born: 1938
140 marathons:
- 1st marathon: 1992 – London
- 100th marathon: 2007 – Edinburgh

I first met Kio (pronounced 'Q') Vejdani in a bar in Prague. He was balancing a shot glass filled to the brim with some bright green toxin on the end of his nose at the time.

But then he is a retired psychiatrist...

And he was on a trip with Running Crazy Limited.

So, in some ways, it made perfect sense. Especially given Kio's personal marathon mantra – 'I don't run marathons to *do* a good time, I run marathons to *have* a good time.' And so he does – all over the world.

Hearing about Kio's marathon experiences as I do, fittingly not in the UK but sitting on a sun terrace of a Mallorcan hotel where he has joined me at Running Crazy's warm weather training camp (and in case you're wondering – no, this is *not* where they teach you how to balance full shot glasses on the end of your nose), is like going on a world tour: from Kenya to China, Norway to New York, Switzerland to Berlin, London to Brighton – oh no, actually that one was a race and Kio did it on foot, at a trot, all 55 miles of it.

Born in 1938 in Iran, Kio moved to the UK in 1968 but didn't take up running until much later when he was in his fifties.

'I knew I was very unfit and unhealthy, and I wanted to change that so I took up squash,' says Kio. 'Then someone said if I ran, it would make me fitter for squash. Initially I ran on my own and got up to 18 miles; I would always run first thing in the morning when there weren't very many people about and to see the sun rise.

'Then a friend of mine started up a small running group. We were visited by a neighbouring club from Lingfield in Surrey and we joined with them in the early nineties; I'd watched the London Marathon on TV for years and envied all those fit people doing it...'

So, in 1992, Kio put his name down for London but didn't get accepted. Despite this, he carried on training with others from the club who had managed to get in. Which turned out to be rather fortunate because about three weeks before the race, Kio had a call from the organisers.

'Apparently they'd had about 500 entries returned from the Germans,' he tells me, 'and they were offering them to people who hadn't got a place, on a first-come, first-served basis,' he tells me, his hooded, Minstrel-brown eyes lighting up almost as if he's re-living the moment all over again.

Kio duly sent in his second application and two days later was told that he'd been accepted. He was then aged 54.

'Everyone was concerned as I hadn't done any specific training for it but I did what I would advise any first-time marathoner to do – don't stop running until you have finished; don't walk, keep running to the end, no matter how slowly; hold back until you get near to home, then you can pick up the pace because you know you will finish.

'It's also a good idea to do your first marathon somewhere special, with good atmosphere and lots going on, such as London,' he adds. 'Then do the next one somewhere with a lower profile.

'Keep steady, don't go too fast,' he emphasises.

Sounds sensible. It certainly worked for Kio.

'There was four miles left to go at Blackfriars and I was passing everyone at that stage and feeling very pleased,' he continues, smiling at the memory. 'The course was different then, the finish was in the middle of Westminster Bridge. I finished in 4 hours and 2 minutes.

'I loved it,' he tells me with evident pride. 'After the success of that first one, I'd got the bug and wanted to do more.'

So he did – in New York.

'It was six months after London,' he recalls. 'I have a cousin living there so I thought it was a good chance to visit him. The race was on my birthday,' he adds.

Funny, really: over the years I've thought of many ways to celebrate my birthday, like a meal at a nice restaurant and champagne, or a trip to London to see a show and champagne, or a party on the beach (only for special birthdays, this one) and champagne, but never once have I considered going for a 26.2 mile run – is it me?

'Again, I loved it,' says Kio, unaware of my inner distractions.

Well, good! Each to his own, I say.

'They say if you like the West End, you'll love Manhattan,' Kio continues. 'It's true. The race was like a tour of New York. It starts on Staten Island and you run the first two miles across the bridge, then you run eight miles straight as a railroad passing through the Jewish and Polish quarters and the streets of New York City before going on through The Bronx and other areas to Manhattan. The last four miles is run through Central Park, which is surprisingly hilly.'

Wow! I feel like I've just been on a virtual tour of New York. Cross that off my list of places to visit.

'I went under four hours, so I was very happy,' says the man who claims times don't matter to him, although he is rightly proud of his PB (Personal Best) of 3 hours 19 minutes, which he did in 1996, at the age of 58. 'I enjoy travelling the world and seeing new sights, and I'm not bothered about PBs,' he reiterates.

'It snowballed from there,' he goes on. 'By 1995/96, I was running a marathon a fortnight and at the height of my enthusiasm, I was doing 22 or 23 per year.'

He eventually became a member of the 100 Club in 2007, when he ran his 100th at Edinburgh. Despite this, the intelligent, articulate, retired psychiatrist doesn't consider his love of running marathons to be an obsession.

'It's not obsessive to do something you enjoy doing once a week,' he says, scratching his swarthy tanned chin thoughtfully before eventually pronouncing, 'I would say it's more of an addiction.'

Interesting. Let's see what *The Oxford English Dictionary* has to say about it:

Obsession – a persistent idea or thought dominating a person's mind.
Addiction – being unable to give something up without incurring adverse effects.

Hmm… So, not running would incur what precisely – a rested body, a freeing of time?

According to our psychiatrist it might mean a decrease in physical fitness and an increase in stress.

Well, yes, okay, he's got me there.

In those early days, though and following New York, Kio did around five marathons a year.

'Each marathon was a stepping stone to the next,' he says. 'As my body got more used to them, I found that two days later I was okay to do another one if I wanted to. I did once actually run a 10K straight after a marathon.'

I'm sure Kio had his reasons…

'That was when I decided to go for the 100,' he explains.

And why wouldn't you?

'I started at Grantham,' he continues. 'It was an ultra-race [longer than a marathon distance] – 33 miles of running along a canal path. It was actually orienteering; we had a map and had to find our own way.'

Eh? I thought he said it was a canal path – why would you need a map? I mean, canal paths just go from one end of a canal to the other, don't they? So long as you stick by the water, you can't go wrong, surely?

'I got hopelessly lost and they sent out a search party,' our intrepid psychiatrist confesses.

And I must admit I am laughing – heartily, inside. Because I am not a naturally rude or ill-mannered person, I keep my merriment to myself, though. Plus, I promise you, I'm not laughing in a mean way. I don't know the Grantham canal personally so it may be that it's different to the usual run-of-the-mill canals; it may be that it stops and re-starts in an entirely different place or has been built over the top of, or to the side of, and the path has to take a circuitous route around some new housing or industrial estate. Either way, I am grateful that Kio (who is the loveliest of men), while having been a psychiatrist, is still unable to see inside my head.

'Actually,' he continues, blissfully unaware of my private jollity, 'I wasn't that far away and was okay once I got put back on track and finished the race.'

I breathe a sigh of relief and am grateful to the search party for getting Kio back on the straight and narrow.

Undeterred, nay encouraged, by his first attempt at ultra-distance running, he decided to up the ante and in 1997, went for the London to Brighton 55-miler.

Don't snigger, I will myself, wondering exactly where a misdirected Kio might have ended up on such an adventurous journey.

'At that time I was running about 120 miles a week. I used to run round a five-mile course near to where I live. It's a small village,' he explains, 'and to prepare for the London to Brighton, I wanted to make it round the course as many times as I could. I'd see other club runners go out for their run while I was running round the five-mile lap, then they would come back and I was still running round the lap.'

Bless him. And might I say how sensible − at least on a five-mile lap he would always end up back where he started.

Being a man of good organisational ability and having discovered there were very few drink stations en route, he organised a support car with two supporters who took food and drink for him (and a map perhaps, Kio, or have I worn that joke to death now?).

'It was a dark and chilly morning in October,' he recalls. 'The race started in Parliament Square, at 7am on the seventh dong of Big Ben,' he tells me with a chuckle. 'We ran down the A23 then it was five miles to Brighton, finishing along the seafront.

'My supporters waited for me every 3 miles, with bananas and Mars bars.'

Yummy! You know, this marathon thing might have something going for it after all. I mean, there's jelly babies, Mars bars, ice creams and, provided you keep on running, you'll never put on any weight.

'I don't usually eat during a marathon,' Kio continues, ignoring my tissue-dabbing antics at the drop of saliva that's just dripped onto my notebook, 'I just drink water before and during the race, and have a sports drink afterwards.

I scribble away, carefully avoiding the wet patch.

He always eats breakfast at least two hours before the start of a race, he tells me.

'I finished the 55 miles in 10 hours and 3 minutes, which was 10-minute miling all the way,' he adds. 'I kept it steady.'

If you *must* run 55 miles, then I reckon steadiness of pace is a really good idea.

'I did a couple more marathons after that and then four weeks later I did a local run of five miles, and my back just went. One leg was considerably longer than the other,' he says. 'I saw a sports therapist and a Chinese medicine person, who was very good. A month later I was able to run again – it was some sort of spondylitis [inflammation of the vertebrae]'.

Now all that sounds not too bad, but in actual fact by the time Kio had the problem properly diagnosed and sorted, he'd been out of running for 18 months. Whether or not the frustration of being injured and having to take so much time out inspired him, who knows, but it was after his back problem that he really took off. And I mean that literally (although not in a rocket, more an aeroplane).

First of all, in 1998 – which Kio cites as his most successful time – there was Paris, quickly followed by the Davos Swiss Alpine Ultra – a race of around 55 miles.

'The run goes through pine forests,' says Kio, 'then it gets more hilly and goes up and down so steeply, you must walk. You have to go right up to the top where there is a small hotel, then you make your way back down again.

'That day, the weather was terrible, boiling hot and we were running in just vest and shorts, but right at the top the clouds came down and the temperature dropped. Then came the rain, snow and ice water.'

Good Lord!

'They were making these poncho-type things for the runners at the top by the hotel. For warmth and safety, we went inside and had a cup of tea, and then started down the hill again.

'The road down the hill is so narrow that the runners have to go in single file down the mountain, like a train. There are lots of boulders and stones, and I stumbled and hurt myself. Ten minutes after I started downhill they stopped the race because the course had become dangerous and the organisers were worried the runners could hurt themselves.

Thoughtful, if somewhat late, at least for our dear Kio.

'They stopped the race and gave people the option to go back the same way and take a bus to the finish, or stay overnight in the hotel on the top.'

But unfortunately for Kio, as he was past the hotel by this stage he had to continue to the finish.

'I was with a group of about 20,' he tells me, 'only two of us made it to the finish. At the meal in the evening, I asked for a brandy and from then on I was known as "Mr Brandy" within the group!'

Undaunted by this experience, a year later Kio decided to broaden his horizons still further, travelling to a 100-mile stage race in the Himalayas.

'The first stage was 24 miles,' he recalls, 'Eight miles up, eight down, eight up again – climbing from 8,000 to 12,000 feet. There was a road with cobblestones and I lost my footing and went down. I tried to get up but fell again, hitting the cobblestones and breaking my nose.'

Ouch!

I wonder whether Kio has ever been described as 'accident prone' and how much he has to pay for travel insurance...

'A doctor came and looked at my nose, and told me that it was broken and needed treatment. So I asked if I went with him whether I would be disqualified and was told I would be. So instead the doctor ran a bandage round the back of my head and across my nose there and then to see if the bleeding would stop. I ran like that for about 20 minutes, but my nose was still bleeding but I wouldn't stop. In the end he put more bandages on and said it was okay for me to continue, provided two conditions were met: I must breathe through my mouth only, not my nose and I must not run, I must walk.'

Kio duly agreed to do this, although he also had to accept having someone walk beside him with a walkie-talkie in case things went wrong.

How very reassuring...

'You could hardly see my face for bandage!' Kio tells me cheerily.

What fun!

'Afterwards I went to the hospital and was given a metal splint for my nose. From then on I became known as "The Man in the Iron Mask", which later changed to "The Bogey Man"!'

Two very lovely names...

'The next morning we were taken up to see the sun rise on Everest. It was one of the most beautiful things I've ever seen,' says Kio, his dark eyes no longer looking at me but disappearing somewhere inside his own head to relive the memory. 'It's hard to describe,' he adds, 'but it was mauve and then it turned to orange.'

That does sound beautiful – almost worth the 100-miler and a broken nose.

Next on Kio's round-the-world trip we move to Norway, where he took part in the Midnight Sun Marathon in Tromsø. Held in June, the race starts at 10.30pm so everyone will be running when the clock strikes midnight. Unfortunately, when Kio competed, it was mainly cloudy so the magical effect of seeing the sun at midnight was slightly diminished.

'It was a strange feeling,' he says, 'you know it's the middle of the night but it's still like the middle of the day. One of the things I really liked about that race was the fact that they give you a genuine Army blanket and a hot chocolate at the finish.'

Ooh, scrummy – the hot chocolate, not the Army blanket obviously! Unless there was a handsome Norwegian soldier wrapped up in it, of course…

'It was also the only time in my life that I went to my room and ate two bars of chocolate and had a shower at two in the morning,' he adds.

Has Kio never heard of midnight feasts? He may be in his seventies and has held down a highly respected, professional job but I feel he has quite a lot to learn.

But we don't have time to stand and stare, we need to get a move on: to Kenya this time and the Kenyan Safari Marathon, held at the Lewa Wildlife Conservancy.

'It's a conservation run,' Kio explains, 'supported by the Tusk Charity and helps to preserve the environment and the animals.

'The course consists of two laps run along dusty brown, sandy roads and there are no barriers between the runners and the wildlife, so you're at their mercy,' he adds with a chuckle.

Uh oh!

'They have a small aeroplane flying over the course, keeping an eye on things,' Kio continues as if to mollify me. 'If they see anything potentially dangerous, they use a walkie-talkie and mention it to the guys who are on the course in Range Rovers, and the animals get moved along so they are out of the way of the runners.'

Phew!

'Elephants are naughty, though,' he adds, brushing my relief away in an instant, as he continues to chuckle, brown eyes twinkling much as I imagine a naughty elephant's might.

'There was an elephant in the way in the middle of the road,' he goes on, 'and a helicopter came down to scare him away, but he came back, as did the helicopter, but this time the elephant got angry and attacked the helicopter.'

Ooh–err…

'Then there were some posts that had been put into the ground to mark the course. The elephants kept coming and taking them out. No matter how many times the officials put them back in again, the elephants kept taking them back out. They never took them anywhere, just left them there!'

Good game, good game! I wonder if elephants can laugh?

'Then there was the rhino,' Kio says, moving on. 'He put his horns underneath the Range Rover once and lifted it up.'

No!

'I also saw many other animals, such as lions, giraffe and zebras, but not during the race.'

No wonder it's called the 'Safari' Marathon. As for the race itself, that started at 7am to avoid the heat.

'It was so hot and very hard to breathe up on Mount Kenya. I'd hoped to do the first lap in under two hours so I could safely finish the second lap before the heat really kicked in, but the first lap took me until 9.30 to finish and by 11.30 the sun was overhead and it was too hot, so I eventually finished the race in 5 hours 45 minutes.'

Marathon over, bags packed. Off we go again: this time to the Great Wall of China.

'I really loved the culture there,' says Kio.

And as for the race itself…

'Unique,' he tells me. 'There are four laps, but they're different distances. The first lap is 10K, with the first 5K on road then you go up some stairs to the wall and run 3K on top of the wall, then you take some stairs back down to the same square for a second time. The main part of the marathon follows an undulating path, then you find yourself back to the same square for a third time and then you go back on the same road, but run it the reverse way round until you find yourself back to the square for the fourth time.'

So, he didn't get lost? Yes, I know the joke's worn gossamer thin, but it seems rude not to ask.

Kio laughs good-humouredly and assures me he didn't.

'It's really difficult to cope with the wall,' he continues, 'because its height changes up- and downhill. On one section of the wall there are uneven boulders and a 200-foot drop on one side, then on the second part of the wall there is a gap on both sides and I had to use my arms to pull myself up from one part to the other.

'It's run on a different part of the wall to the normal tourist bit,' he puts in necessarily, possibly because my face is telling its own story.

Like, that's the Great Wall crossed off my must-visit list – unless I get to the gym and start doing 100 chin-ups a day. The very idea makes me shiver so instead we take a flight to the (hopefully) warmer climes of Florence, which Kio says he really enjoyed for the scenery, and then it's off to Athens.

'An interesting route, historically,' he tells me, 'it follows the same path as that taken originally by Pheidippides through the mountains, although the weather wasn't too good when I did it so I didn't see much, which was a bit disappointing although I did get a glimpse of The Acropolis.'

The one that got away, though – as far as Kio is concerned – is the Marathon des Sables.

'I wish I'd done that one,' he says, 'but it's too late now.'

Oh, I don't know... Running 151 miles over six days, carrying everything you need across a barren desert broken only by sand dunes, sometimes in the dark and in temperatures of up to 120°F might just be the thing for a man in his seventh decade. But for all the unusual places Kio's marathons may have taken him, his favourite overseas races remain the ever-popular Paris, New York and Berlin.

As for any advice he would offer to anyone else aspiring to do the 100, he would say: 'If you want to do it, you will do – so long as you like marathons.'

And when it comes to food, Kio is a man after my own heart.

'I eat anything I like, and I like a drink...'

And not just on the end of his nose either.

'I ran a marathon in Nottingham with a hangover after a night of heavy drinking – beer, red wine and brandy,' he tells me.

Don't ask me why, but I feel certain this is no idle boast.

'I told my friend (who was also suffering) that once he broke into a sweat, he would start to feel better. And he did! We both completed the race and finished ahead of many other runners in the Club who hadn't been drinking!'

Hmm...

'Over the years I've tried running having eaten and drunk lots or a little, good or bad food, and really it makes no real difference, although I guess at a higher level it might do.'

I tend to agree, though I somehow cannot imagine top international runners getting away with it. Of course they may not have Kio's sheer bloody-mindedness when it comes to carrying on against all odds, for he has received many setbacks in his running career. His old back injury flared up a second time, causing another long lay-off, and then just as he was getting his fitness back, he was struck down by pneumonia in 2010, from which he's only just recovering. But every time something comes along to test him, Kio bounces right back like the proverbial rubber ball, showing guts, determination and an incredible strength of mind.

So, let's have one final comment as a psychiatrist please, Kio.

'Marathon running is a very good hobby. It keeps you physically fit, is a very good anti-stress device, also boosts your morale and self-confidence.'

So, who am I to argue?

SUMMER SHORTS

Drinking alcohol prior to running a marathon is not to be recommended due to the dehydrating effects. Running steadily over the first part of a marathon, however, is.

If you've been inspired by Kio's ability to balance alcoholic beverages on his nose and wish to emulate him, practise at home first using a plastic glass and water – preferably in the shower. You can even add a splash of zingy lemon juice to banish skin problems at the same time – just keep your eyes closed, though!

MILE 20

BEER, BABES AND THE PERFECT
PRE-RACE HANGOVER CURE

Despite collapsing on the finishing line of a marathon a few years ago, Martin Bush has no intention of giving up running – at least not so long as there's beer to be drunk!

MARTIN RICHARD BUSH
Born: 1958
580 marathons:
- 1st marathon: 1990 – Abingdon
- 100th marathon: 1995 – Apeldoorn, Holland

'Hello, Gorgeous!' These were the words that greeted me when I telephoned Martin Bush to chat about his marathon experiences.

I was all ready to be flattered, especially as I'd met Martin on several occasions so he knew what I looked like, but more especially because he's rather gorgeous himself. Not overly tall but with a proportionate, taut, sinewy body, year-round natural tan set off by a single square of silver set into his right ear lobe, permanently twinkling deep brown eyes and a dimpling smile that would give George Clooney a run for his money. Oh yes, I was ready to be flattered all right, ready to forget I had a job to do, to forget professionalism, lay down my notepad and pen and offer up my best come-hither look…

But then I remembered the beer. And the fact that he was not actually in the room with me and there is absolutely no point in giving a man your best come-hither look when he's 100 miles away and on the end of a telephone line.

It is simply wasted, which, while I'm not for one moment suggesting that's what Martin was, I couldn't help but suspect there was the teeny tiny possibility that a delicate drop of fizzing amber nectar may well have passed his luscious lips and was responsible for his attributing such a delightful and hitherto unheard-of adjective to plain old me.

So, returning rapidly to reality, I gathered up my notebook and my wits, then plunged in with the first question.

'If you're asking me why I run marathons,' he says, which, unsurprisingly given this is a book about running marathons, I am, 'beer is certainly one of the main reasons.'

Told you so.

'A marathon in a different country means a new beer,' he states, leaving no room for argument.

Not that I was planning to offer any.

It's not that Martin is an alcoholic – he's not; it's just that he enjoys trying new beers. Admittedly for most people a jaunt to a local real ale pub or brewery would suffice, but Martin prefers to jump on an aeroplane, disembark in a foreign land, run 26.2 miles and then check out the local beverages in a friendly hostelry in the company of his marathon mates.

'You're never alone once you start running marathons,' he says. 'There is always someone at a race who you have met before.'

Actually that sounds rather nice, apart from the marathon bit.

Dedication is, of course, key. And I'm not talking about the beer drinking. When most people are kicking back on a Friday night after a long week at work, Martin is packing a bag, taking care not to forget his selection of favoured racing shirts – his 100 Marathon Club vest, his Manchester United shirt and his England Rooney shirt – before heading off for the nearest airport and boarding a flight to his next marathon.

'It's what most 100 Club guys do,' he tells me, modestly. 'In the old days they used to do it in one day, travelling overnight, racing in the day and travelling back again straight afterwards. But these days, with cheap flights and hostels or B&Bs, it's fairly simple and inexpensive to make a weekend of it.'

And the more you save on flights and accommodation, the more beer money you have, too.

What? I'm just saying… Of course such commitment requires dedicated training.

'I don't do much training because I'm racing most weekends…'

Or not, in some cases…

'I tend to rest completely for a couple of days after a race,' Martin continues, 'and then I only do about five miles mid-week and three miles on a Saturday if I'm not racing.'

I see…

'It's a lot less than I used to do,' he adds, as if he can feel my disappointment pulsating its way through the telephone line and feels the need to explain his laxity.

'I don't belong to a club, apart from the 100 Club,' he adds, 'so all my training is done alone.'

All of it?

'Occasionally, I'll do a 2-in-2 [two marathons in two days] or a 3-in-3,' he tells me, as if he thinks that by changing the subject from training to racing consecutive marathons over consecutive days, he can distract me. 'I once did the Seven Sisters Marathon at Eastbourne on a Saturday, the Snowdonia Marathon on the Sunday and the Dublin Marathon on the Monday. Amazingly, my times actually got faster with each race!'

Consider me distracted…

So, if he's doing a 3-in-3, say, what does he do about work?

'Even when I'm not doing a 3-in-3, it's not always possible for me to get back in time for work on a Monday, especially if the race is on a Sunday,' he explains, 'so I just take the Monday off as holiday.'

Simple.

Of course it's not just the beer that keeps Martin running marathons. At least that's his story.

'It's a bug,' he admits. 'Once you start, it's difficult to stop.'

I'm trying hard to imagine it, but…

'I get serious withdrawal symptoms if I'm forced to stop running through injury or illness,' he confesses. 'If I can't run a marathon even for a short time, I quickly become depressed.'

Actually, that's not so surprising given the endorphins ('feel-good' chemicals) that are released in the brain during exercise to produce a 'natural high'. If you give yourself a weekly fix, it can come as no surprise that if that fix doesn't arrive as expected — there's bound to be a low.

'It will have to give me up,' Martin continues, quite animated now, 'I will run until my body can do it no more.'

Okay, I think we get the message. And so, no doubt, does his body. For it very nearly made the decision for him, back in 2003.

'It was at the Malta Marathon,' he explains. 'I'd been running along quite happily, feeling okay and was nearly at the finish when suddenly my body just went numb on one side.'

That sounds very frightening.

Frightening it may have been, but Martin, determined as ever, continued to run across the finish line before he finally gave in to it and collapsed. Even then he wasn't prepared to accept anything was wrong and instead managed to convince concerned onlookers and the Maltese equivalent of the St John's Ambulance that he was perfectly okay minutes after he'd returned to full consciousness.

Of course, being a man he didn't bother to pay a visit to the GP on his return home to get himself checked out, did he? Oh no, he waited until he'd mentioned the incident to his boss at the screen printers where he works, who suggested he might seek medical advice.

'I had to go into hospital,' Martin tells me, as if this came as something of a shock to him. 'They did loads of tests and I was unable to run for eight months. I got very depressed at that time – I was doing nothing, I couldn't work and just had to rest. I'd had all my races planned for that year and paid for flights and hotels.'

The frustration he must have felt at the time of this 'marathonus interruptus' is still evident in his voice.

'And then they said it was all okay,' he goes on, his voice lifting. 'It turned out to be a vein in my head that was too narrow and wasn't able to let the blood flow through to the brain. They put me on medication and aspirin to thin the blood, and that was that. I was able to run again!'

He assures me apart from having to continue with the medication, there have been no after-effects and no affect on his running. I get the feeling that even if there were, he wouldn't tell me. Clearly this is a man who loves his sport and nothing will stand between him and it. Certainly, he is honest enough to admit that his love affair with the marathon might be described as an obsession, one he has no intention of giving up.

Love affair, eh? That reminds me – how come a man with such a finely honed body (and despite all those beers, no middle-aged paunch), finely chiselled jawline and captivating smile, is still single?

'I can't keep a girlfriend,' he 'fesses up straightaway.

But pray tell, why not?

'It's pretty well impossible to maintain a relationship with someone when you spend the week at work and virtually every weekend away,' he says, candidly.

Well, yes, I suppose it's not ideal…

'Even if she came with me,' he continues, 'it wouldn't be much fun for her, standing around for four or five hours sometimes in the cold and wet, waiting for me to finish. It just wouldn't be fair on her.

'Maybe if she was a marathon runner herself,' he muses, 'then I suppose it may be possible…'

So, he doesn't fancy the idea of cutting back on his marathons and giving himself the chance of finding someone to settle down with into his dotage, then?

My phone positively vibrates as Martin explodes quite noisily with laughter. I worry a bit about the vein in his head, but I'm actually more concerned about the sensitivity of my own eardrum.

Okay, I was just asking. Not for myself, of course – just generally. And now we know…

'I'm not saying I wouldn't like that,' he eventually tells me once he's finished guffawing, 'I'm just saying I don't see it happening, at least not while I'm running marathons.'

Oh, okay then. Patience is a virtue and all that…

Maybe a girlfriend would also get in the way of his quest for discovering new beers? I tentatively suggest.

'Maybe she would,' he admits with a boyish chuckle that I know will dimple his eyes and twinkle his cheeks.

So, I probe, just as a matter of interest, does he ever drink before running?

Merriment abounds.

'I may have been known to down the odd one or two,' he

admits, still chortling heartily, 'but I've found the perfect pre-race hangover cure…'

Really?

'Yes,' he confirms, 'having a shower before a race really helps. I discovered that when I was in Mallorca in 2009.'

Go on…

'Well, I'd been enjoying the hospitality of several local hostelries in Calvia, the night before a race, and was having difficulty finding my hotel. I ended up walking round in circles in the pouring rain for about five hours before finally managing to relocate my accommodation at 4.30am!'

It's not big and it's not clever, Martin…

'About four hours later,' he continues, clearly unfazed by my smote, 'I got up, had a shower and made it to the start line in time for the 9.30am start. I felt fine,' he boasts. 'And I finished the race in 4 hours 46 minutes and 9 seconds,' he brags some more, seemingly plucking the figures from the air at will. Unless of course he has a list of his marathon performances sitting in front of him as we speak? Hmm… Hadn't thought of that.

I'm waiting for the 'so there' that must surely follow such a story, but he manages to resist.

So, if there's one piece of advice he has to offer potential 100 Marathon Club members, does he have any others that don't involve, er, say, beer?

'Don't worry about times,' he advises straightaway. 'It's more about completing the distance. Of course everyone's different and has different goals, but for most of us it's about doing the distance and enjoying the weekend.'

You don't say!

Unsurprisingly, he cites the Medoc Marathon in France as being his favourite, swapping his usual favourite beverage for wine.

'It's a fun marathon,' he tells me. 'It's run in the Medoc wine

region of France and the water stations serve wine as well as water
and most runners wear fancy dress!'

Fancy dress? Wine on the run? Now that sounds like my kind
of marathon!

'Less than half the participants actually finish the race,' Martin
continues, sounding really quite gleeful, 'most drop out or pass
out long before the finish!'

Or maybe not…

'I have never not finished,' he tells me with obvious pride,
before adding, 'although it does take me about two hours longer
than usual.'

Only two hours?

It is apparent from Martin's energetic enthusiasm as he talks
about his marathon experiences and his life as a multi-
marathoner (because to someone like him, that's exactly what it
is – a way of life) that he loves every minute of his chosen path.

'Most people when you tell them what you do react with
shock,' he says, 'asking you at least twice if they have
understood you correctly, before going away with that look in
their eye that tells you they know you are nothing short of
completely mad!'

Oh, come now, Martin, not *completely* surely?

'But,' he continues, undeterred, 'the way I see it is that it's a
great life, and a great way to stay fit and see places you wouldn't
see, if it were not for the marathon.'

Hmm… Maybe he has a point. But after 580 marathons and
21 years, what inspires him to stay motivated?

'The other guys in the 100 Marathon Club,' he says without
a moment's hesitation and as if it should be obvious, 'they are the
people who inspire me most and keep me going.

'And the medals,' he adds. 'I do love my medals – I have them
displayed on a corkboard covering the whole of one wall. Each
one brings back a different memory.'

Like wandering around Calvia at 4.30 in the morning, perhaps?

'Amongst other things,' he tells me with a soft chuckle.

Okay then, let's check out his memories. What's his favourite marathon?

'New York,' he says instantly.

Why?

'Because it's such a vibrant city, and the race has such a great build up and then you run through the city and see all the sights. The whole thing is really exciting.'

And he doesn't have a least favourite.

'They are all good,' he says, but then adds, 'The hardest one I've ever run, though, was a new marathon in 2010, in North Devon – which was partially off-road.'

Now see Coach Summer would have thought this was a good and helpful idea, preserving the joints from the jarring of the hard road surface on which most marathons are run.

'The softness of the ground really saps your energy,' says Martin, conversely, 'it was the worst I've ever felt after any marathon.'

Oh dear! I guess to be the worst out of 580 must make it pretty bad on a scale of 1–10… Presumably he won't be rushing back to repeat the experience, then?

'It was a one-off,' he says, 'not by me I don't mean, but by the organisers.'

Do I detect a note of relief in his voice?

'Actually, I believe they're bringing it back again this year [2011],' he informs me, sounding somewhat cautious, as if he's afraid that by telling me this, it might mean he'll have to do it a second time.

I might just play devil's advocate for a moment, just to check out the theory. So, I press, would he do it again if it did come back?

'Yes,' he admits after the slightest of pauses, 'I would.'

And thus any thoughts I might have had about having discovered Martin's limitations are instantly dispelled.

Despite this, and despite his love for all things marathon, it's really quite intriguing to discover that Martin wasn't so keen on running as a schoolboy.

'I didn't like running at school at all,' he admits.

In fact, he didn't take up running until 1983, when he was in his twenties.

'My first race was the Reading Half Marathon,' he tells me, 'A mate asked if I'd do it with him as it was in my hometown and I said I would. We did a little bit of training for it, but not much, but I knew then I'd got the bug.

'I only ever did one half marathon a year,' he continues, 'but then I moved up to marathon distance in 1990 and things changed. Once I started talking to others who were into running marathons and listened to their stories of the places they'd visited and where they planned to visit next, the people they met on their travels and the stories they told, I thought, this is for me.'

These days he runs an average of 30 marathons a year, with the occasional half marathon and 10K thrown in for good measure.

'I didn't set out to run 100 marathons,' he tells me as if he feels the need to defend himself, 'it just sort of happened.'

That's what they all say, Martin.

However it happened, he has never looked back and today is a man with maybe not so much an obsession as a true passion for his sport, the people involved in it and all that it offers him. Certainly, marathon running has opened the world to Martin, bringing with it many good friends from all sorts of places, cultures and backgrounds, and has kept him happily optimistic about life in general. He also knows to value his health, but is not afraid to enjoy life at the same time.

Somehow I just can't shake off the feeling that if Martin were to die during a marathon, he would die happy – almost. Ideally, he would also be wearing one of his favourite racing shirts and have a belly full of beer.

SUMMER SHORTS

Running has something of a reputation for being a solitary sport. Martin's experience, however, suggests otherwise. There can be nothing more certain to bring people together than a shared experience, especially one that tests them to their limits and may necessitate the support and camaraderie of those around you. Friends made in such circumstances are nearly always friends for life.

And if you want to drink copious amounts of beer without getting a beer belly, take up marathon running!

MILE 21

BOG TROTTING IN IRELAND

Jerry Forde was born with spina bifida and spent the first 12 years of his life on his face and hands in a hospital bed. By the age of 56, however, he'd completed 100 wheelchair marathons.

JERRY FORDE
Born: 1950
196 marathons:
- 1st marathon: 1992 – Dublin
- 100th marathon: 2006 – Connemara
Records:
- Most Wheelchair Marathons in Northern & Southern Ireland and the UK

Jerry Forde is one of those people who has had the sort of life most of us only ever get to hear about through television documentaries – you know, the ones about the child unfortunate enough to be born with a disability, who then gets put in an institution by his parents because they have four other able-bodied children to look after. Of course you want to condemn such parents but you can't because you honestly don't know what you yourself might do in the same circumstances. More than that, your heart goes out to the little boy.

And when that little boy is all grown up and tells you quietly in a gentle Irish brogue that actually he didn't go to school because he was stuck in hospital and unable to move other than if someone was willing to push him around in his wheelchair – a wheelchair too small-wheeled and heavy for a child to operate himself – you can only feel unbelievably humble because your own childhood, by comparison, was like a joy ride on a rocket to sweet factory heaven.

The first bit of respite Jerry had was when he was 10 years old and he moved to a different hospital, where he was given a larger-wheeled chair which meant he could push himself about.

'That wheelchair meant real freedom,' he recalls today, the relief and joy he must have felt at being given his first real bit of independence travelling clearly down the telephone line, all the way from Ireland. 'It was like getting your first car!

'The only trouble was it was such a novelty and I was so excited, I wanted to go everywhere quickly rather than slowly, and so kept getting told off for speeding. Luckily,' he goes on, 'this didn't earn me any penalty points or a fine – just a remonstration and an order to stay in my room!'

Eventually, when Jerry was 12, he was discharged from hospital and sent to a Cheshire Home (an institution for those who are unable to look after themselves or be looked after at home), where he was supposed to stay for good.

'I hated it,' recalls Jerry. 'I knew straightaway that it wasn't for me. Then, when I was 20, I had a disagreement with a member of staff and decided I'd had enough. Completely on the spur of the moment and without telling a soul, I walked out – on my crutches.'

Nothing like a dignified exit, Jerry!

'It was worse than that,' he says with a soft chuckle, 'I'd recently had an operation on one foot, which meant that I could only really hop on one leg. Of course I didn't want to be spotted leaving the home, so I had to go via some concealed steps that ran from the playground to the gate – that was a real problem!

'With my parents in Galway and me in Cork,' he continues, 'there was only one place I could think of to run – or rather hobble – to, and that was a kindergarten some three or four miles away. I happened to know the owner there because I'd been working with her son at the Cheshire Home repairing antique furniture.

'So, there I was with only one leg fully functioning, swinging along the dual carriageway, wondering how I was going to negotiate the approaching roundabout on one leg, when a car suddenly pulled up alongside me. I was lucky: the driver turned out to be a regular visitor to the Cheshire Home, who'd recognised me hobbling along. I told her what had happened and she very kindly gave me a lift to the kindergarten.

'I felt like someone on the run,' he says. 'I spent a couple of nights staying at the kindergarten and then my parents came to get me. They'd been informed by the Cheshire Home that I'd run away, as in those days you weren't considered an adult until you were 21. They took me home with them, thinking I'd be okay after a couple of days' holiday and would then go back to the Cheshire Home, but I wouldn't.

'Instead I was with my parents for about four months and then the person who ran the kindergarten contacted an agency, who arranged placements for disabled people, and I was given one in a sheltered workshop working on a sewing machine putting clogs together, then I moved on to putting elastic bands into baby's pants. I didn't earn very much money, but I enjoyed it because it was so good to be out. Because I was on such a low income, I was put into digs that were paid for by the Health Authority. It was another step towards independence.

'Later on, I got a job with a small business outside of the sheltered workshop and worked as a trainee ladies' tailor, shortening coats, slacks and shirts. I was there for about two-and-a-half years. That job and the training have proved very helpful,' Jerry adds, 'because whenever I buy myself a new pair of pants, they always need shortening and I can do it myself!'

I wonder if he does alterations by post?

'Then, one day,' he continues, 'I was watching television and they started showing live scenes of a marathon being run in Dublin. I remember thinking how much I would love to do that. But of course I didn't have a chair I could race in and certainly not enough money to buy one.'

Neither, sadly, was there a kindly fairy godmother on hand to make Jerry's dream come true.

'But then I was at this spina bifida meeting and they mentioned that they were buying racing wheelchairs for two of their members. So I asked if I could have one too and they agreed!' His voice positively simmers with excitement as if re-living the moment.

And so it was that in 1992 at the age of 42, Jerry was able to make his dream come true for himself and take part in a marathon. And not just any old marathon, it had to be Dublin, the very race he'd seen on television, the one that had set alight the initial flickering flame of inspiration.

'The first thing I did was to go and see my doctor to get checked out,' he tells me. 'He told me I had to take one day complete rest every week.'

I confess to feeling a little confused. Was Jerry really planning to train every single day?

But Jerry chuckles – it's a soft, soothing sound, like water tumbling gently over a small, smooth boulder in the middle of a slowly coursing stream.

'Not at all! It was because I tend to walk a lot using my crutches and the doctor must have seen me walking to the shop for milk or whatever and he told me to take the car to the shop instead.'

Oh, good, very sensible doctor!

'My doctor had run a marathon himself,' says Jerry, 'and he recommended that I start off by taking part in some local 5K and 10K races and build up to the marathon distance gradually. It was through those races that I got to know other runners – they were all doing at least two marathons in the year because at that time there was only Dublin and Belfast that had marathons in Ireland.

'My doctor also recommended that I should do the full marathon distance before taking part in the actual race.'

Is it me, or is Jerry's doctor beginning to sound more and more like he's doubling up as his coach?

'I did what he suggested and was glad I did,' he continues, 'because when I was at the race there were 12 wheelchair racers including me and they'd all done a marathon before and I didn't want to look an eejit! Of course, when I did that first marathon in Dublin in 1992, I thought that would be it – I had no idea I would get to do over 100 of them!'

Ah, that soft chuckle again! It really is quite musical.

'Initially, I was happy just to run in Dublin then I started getting to know people at the shorter races and they kept asking me if I was going to do another marathon, so then I started doing Belfast as well as Dublin and I've done them both every year since.

'Then, as more and more races appeared, I thought I would branch out a bit and run a race in every county in Ireland. I really never had any idea I would get to 100,' he reiterates, 'until

I'd run just over 30 marathons then I thought I would go for it! By then, I'd met a lot of the UK members of the 100 Marathon Club, not only in Ireland but in the UK, including the Isle of Man every year and in various countries all over the world.'

Have wheelchair, will travel.

'I race mainly in Europe,' he adds, by way of confirmation, 'but I've also raced in America, Sydney and the Gold Coast in Australia, as well as Beijing.

'It wasn't very hot in Beijing, but it was very hilly,' he recalls.

I wonder whether there's a special knack for going uphill in a wheelchair?

'Not really,' says Jerry, 'although some people like Mike Marten, who's also in the 100 Club, go up backwards.'

Interesting...

So, has Jerry ever had any coaching in relation to wheelchair racing?

'No, not at all! I've taught myself and push it as well as I can. Although once I was doing a marathon that was really hilly and was having a lot of problems, so I asked some walkers who were doing the half marathon to stand behind the chair so I could lift both my arms to push myself upwards. I would never ask anyone to actually push me.'

I would – and that's without the encumbrance of a wheelchair!

'I just needed them to stand behind me so I wouldn't roll back down the hill in between each push,' he continues as if afraid I might accuse him of cheating.

'Last year I did the Bog Trotter,' he suddenly adds, whether to distract me I'm not sure, but how could one *not* be distracted by such a delightful sounding event? 'It's the only marathon I've done that wasn't purely on road. Instead, it's a mixture of grass, mud, stones and peat briquettes...'

Eh?

'Turf made into briquettes by machine,' he explains succinctly, with which to be honest, I'm a little disappointed. Whenever I've come across Irish people before – which isn't often I grant you, but even so – they always offer up lovely long explanations about anything and everything, ending with me more confused than before they'd started to explain.

'They dig the bog with big machines,' Jerry goes on, as if he's suddenly remembered his origins and has no wish to disappoint me. 'There is a field and across the way another field, and because of the machines being so heavy and because they have to go between the two fields where it is very boggy, they put in stone or blocks to help the machines get across.'

Ah ha, I think! But I'm not sure. Whatever, it's a proper Irish explanation and I'm now quite satisfied, even if I'm not entirely sure what he's on about.

'It was hard work in a wheelchair,' he continues, unaware of my Gaelic observations, although that bit I can easily understand. I mean bogs and wheelchairs, not a good mix. 'I had to do an extra half-kilometre or so because there was one part that was extremely bad and the wheelchair would get stuck so to avoid that bit, I had to do the extra distance to get around it.'

Now that's just unfair, but Jerry, as you might suspect, isn't one to complain.

'I've just got a new chair,' he says, swiftly moving on from the unfairness of bog trotting. 'I'm trying to work out a way of carrying water with me. Normally, I just take it on the go or someone will pass me a bottle if they see me with my hand out, but it would be much easier if I could actually carry it with me and not have to bother with all that.

'Most people are very good when they see you in a chair,' he goes on. 'I've never had any problems. I suppose really I'm quite well known and people make it their business to talk to me. Even people I've never met before will come and talk to me after marathons. Able-bodied runners often tell me I've kept them going. Last year, there was this young girl in her early twenties who was at a marathon in Ireland. I was walking back to the car after prize-giving and she was coming towards me with her mother, but then she stopped and asked me if I was Jerry Forde.

'I said I was, and she said she'd seen me on TV or heard me on the radio or something, and that I was the cause of her doing marathons. I was overcome.'

Jerry still sounds overcome as he recites the story, almost as though he can't believe that he, plain old Jerry Forde, should be responsible for such a thing.

'The mother had a camera and asked for a photograph of me with her daughter, which of course I was happy to go along with. Then this reporter, who was there from the national radio station, talked to the girl and the girl told her the story about why she was running – because of me,' (he says the words as though he's still wondering how someone like him could possibly influence someone like her to do something like run a marathon), 'and that came out on the radio, so then the lady from the radio came down to talk to me, too.'

Jerry is still talking in hushed tones as if he can't quite grasp the concept of being the type of person who is able to inspire others to do things, yet there is also in his voice a quiet pride in the knowledge that actually he can and he does.

Not only is he an inspiring individual, he is also, in true Irish fashion, blessed in being able to tell a funny story or two. Such as the time he was taking part in a marathon in County Cork.

'Everyone had a number on their bib, both back and front, but I also had my name on mine and people were passing me and saying, "Well done, Jerry". And this was going on and when someone was about to pass me, they remarked that I was very well known around there, to which I replied, "No wonder, haven't I got me name on me back and front?"'

Only the Irish…

'And then in a marathon in America, someone passed me and said "Well done, Jerry" and I was saying to myself, "Ah, who knows me in America? I don't know anyone in America," and I only realised when I took off me number that everyone's names were on the number bibs!'

Ah yes, *only* the Irish.

So, if Jerry inspires others to run marathons, what encourages him to keep on running them?

'The members of the 100 Marathon Club – they have always been and still are a huge influence on me,' he acknowledges. 'They are an amazing bunch of people and whenever the weather is warm enough, I wear my 100 Club vest with pride.

'It's also about the travel, meeting people and a determination to keep challenging myself and achieving my own personal goals,' he goes on. 'I get far too much out of marathon racing and racing generally to want to give it up. I met a man of 80 at a 5K race. He'd had a hip operation and was still recovering, but he was still running – I'd like to go on like that. I won't make a decision to stop, I will have to be forced.'

Hardly surprising then that his ultimate goal is simply to keep going and finish as many marathons as he can. Therefore he continues to train as well as race.

'Currently, I'm training six days a week, five of which I do about five miles and then the sixth, on a Saturday or Sunday if I'm not doing a race, I'll cover another seven or eight miles over harder, hillier ground,' he explains.

And what do others make of his exploits?

'When I tell other runners I've done over 100 marathons, they take a big breath of disbelief and think I'm amazing and inspirational. People who are non-runners simply think I'm crazy.'

Away from marathons, Jerry, now 60, is no longer working although he busies himself with his own show on hospital radio.

'I play music and interview people,' he says. 'It's FM radio so it can be heard outside the hospital as well as inside but don't tell the authorities that because it's only meant to be for the patients,' he adds, almost in a whisper, as if he thinks they might be listening in. 'Of course there's nothing they can do to stop it. I actually get people ringing me up who aren't even in the hospital!'

He sounds quite gleeful about this, like a mildly mischievous schoolboy.

'Normally I do the show for two-and-a-half hours, five days a week,' he tells me. 'I love it – I *love* chatting!'

And right then a thought hits me smack-bang between the eyes. Actually it's more like between the eyebrows – I mean, the nose is between the eyes so I'm hardly likely to have a thought there, am I? But that's not important right now, what matters is this: could Jerry be the next Terry Wogan? Something tells me not to discount it – with Jerry Forde I rather suspect anything is possible.

SUMMER SHORTS

Jerry's story made me realise you don't need a fairy godmother to make your dreams come true. What you need is, to quote Rudyard Kipling, 'the heart and nerve and sinew' to realise them for yourself. And how much greater the joy and satisfaction in knowing that it's you who made it all happen.

And if your trousers need shortening, contact Jerry.

MILE 22

NAKED MEN AND CAKEWALKS

Jim Manford was quite happy trotting out a handful of marathons each year – until he had a serious eye injury that made him realise tomorrow might not always come.

JIM MANFORD
Born: 1945
154 marathons:
- 1st marathon: 1985 – Perth, Western Australia
- 100th marathon: 2008 – Connemara

Described by his friends as outgoing, determined and loyal, 66-year-old Jim Manford, a retired parole officer for the Crown Law Department of Western Australia, among other things, would add that he also enjoys a challenge and always tries to do things correctly.

As if to prove the point, this six-foot, twelve-stone gentle giant of a man has taken two of the 100 Marathon Club's main aims – to promote marathon running in the UK and encourage newcomers to the sport – very much to heart and has helped found a new club in the North East exclusive to marathon running.

'The North East Marathon Club – or 'NEMC', for short – was set up in 2010 and is the first regional marathon club in the UK,' he boasts proudly.

And who can blame him? With over 70 people applying to join in the first three months of the Club's existence, clearly there is a real demand for such a club.

'After decades of having no marathons in the North East, we're organising four this year [2011]. The details are on the Club's website,' Jim adds, unashamedly guiding me to www.northeastmarathonclub.co.uk.

Taking the unsubtle hint, I check out the website immediately. I'm impressed: the site is well organised, informative and also has several photographs of Jim presenting various trophies in his role as secretary.

Born in 1945, in Durham City, Jim became actively involved in sport at a relatively early age, primarily playing soccer before turning his attentions to tennis and squash. Then in 1972 he got married and emigrated to Australia for £10.

Oh, those halcyon days!

'My wife and I emigrated to Australia for our honeymoon to travel and see the world on the premise that for £10 it represented much better value for money than whatever it cost to go to Europe in those days. We ended up staying for 15 years. Some honeymoon!'

Yes, indeed.

'It was a good base to travel from, particularly for visits to countries in South East Asia,' he continues. 'I lived next to the beach in Aussie and would jog there to train for the other sports. As I got older and started running out of tennis/squash partners, the running gradually took over. The marathon seemed the natural progression from the 10k/10 mile events I competed in.

'I ran my first marathon in Perth, Western Australia on my 40th birthday in 1985, but it took me 23 years to run my 100th, which I did in Connemara in April 2008, although I joined the 100 Marathon Club as a "wannabe" in 2006 when I'd done my 50th. It was my incentive to keep going to the century. I certainly didn't start off with the intention of running so many marathons, though.'

They all say that, Jim.

'I was coming back on the train after my fourth marathon and I met someone who'd run 100. My first thought was, why not? That gives me something to aim for.'

They are everywhere – those people who have run 100 marathons. And they will find you, even if you've only just lost your virginity. When it comes to hunting out willing marathon masochists, they're as efficient as an undercover agent for a Stephen Fry fan base. At least in Jim's case it would appear that he didn't go hell for leather (or trainer for tarmac) at it, instead building up the numbers gradually over the years.

'The numbers have varied a lot since 1985,' he admits. 'I didn't do too many annually at first and actually stopped running them altogether for six years when my travel companions packed in. Then a serious eye injury in 2005 persuaded me to start again and complete the 100 while I still could.'

Ah yes, the sudden realisation that good health is not something to be taken for granted. Same thing happened to me when I was stuck in a hospital bed after having a kidney removed. I remember thinking then that I would run a marathon when I got out of there, even started planning my training; I think I got up to two miles before I realised I had neither the strength of mind nor the desire to go any further. However, back to a man with plenty of both...

'It was just after my 60th birthday,' Jim continues, 'and I got a badly detached retina, though nobody knew why. The surgeons were unable to fix it initially and it eventually required a series of operations before minimal sight was restored in that eye, but the lens was so badly damaged it had to be removed. I was under doctor's orders not to run for six months.

'Fortunately, my consultant is a runner himself,' he adds. 'He's done all but one of the Great North Runs and he took it on himself to ensure that I was able to run again and complete my 100th marathon.'

Praise be for such surgeons!

'He was so supportive that I organised a marathon, the Northumberland Coast Marathon in 2010, with all proceeds going to his charity: the Tynesight Charitable Fund,' Jim goes on. 'The only real long-term effects on me have been that I'm not able to drive long distances so can't go to distant races and I'm not confident in crowds due to lack of peripheral vision, which makes the busy Spanish marathons a bit of a nightmare!'

Only a bit?

So, why 100 marathons?

'Why not?' argues Jim challengingly, yet leaving me in no doubt that his question is purely rhetorical and he's not really expecting me to come up with an answer. 'I actually enjoy the challenge of the distance and knowing that I'm going to have to "dig deep" each time to finish the last few miles – you don't get that with shorter events. It also gives me the opportunity to meet up with all the friends I've made through marathon running.'

Well, yes, I suppose so but couldn't you do that over a nice cup of tea and a scone?

'You wouldn't get the same sense of achievement or satisfaction,' he tells me, quite seriously.

To be completely honest and speaking from actual experience (not of a marathon obviously, just running generally), I know he is right. Tea and scones taste far better after a run, even a short one. No guilt for a start!

At the moment, Jim is hoping to run around 24 marathons this year, the same as last year, which equates to approximately two a month, which I guess must have some impact on his family life?

He agrees that it does and makes no bones about his thoughts on the matter, saying: 'Marathon running is a selfish, time-consuming and costly pastime, which I'm sure will have contributed to at least a couple of marriage breakdowns/family disputes!'

Ooh err, yes, well… tell it like it is, Jim!

And he proceeds to do just that, at least in respect of the financial aspects.

'Something a lot of us are concerned about, given the ever-escalating costs of marathon entry fees is the financial implications and commitments of running marathons. I actually wrote a report about it on the North East Club's website,' he says. 'Basically, people need to differentiate between marathons arranged by private companies or individuals purely for profit purpose and those put on *by* runners *for* runners with the primary aim of providing a satisfactory, low-cost, friendly running experience.

'Take the big city marathons, for example,' he continues. 'They tend to cost anywhere between £30 and £50 at the moment, although New York is nearer £200! Compare that to running club organised marathons with no celebrity-attachments, which cost between £7 to £20.'

That's quite some difference – but why?

'Personal greed and celebrities,' says Jim, unequivocally.

'I'm speaking from experience,' he assures me. 'Last year I helped organise Newcastle's Town Moor Marathon. There was an entry fee of £16, based on an expected entry of 100 to cover the usual costs associated with such an event, such as permits, timekeepers, judges, officials, insurance, St John Ambulance, race HQ, refreshments, etc. In return, runners received quality mementoes, trophies to winners and awards to the first three in every age group imaginable and a decent goody bag with energy bar and drink.

'We still ended up with a surplus,' says Jim, 'despite trying to give it all back to the runners in the form of a £2.50 drink/food voucher. Next year's entry fees are therefore being reduced and any surplus being used to provide more portaloos for the runners' comfort.

'The Kielder Water Marathon in Northumberland is another good example,' he continues. 'I organised that one on behalf of the 100 Marathon Club. Entry was free and there was even free accommodation on the Saturday night, courtesy of the Youth Hostelling Association. However, interestingly, another marathon is being organised next year by a well-known public figure using the exact same public footpath around the exact same lake – but they are charging £35 per entry!

'I think people may be swayed by the celebrity factor without realising they're helping to push up the cost of marathon entry,' he adds.

So, what of his family then, what do they make of his running?

'My family are all outwardly very supportive,' he says, appreciatively, 'although secretly I feel they all think it's time I gave it a rest!'

Do any of them run?

'My partner isn't a runner,' he tells me, 'although she has walked a marathon with me. Both my sons, who are grown up now, have run marathons and I think that helps them to understand what lies behind my interest.'

So, aside from his own desire and determination and the

'outward' familial support, is there anything else he relies on to get him through each race?

'Not really, other than making sure I have the correct kit, Vaseline and gels.

Note to self: buy shares in Vaseline…

What about any marathon runners or others who have influenced him?

'Again, not really, though it's hard not to be inspired after reading the exploits of people like Tom McNab, (*Flanagan's Run*), Dean Karnazes (*Ultramarathon Man*) and Tony Rafferty, (who ran across Australia and back). What these men did makes marathon running seem like a cakewalk!'

A cakewalk? *Cake Walk…* I'm excited. I can see it now, thousands of people lined up at the start, cakes in hand, ready to walk – *and* eat. Only problem I can foresee is indigestion. Will have Rennie at the ready.

Note to self: buy shares in Rennie.

And so, Jim, any marathons that stand out from the rest?

'Connemara in Southern Ireland is my favourite,' he says, unhesitatingly. 'It has such beautiful scenery, even in a snow blizzard. Rotterdam in 2007 stands out as having the worst weather conditions I've ever run in – it was so hot, they stopped the race after 3 hours 30 minutes.

'Most unusual has to go to the Bilbao Night Marathon. It was really different running through the streets of a strange city in the pitch-dark. Some of the Spanish runners were running in the nude for a laugh!'

Note to self: write article on the Bilbao Night Marathon – pack night vision goggles, extra-powerful LED light torch and zoom lens.

Any funny stories, I venture.

'Actually, yes, I do have one,' he says, 'at least it's funny in retrospect, it wasn't so funny at the time.'

Never mind that, if Jim has got over it, I'm sure we can, too. Besides, funny stories are my favourite kind…

'It was at the Pennine Marathon,' he begins, 'I was running and talking away to a friend, who was running slightly behind me. We were at about the 22-mile mark and I didn't realise that he'd stopped answering until a police car pulled alongside to say that he was lying in a ditch a mile back, having been side-swiped by a caravan! I had to jog back to him. Fortunately he was okay and we eventually finished together.'

Now *that* was funny! Though possibly not so much for the friend, but still…

So, aside from his most memorable and funniest marathons, I wonder if Jim has an easy marathon he might recommend for people like, oh, say, me.

'None of them are easy,' he tells me in his forthright way, shattering any potential desire I might have had to write the Bilbao article from the perspective of an actual participant.

'Those that describe themselves as flat usually end up being boring,' he goes on.

Now you see I'd have thought the exact opposite, although I guess living among Hadrian's hills, Jim must have grown familiar with the ups and downs of training on that sort of terrain.

'Actually, I do most of my training along the beaches of the Northumberland coast,' he corrects me. 'I think that's why I haven't suffered much from injuries.

'In fact,' he continues, unbidden, 'the only serious injury I've ever had was Popliteus (an injury to the muscle behind the knee) in 2001. I had to miss the World Veterans Championship Marathon in Brisbane because of it. I'd already paid the air fares and everything, so had to go anyway just to be a spectator – it was so frustrating!'

Frustrating it may have been, but to have run so many marathons and only to have suffered one injury is pretty remarkable and so I shall now rename him 'Lucky Jim', not only for his lack of injuries but also for being able to train along a beach. Which leads me rather neatly to asking him exactly what sort of training he does along the shoreline.

'When I'm running marathons on a regular basis I tend to do only about 45 minutes/1 hour running each day,' he explains. 'I find it easier to continue to run marathons on a regular basis than to start from scratch each time. If you do it that way, you never lose your state of "marathon preparedness" and only need to do ticking-over miles in training.

'I recover very quickly from racing and tend to start jogging the next day after a race. Mind you, I no longer "race" each marathon. The greater the effort I put in, the more I ache after a race. Strangely, I tend to ache more in hot weather.'

The coach in me can't resist asking whether he does a warm up/warm down before/after racing.

'No thanks!' is his prompt response.

My equally speedy response is in that case, he can probably expect to carry on aching, then!

It would appear that Jim applies the same sort of uncomplicated approach to running nutrition.

'I eat and drink what I like. My favourite post-race recovery drink is a couple of beers.'

Why am I not surprised?

At this stage, I'm wondering whether it's wise of me to ask this non-stretching, beer-swilling (okay, so two pints probably doesn't count but it works well in a literal sense so please don't sue me, Jim!), straight-talking guy for one piece of advice for aspiring 100 Marathon Club members, but what the hell...

'Stick at it, you'll get there in the end!'

Oh, okay, that wasn't too bad and it does actually make sense.

I feel certain my next question is liable to elicit a rather more explosive reaction, but as there are approximately 400

247

miles of roadway between Jim's house and my own, I decide to take the risk.

So, does he think he is obsessed with running marathons?

'Definitely not!' he responds immediately, pretty much as I'd anticipated.

'I've a variety of interests,' he continues, 'music, travel, literature, etc. [a very popular pastime in Northumberland], as well as running marathons. I also cycle and play tennis. How can something you do at the most once per week be described as obsessive?'

Well, I didn't say it could be, Jim. I was merely posing the question.

With a deep breath I form the words for my next question and I'm beginning to think I should be receiving danger money as well as royalties from my publisher.

How do other people react when you tell them you've run over 100 marathons?

Again there is an immediate response but this time milder in tone.

'You tend to get respect from fellow runners and those who know what's involved, but mixed reactions from the general public. I've been called everything from a "nutter" to "insane" – you learn to ignore these remarks.'

How very wise. And I know exactly what he means. As a young woman running the streets in shorts and T-shirt, I learned early on to ignore the remarks of passing males stuck in adolescence.

And what of the future? Does he have any ultimate running goals or ambitions?

'I simply want to keep on running marathons while I can, visiting as many countries as possible and to run a marathon in each of the regions of Spain. I have an apartment there,' he explains.

Ah, somewhere to lay his aching body after another hot marathon then – and why not?

SUMMER SHORTS

None of us know what lies ahead or whether today is our tomorrow. While it's not practical to treat each day as if it were our last, it is perhaps possible not to put the things that we really want to do into the 'pending forever' tray. Sadly, we are not the masters of time, merely its puppets.

Buy Shares in Vaseline (and Rennie).

MILE 23

BIN LINERS, NOSEBLEEDS AND MARITAL DISHARMONY

Allan Rumble almost lost his wife due to his excessive marathon running and he doesn't intend making the same mistake again. He also caused a sensation at the 2010 London Marathon.

ALLAN RUMBLE
Born: 1968
130 marathons:
• 1st marathon: 1994 – Edinburgh
• 100th marathon: 2010 – Zurich

It's nearing the start of the 2010 London Marathon. The BBC team have taken their places in the commentary box when one of them notices something odd in the elite start area. It's a man wearing a black bin liner, sipping tea from a plastic cup.

'Who the hell is that?' asks one commentator, picking up his binoculars for a better view, unable to believe even an experienced elite athlete would have the audacity to treat the

London Marathon with such casual indifference. A colleague squints through the window and shakes his head then picks up his notes, flicking through the list of elite athletes, but is unable to find any clues as to the identity of the mystery man.

Meanwhile, down at the start, there's a distinctly nervous rumbling among the Kenyans and Ethiopians. 'Who is he?' they mutter, knowing the man in the bin liner must be someone special to be acting so cool, even though none of them recognise him.

As for the character causing so much concern, he is keeping his head down, determined to avoid making eye contact with any of his rivals, wondering how the hell he, Allan Rumble, 100 Marathon Club member, has ended up on the elite start line of the 2010 London Marathon and closing his ears to the chit-chat of professional international athletes debating whether today is a good day to have a go at the Olympic qualifying time.

'I found out later,' he tells me, his voice ringing with laughter potentially loud enough to shake his 15-stone, 5-foot 11-inch frame, 'that I'd been sent an elite number by mistake. I had no idea, not even when I was looking around for where to leave my kit and was directed to the elite kit storage area – I wasn't allowed in anywhere else!

'When I walked in, there were all these professional athletes stretching and warming up with all their sponsorship kit on and with their own personal coaches, and there was me wearing a bin bag and carrying a cup of tea in a plastic cup! When I got on the start line, I was right at the front with all these elite athletes who were saying things like, "I'm going for the Olympic qualifying time," and I was thinking, oh my God, don't talk to me, *please* don't talk to me! Please don't ask me what I'm going to do, and keeping my head down – all I wanted to do was finish in under three hours.

'The gun went off and I took off like a bat out of hell,

sprinting as hard as I could, but I must have looked like I was going backwards. I was thinking, oh my God, I hope nobody's looking at me and thinking what an idiot! I told myself to just keep my head down and run. As about 5,000 people had gone flying past by then, I just hoped the TV cameras didn't pick me out.

'After one mile I felt totally cracked, at 19 miles I hit the wall – I eventually finished in 3 hours 17 minutes.'

But for Allan, running marathons hasn't been all fun and games. Indeed, he tells me quite openly, it almost cost him his marriage.

'I did my first marathon because running a marathon before I was 40 was something on my list to tick off. I really enjoyed it and was determined to do another one, and did so a year later in Essex, where my in-laws live. When I was there, I saw a guy wearing the 100 Marathon Club T-shirt and asked him what that was about. When I heard, I said to my wife, "I'm going to do that, I'm going to run 100 marathons!"'

I ask what his wife had to say about that but before he has a chance to answer, a dog barks in the background.

'Sorry,' says Allan, 'that's my wife just come back with the dogs. We have two Cocker Spaniels. One of them used to run with me,' he adds, 'but he has a bad back and he's glad now not to have to go out with me.'

So, I venture carefully, talking about your wife…

'You can ask her yourself,' he offers, 'if you'd like to.'

I say that I would and the next moment I hear a woman's voice. She sounds slightly nervous, but also keen to give me her side of the story.

'I thought he was mad,' Allan's wife (whose name turns out to be Jill) says straightaway. 'The whole running thing has been a bone of contention between us and actually led to us breaking up a couple of years ago, although we are now back together. He's promised me he's going to retire after he's done the Spartathon race,' she continues. 'If he doesn't…' She leaves the unfinished sentence hanging significantly in the air.

I wonder how she views what her husband and other members of the 100 Club do on a general basis?

'I don't think anyone is necessarily insane,' she starts off tentatively, 'but they are selfish.'

Those last words are spoken with complete conviction.

'I think what Allan has done is selfish,' she repeats, 'and I honestly don't understand the obsession. I actually ran before he did – with a friend, just three or four miles a couple of times a week – but I would never have let it take over my whole life, like he did. Maybe if you were single, it would be okay,' she adds, 'but when you're married, it affects the other person, too.

'I feel excluded,' she goes on. 'He invited me to races to watch and I went, but it's a long time waiting for them to finish. Now he has promised me that the Sparta will be his last race and I believe him: we need to spend more time together.

'Also, when he has raced or run long distances, he is too tired to be interested in me or anything else, or to help around the house or with any other jobs that need doing.'

Despite this, Jill admits to being very proud of everything Allan has achieved, although she does worry about the effect so much running may have on his health. Having established that running marathons isn't necessarily a recipe for marital bliss, I thank Jill for her extremely frank and eye-opening input and am duly handed back to Allan.

'I admit I felt driven to get to the 100,' he continues, 'especially once I'd completed the first 50 and became a "wannabe". My whole mindset changed after that and between 50 and 100, I completed 47 marathons in one year.'

That's quite a lot – as in, there's quite a lot of Chinese people living in Hong Kong.

'I did have one month off for a total rest,' he says, as if admitting to a cardinal sin. 'It was all-consuming.'

I assume he's referring to the running and not the rest.

'I've cut down the number of races now to once a month and I've promised Jill that Sparta will be my last race – and I mean it. I do recognise how selfish I've been, although it was something I needed to do and I don't regret it.'

However, he does go on to say that although Sparta will be his final race, if he fails to complete it, he will have to do it again – and again if he fails a second time, until he has achieved his final goal.

'It's on the list,' he adds, 'and as Jill knows, if it's on the list…'

Well, if Jill didn't know, she certainly does now!

'But I do feel ready to retire,' he reiterates. 'I've done everything I wanted to do – I don't want to do anything else, running-wise.'

Despite these assertions, his friends see it differently.

'They tell me I won't know what to do with myself when I give it up, but I tell them I don't need anything else – I want to spend more time with my wife.'

Assuming he applies the same dedication to the time he spends with his wife as he did to running 100 marathons, I'm sure their marriage will reap the benefits. Certainly from the way he talks and the things he says, Allan would appear to be a man who knows his own mind.

'The Spartathon will be my retirement race,' he tells me yet again, as if feeling the need for further affirmation. 'It's my main target this year [2011]. The race goes from Athens to Sparta – 155 miles non-stop and has to be done in under 36 hours.'

Running ultras [races longer than marathon distance] is something that has featured quite strongly in Allan's running career.

'I run ultras as well as marathons because I enjoy doing

them – there's not the same competitive edge to ultras as there is to marathons. Last year, when I ran in the 145-mile Grand Union Canal Race [GUCR], my support crew had changed and moved, and I ran out of food and water, so I nicked some from another crew and nobody minded! It's friendly rather than competitive.'

Let's hope the other crew saw it that way, too.

While I hear what Allan is saying about cutting down his racing and retiring after the Spartathon, I can't help but think if he's planning to take part in a 155-mile race, he must still be doing quite a lot of training.

'I usually do 10–15 miles a day when I'm training for a target race,' he explains, 'although for Sparta, I've had to up it to 20 miles a day. The day after a race I'll do six or seven miles to loosen my muscles. Friday is my rest day and one week a month, I'll rest for the week.'

As a coach who believes in rest being as important as running, I'm kind of glad to hear this.

'Because of the difficulties with my marriage,' Allan continues, 'I was trying to fit my training into my daily life by running to work and back.'

Good plan!

'Unfortunately, I was made redundant from my job a couple of weeks ago, so that's no longer an option.'

Okay, good plan gone wrong.

'However, whilst I'm looking for another job, I'm going to be doing some building work on our other house and intend running there and back so I can keep my running time to a minimum and lessen the impact on the rest of my life, although realistically, I know I will have to be selfish sometimes.'

Good contingency plan, but at the risk of sounding like his wife – why the 'selfish' bit?

'Well, for example,' Allan begins, 'there's this guy I'm

mentoring to do the Grand Union Canal Race, who wants to do a 50-mile training run with me, which will take pretty much a full day.'

Ah, yes – I see what he means. But how did he come to be mentoring?

Allan laughs, it has to be said, quite uproariously.

'It was because I wrote a blog about my disastrous attempt at the Grand Union Canal Race last year which I, possibly stupidly, [let's ask Jill, shall we?] entered just seven days before race day with horrendous results [such as nosebleeds, coughing up and peeing blood, of more later].

'The blog I wrote recording my race was used by the race director to warn potential participants what can happen when people don't prepare or train properly for the race. Normally,' he adds as if by way of defence, 'I pick my target races and prepare specifically for them. If I'd had time for the Grand Union Canal race, I would have just run loads and loads of flat miles as obviously it's a totally flat race. I really prefer races with hills in as it changes the stress on muscles and is more comfortable. Anyway, Spencer (my protégé) read it and asked me to mentor him.'

Presumably because he thought Allan would be able to teach him how *not* to do it?

'When Spencer asked me to do a 50-mile training run with him, by taking a train to Brighton and then running home again, I agreed but only on the condition that the route we take must have shops and churchyards.'

Shops, I get – but churchyards?

'They nearly always have taps in them,' he tells me, 'for the flowers.'

Now that's something I would never have thought of. For some reason my mind had gone along the lines of using gravestones for peeing behind – don't ask me why, it's not something I've ever done or would ever do – honestly!

'I'm not a religious man,' Allan says, unaware of the extremely irreligious thoughts running through my own mind, 'but I have to say there have been many occasions when the Church has saved my life.'

In his mentoring capacity Allan has also been asked for advice on sports drinks and nutrition.

'When I run a marathon or anything up to 30 or 40 miles, I will only drink plain water and I never take on energy drinks or food. Anything over that distance, I stick to plain water but will also take on food. I buy my own and have found the best things for me are total junk food! Things like sausage rolls are perfect – full of fat and salt.'

Coach Summer swallows a shocked gulp.

'I don't know whether it will be right for Spencer,' Allan admits, 'but it's right for me. The rest of the time,' he adds, as if he may have heard me gulping down the telephone line, 'I eat healthily, with frozen vegetables and meat, cooking proper meals…'

'I'm not fat,' he assures me, but then checks this fact with his wife, who apparently is in agreement, 'I'm just a big bloke.'

A big bloke, whose weight fluctuates between 14 and 15 stone depending on how much running he's doing and with a Personal Best of 3 hours 10 minutes and an average time of 3 hours 30 minutes, so he must be doing something right. What's more, a bloke who is also so proud of his 100 Marathon Club vest that he will only wear it when racing marathons, never for running an ultra.

'I wear a rucksack when I'm doing ultras,' he explains, 'and the rucksack will rip a T-shirt to shreds. I worked too hard for my 100 Club vest, I'm not ruining it. I'll buy a shirt for a tenner and wear that, and chuck it away afterwards if it's no good. But the 100 Club vest – never!'

So, aside from the GUCR, obviously, what are his most memorable races?

'The Trail Marathon at Exmoor,' he says immediately, 'although it was also the hardest trail race I've ever done.'

I'm sensing some mildly masochistic tendencies here...

'It's a coastal run,' Allan goes on to explain, 'very hilly, with around 10,000 feet of ascent, but without doubt the most scenic race I've ever run in.'

Oh, I do apologise! No masochistic tendencies at all. It's all about the views, because, obviously, when you're running up 10,000 feet of ascent, you'll be taking in the views.

'The hardest one on road, though,' he says, 'has to be the Dartmoor Discovery ultra, although actually,' he adds, thoughtfully, 'that turned out to be less arduous than the Hard Moors, 114 miles along the Cleveland Way but that was only because we ran it at a time when Scarborough was suffering from the worst storms it had had in 100 years and despite that and the fact that the waves were 30–40 foot high and crashing over the sea wall onto the promenade, we were told we still had to run along the seafront because loads of people had come out to watch the race and if we didn't, we would be disqualified. We all got utterly drenched and were lucky not to get washed away into the raging sea!'

Ooh, err...

But Allan's all-time, hands-down favourite marathon is London.

'It *has* to be London – you just can't beat the atmosphere,' he enthuses. 'Where else would you get three million people cheering you round a course? There are people all the way, no bits where you are on your own as in so many other races.'

What about injuries?

'I've been very lucky, injury-wise,' he tells me. 'There was the stress fracture due to the Grand Union run, but otherwise nothing serious – just the odd twisted knee or ankle. Also, I never run without putting Vaseline between my toes and I always wear two pairs of cheap socks to keep blisters at bay – and it works, no problems.

'To be honest, when I was going for the 100, I would have run through anything anyway – no pain would have stopped me, especially on the second 50. I was so possessed, I would have carried on no matter what.'

Does that mean he considers himself to be obsessed by marathon running?

'Yes, I definitely was,' he readily admits, 'but not now – it took over my life.'

So, what advice would he give to others who want to become 100 marathoners?

'I would encourage them to go for it, but try not to be as selfish as I was.'

I have a feeling that this is one statement his wife would definitely agree with.

Having checked out Allan's blog report about the GUCR for myself, I decided this chapter would not be complete without at least an abridged version, together with my reactionary comments, of the events that transpired on that fateful day. So here it is.

'It was in May 2010…' Allan begins.

Ah, 2010 – what a year it was!

'The Grand Union Canal Race (GUCR) covers 145 miles of canal path from Birmingham to London and has a reputation for being relentlessly tough, both physically and mentally, with a 60 per cent attrition rate.'

Loving it so far, *do* go on!

'Normally the entrants in this race are selected on a first-come, first-served basis and having missed the deadline by just one day the previous year, I was determined not to miss out again, so I drove my application to the race director's house on the same evening the forms were sent out. However, postal strikes meant that the race director decided that entrants would be selected in an email ballot instead,' he goes on. 'I'm the unluckiest person in the world when it comes to things like that and this was no exception – I wasn't selected.

'That was in November 2009. In May 2010 I received an email from the race director saying a couple of people had dropped out and offering me a place. The race was only a week away and my training had been pretty poor due to a knee injury, so my first reaction was to say no.'

Excellent idea…

'But…'

Uh-oh! 'But…' – an innocuous enough word, but within its syllables lurks unimaginable danger.

'Then I posted about it on Fetch [the online site for runners, cyclists, swimmers and triathletes] and I got a response saying I'd be mad to even contemplate it at such short notice.'

How sensible…

'But…'

Double uh-oh!

'If I did, then they would help out as much as possible.'

As in they would run the race for him, perhaps?

Alas, no! Allan explains that in races such as these, each entrant will have a support crew to help with preparation and throughout the race – supplying fresh clothing, food and drinks, and generally keeping the runner going.

'I really needed to do the race because it was to be my qualifying race for Spartathon and so I grabbed it, reasoning that even if I didn't finish, it was worth the gamble. I sent a quick email to the race director to confirm my entry and I was in!

'A week later it was race day and I was up at half past four in the morning for a quick breakfast of coffee and a banana. I knew I should eat as much as possible but I just couldn't face anything else. As I hadn't had time to prepare and train properly for the race, I decided to settle into a 25-minute run/5-minute walk routine.'

Sounds reasonable.

'I kept this up for the first 36 miles, meeting up with my crew at checkpoints along the way. They would wrap me in a blanket to keep me warm and refuel me with coffee and pot noodles or a sandwich. This would take about 15 minutes and had to be kept to a minimum as the longer I stopped, the colder and stiffer I became.

'Then it started raining and I was also beginning to find it hard to digest food properly, so my stomach started to bloat and I felt a little sick.'

What fun!

'At the next checkpoint, someone in the crew removed my sodden trainers and socks and dried my feet, while another forced me to drink and eat. This may sound odd, but when you're worn out you really do need someone to bark orders at you and make sure you're still doing the right things.

'As the race went on I spent longer at checkpoints and it was becoming more and more of an effort to get going again as my legs had stiffened up quite a bit by then. It probably took me about two or three minutes just to be able to get running properly again.

'At the 70-mile marker, which is commonly thought of as halfway even though there is still another 75 miles to go, I changed into my night running gear. Then it got so dark I had to wear a head torch. The crew kept popping up at various points, shouting encouragement and generally keeping me sane.'

According to the *Oxford English Dictionary* 'keeping' means 'to retain possession of', implying it (sanity) was already there in the first place. Just thought I'd point that out…

'I can switch off during really long runs so I never get bored and this was worth its weight in gold during the night as you couldn't see a damn thing anyway,' he continues.

That's generally what happens at night.

'By 85 miles, I was very tired…'

Lightweight!

'I had to change to a 20/10 minute walk/run rhythm. I was really just keeping going, forcing one foot in front of the other and making sure that I never stopped. At about 3am, I saw my first elephant – not literally of course, just the result of running non-stop for such a long time in the dark. Turned out it was just a tree across the canal! Later, I saw an evil-looking pixie staring at me from the fence of a lock-keeper's cottage.'

Of course you did, Allan.

'It was so scary that if I hadn't been running a race, I would have turned round and gone the other way! Drawing level with it, I was preparing for it to pounce out on me but was relieved when I saw that the "pixie" was just a clump of weeds.'

No kidding!

'By dawn the elephants and pixies had gone, but my body was starting to complain about the abuse it was under and things were starting to go wrong. At the next checkpoint, I had to have a massage and take painkillers – I didn't mention the elephants or pixies to my crew in case they thought I was losing it and wanted to pull me from the race.'

Losing it? Long gone, Allan, long gone!

'Leaving the checkpoint at 108 miles, my legs were so stiff the crew had to physically push me just to get me moving but at least the sun was shining.'

That's all right, then.

'Any idea of pace routine had gone by now – I was just running for as long as I could before walking, although I did try to keep to some sort of timing strategy so I could keep my mind active and not fall asleep. By the time I reached the 120-mile checkpoint, my leg was so bad that I had to have treatment on it and another massage. My body was definitely starting to rebel. I was peeing blood, though I didn't panic as I know this happens to long-distance runners – something to do with your bladder wall rubbing. But the pain in my leg was getting worse and I'd also started to cough up blood. Lots of things were going through my head.'

Like, where's the nearest hospital perhaps?

'I knew I could be in trouble…'

No fooling this guy.

'…and a DNF [Did Not Finish] was becoming a real possibility. But the idea of having come so far and not finishing was unthinkable at this stage.'

Absolutely. Unthinkable.

'I was very emotional by then and told my team captain, Nicole, that she wasn't to let me quit, no matter what happened. She was great, spraying up my leg, giving it a quick rub down and telling me she was going to buddy run me in [run alongside Allan] just to keep her eye on me, so if I did get in trouble there was someone there to get help. I readily agreed to this as I just wanted to keep going.

'By then, just moving my body was a huge effort and I was probably only going about three miles per hour and every part of my body was screaming at me to stop. I ignored it and kept going – I wasn't going to stop as long as I could just keep putting one foot in front of the other. Nicole ran about 20 feet in front of me as she knew I needed as much space as possible, then the nosebleeds started.'

Fab!

'By the time I reached the last check point, it was all I could do to take on water but my crew force-fed me, gave me a rub down, emptied my backpack and gave me a bottle of water to carry for the last few miles. The sun was now beating down and I was starting to suffer from that as well…'

But I thought he liked the sun?

'Again, the crew were brilliant. Knowing I'd stiffen up the longer I stayed but also knowing I needed to rest, they timed it perfectly and got me on my way by dragging me out of my chair and push-starting me again.'

Give me their names and I'll sort them out for you…

'I'd run 133 miles and had just 12 to go. Those were the hardest 12 miles of my life – less than half a marathon and about 3½ hours to finish it! I had my head down and was just going for it as best as I could. The slightest incline felt like I was climbing a mountain – my quads were shot, it was pure agony; up or down, the pain was intense. Thank God for painkillers!

'I kept telling myself to ignore the leg, the blood, the pain and get to the damn finish. Six miles is nothing when you've already run 139, but they can be the most emotional of your life! I allowed my mind to wander and thought about how much everybody on my crew had done for me. I felt a duty to get to the end and cross the line – I admit a couple of tears may have dripped down my face.

'But the most emotional moment was when my running mentor, Terry, appeared walking towards me along the canal path. I went to shake his hand but he just grabbed me and gave me a big hug. That nearly did me completely and I had to use all the strength I had left to stop from bursting into tears, there and then.

'And then I turned the corner and could see a big white banner with the word "FINISH" on it. I was probably running faster then than I had in the last four or five hours as familiar faces appeared, cheering me and clapping me in. I crossed the line and the race organiser, Dick Kearn, shook my hand and handed me my humongous medal. I told him there and then to put my entry in for next year as I wanted to see what I could do if I actually trained for the event. He just grinned.'

And then he fetched the men in white coats...

'Total mileage – 145; time taken – 34 hours 42 minutes; position – 10th.'

What amazes me as much as anything is the size of Allan's gamble: if he hadn't completed the race, not only would he not be able to qualify for Spartathon, he wouldn't be able to count it towards his total number of marathons run. And that was worth five marathons, wasn't it – or however many he'd got up to if he had dropped out before the finish?

'Oh no,' he tells me cheerily, 'it would only be worth one. And if I hadn't finished the whole race, it wouldn't even count as one.'

Hmm... The debate rumbles on.

SUMMER SHORTS

Bin bags... a runner's best friend. Not only for use as a cunning disguise from BBC commentary teams and elite athletes, but also for wearing (having first punched holes for arms and head) over race kit at the start, keeping you warm and/or dry for the moments between arriving at the starting line and actually stepping over it. The bin bag can later be removed and chucked away at the side of the road, unlike a favourite piece of kit which you may feel obliged to carry all the way round with you.

Also ideal for kit storage – minus holes – on a wet day!

MILE 24

CAMEL DUNG, BEAUTY CONTESTS AND FUND RAISING

David Phillips runs marathons for charity. By 2012 he will have run over 400 marathons and raised £55,000, most especially for the Brain and Spine Foundation (see www.brainandspine.org.uk).

DAVID PHILLIPS
Born: 1944
400 marathons:
- 1st marathon: 1982 – Coventry
- 100th marathon: 1991 – Stratford
Records/Honours:
- 1st in World to Run 100 Marathons & 100 Half Marathons
- 1st Welshman to Run 400 Marathons
- Twice Gold Medallist Welsh AA Marathon For Age
- Bronze Medal British Veterans Marathon

The first time I met Dave Phillips was at an Oxfordshire Service Station off the A34. He'd told me I would have no difficulty in recognising him and he was right – he only has one kidney, and so do I!

Actually, to be totally accurate Dave still has two kidneys, but one is shrivelled and useless while the other has grown to almost twice the normal size to handle double the workload, just the same as mine, although my wizened old thing was removed many years ago.

So, naturally, we recognised each other instantly and it had nothing whatsoever to do with the fact that Dave happened to be wearing a rather fetching, pale blue Swiss Alpine Marathon top that complimented his baby-blue eyes and vaguely greying hair, together with a pair of running trousers and trainers. Or the fact that despite his 67 years, he still has the body of someone who played rugby between the ages of 14 to 44 and has hardly missed a day's running or circuit training for the past 50 years. Nothing whatsoever.

Having hauled the 99 volumes of ring binders and photo albums containing Dave's personal collection of newspaper cuttings, club newsletters and magazines dating back to the early days of the Club from the boot of his car into the cosy cafeteria, much to the astonishment of onlookers, Dave and I proceed to take over a table meant for a family of 10 and lose ourselves in our Gulliver-sized coffee cups and a world of marathon memorabilia dating back to the formative years of the Club during the early-80s running boom.

As a chartered management accountant running his own company (set up in 1975, after he failed to secure a job) and one of the founder members of the 100 Marathon Club, Dave was entrusted as the Club's first ever treasurer. He was also its first secretary and magazine editor/printer. Leafing through his personal paraphernalia, it turns out the former Kenilworth Club and Warwickshire County Rugby Union hooker (his father, Dewi, won a Welsh rugby cap in 1921 against France) took up running in 1983 when he retired from rugby.

'I joined the Massey Ferguson Running Club,' he tells me, 'because their social scene was similar to that of rugby.'

And what better reason could there be?

'I also belong to Pembrokeshire Harriers in Wales,' Dave adds, 'as my wife and I stay there for about three months each year.'

Since taking up running, Dave, who is married to Robina (a non-runner) and has two grown-up children, Gareth and Anna (who enjoys fell-running in the Peak District and has run three marathons with her dad, including his 300th) has not only run 400 marathons, with a Personal Best time of 3 hours 21 minutes, but also hundreds of other races, from 10K to 100 miles.

Indeed, he gained a place in the *Guinness World Records* for becoming the first man to have run 100 marathons and 100 half marathons. He is also the first Welshman to have completed 400 marathons and was named 'Club Athlete of the Week' in the prestigious *Athletics Weekly* magazine of 1994 and also got a mention in *Runners World* for his endeavours. Currently, he runs about 50 races every year at various distances and plans to reach 300 halves by 2012.

While Dave may have travelled the world to run marathons, many of his most memorable races have taken place on home soil, though.

'I ran my first marathon at Coventry because of a drunken bet with some rugby mates,' he says, picking up the story. 'Ten of us were meant to do it, but only two of us actually made it to the start line! It was a great occasion, though, as it was also the first marathon Coventry had ever held. When I finished, I said, "Never again!" I've run every Coventry Marathon since then – 30 in all!'

Aside from that, prior to becoming an accountant he was an indentured apprentice at a Coventry machine tool company for five-and-a-half years and was voted Coventry's Apprentice of the Year. Subsequently, he was awarded the Freedom of the City of Coventry.

Another marathon that Dave has loyally attended for 30 years is the Shakespeare Marathon, held at Stratford, which is also where he ran his 100th.

'It was fantastic,' he says. 'Because I was the first in the area to do 100 marathons and only the 25th person in the UK to do so, there were huge crowds and it was a really big thing.'

Of course being a Welshman, Snowdon also gets a special mention, although Dave has only run there a mere 23 times!

'I never tire of the scenery, it's amazing. The Hastings Marathon is noteworthy, too,' he adds. 'I've only done it once and will never do it again.'

Oh dear! Not a good experience then?

'It's not that,' he explains, 'it's because they only hold the race every 100 years! Last time was 2008, so, naturally, lots of the 100 Club did it.'

Naturally. Equally, none will ever do it again – unless, of course, running multiple marathons is the as yet unknown answer to everlasting life. However, Dave is not content just to run marathons – oh no, he has also completed many ultras (further than a marathon), as well as once running 100 miles – yes, that's what I said – 100 miles. It took him 29 hours.

'It was in the Cotswolds,' he recalls. 'They hold an annual relay race known as "The Hilly 100" for obvious reasons. Each team consists of 10 runners, who each run 10 miles. As each runner finishes their leg, they are picked up by a support vehicle and follow the runners, cheering them on, so by the end there is a huge crowd of people to see the last leg runners finish the race. One year I decided to run all 100 miles by myself and another year I did 50 in a relay with another runner – it's good to ring the changes.'

If you say so, Dave...

But it's his tireless commitment to raise money for charity through running that really stands out and has turned him into something of a media star in his local area, including a recent nomination as a torchbearer for the 2012 Olympics.

'Carrying the Olympic torch would be the highlight of my running career so far!' says Dave.

Since 1988, he has raised over £50,000 for various charities, including Snowball, Crimestoppers, Barnados and the MS Society, as well as a sports centre for the disabled in Coventry. But his main beneficiary is the Brain & Spine Foundation, a charity that provides trained nurses to give telephone advice and support to those with neurological conditions, such as brain tumours, strokes and epilepsy.

The charity is supported every year by the *Daily Telegraph's* London Marathon Team, which has so far raised a massive £1.2 million with £100,000 raised in 2011 alone. It's a team led by Dave, whose honorary captains feature A-list celebrities, all of whom have been captured on film and stored in his impressively well-organised photograph albums.

Ex-professional boxer Michael Watson, who was Dave's initial inspiration in supporting the charity, is one such who has served as honorary captain. Following the well-documented injuries suffered as a result of the final fight which very nearly cost him his life, Watson received treatment from the charity's founder: the highly respected No. 1 neurosurgeon in the UK, Peter Hamlyn.

Because of Dave's commitment to the charity, the *Daily Telegraph* provide him with a guaranteed place on the London Marathon Team every year. In return, he heads up the team, offering running and fund-raising advice, as well as general encouragement at the launch held every January at Arsenal's home ground in London. Olympic year will be the 11th year Dave has run for the team and will coincide with his aim to raise £50,000 for charity and run 400 marathons – a target which he actually reached two days after I met him (at Nottingham) and following which he raised the bar to running 407 marathons and raising £55,000!

Aside from his epic fund-raising efforts, Dave has some amazing stories – 'None of which would have happened if it hadn't been for running marathons,' he tells me.

Never mind that, man! Get on with telling the stories.

'Well, in 1990,' he begins obediently, 'I ran in Cairo, Egypt – it was the first marathon they'd ever held there. The race started at the top pyramid, then we ran past the Sphinx and then back to the top pyramid, but the course passed through some areas of abject poverty. The filth and squalor were dreadful, with mud huts, garbage mountains and even open sewers beside the dusty, unmade-up roads. In some parts there were gangs of barefoot children who ran alongside us, throwing sticks and stones (and even camel dung), demanding money. When I told them I had no money, they went for my camera but I managed to hold on to it!

'The children had also pinched all the water from the water stations so a van had to follow us round and if we wanted water, we had to stick out our hand and grab a bottle, then hand it back! Trouble was, they were two-litre bottles and far too heavy to run with, so we would tip enough water away till they were light enough to carry!

'Also, because I was the only English-Welshman in the race and it was my birthday, the organisers made a cake for me and invited me to help judge the Miss Egypt Beauty Contest, which was being held at the same time for entry into Miss World.'

It might have been rude to refuse, Dave...

'I took some photos...'

I bet you did!

'But when I was changing my film, I must have dropped that reel because a cleaner later found it. Not knowing who it belonged to, she handed it to the event organiser, who assumed it belonged to the official photographer and duly posted it to him – in Texas! Some months later I happened to write to the photographer, whom I'd met at the Beauty Contest, and he – having already realised it was my film, but not having my address until then – immediately sent it on to me, six months after I'd returned from Cairo!

'Then in Paris,' Dave continues with his Tour of Tales, 'I was running along quite happily when I saw this large group of people blocking the pavement up ahead. Forgetting for a moment that the traffic would be coming from behind me and seeing the road ahead of me clear, I stepped out into the road to be given rather more than a glancing blow by the side of a passing bus. Of course the driver didn't even notice and just carried on. Luckily, I wasn't too badly injured – more shaken than anything – and carried on as well, but if it had been a second earlier it would have been the front of the bus that hit me and I would have been killed.'

And I would be a chapter short for my book, so you see how these things are just meant to be…

'And in Davos,' Dave continues, 'during the Swiss Alpine Marathon, one of my favourite marathons – well, actually, it's not a marathon at all. It's actually a 72K trail run or a 42K.'

Hmm… Now let me think, which one should I do?

'But the 42K involves a 2,700-metre climb…'

Thank god he mentioned that before I put my entry in…

'I've done both,' he says.

I'd expect nothing less…

'The event was thought up by an Englishman,' he adds. 'I've actually run there 20 times.'

I want to say I'm surprised on both counts, but…

'Anyway, back to the story…' says Dave.

Good plan.

'One time I was running there with another guy on this path that runs alongside a live railway line and you have to cross a fairly high viaduct…'

At this point he shows me a picture of a narrow footpath along which runners run (oddly enough) in single file, while a train chugs past them no more than an arm's length away.

'They have men with flags at either end of the viaduct,' he goes on, 'to slow the trains down as they go across.'

Oh well, that's all right then.

'Anyway, this one guy was really nervous about crossing the viaduct…'

Can't *think* why.

'He didn't like heights so we had to blindfold him.'

What?

'And then I went on one side of him, another competitor went the other side and we walked him three abreast, actually on the railway line, across to the other side of the viaduct.'

Err… What about the trains?

'The flagmen made sure we crossed at a time when there were none due to come.'

That's a lot of faith going on up there on that there viaduct!

'Anyway, we all made it and finished the race!'

Praise be to God – and railwaymen with flags!

'It's one of the reasons I love running,' adds Dave.

Really?

'Yes,' he assures me, 'the friendship and the camaraderie, it's really special.'

Oh, *that*.

'None of these things would have happened if it hadn't have been for running a marathon.'

How true.

'It's one of the few things in life that makes no differentiation between what job you do, what sort of house you live in or what sex you are.'

True again.

'Take the Jungfrau Marathon in Switzerland,' he goes on.

'There, they have a specially erected tented area at the base of Mount Eiger, with mixed toilets and mixed showers.'

Mixed showers?

'Yes,' says Dave, 'and it's fine, nobody could care less. Of course,' he adds, with a wry grin, 'unless you've done it before, you don't know they're mixed until you're in!'

Ah well… If you're a marathon runner with a penchant for Swiss marathons (and don't buy this book and read it), enter at your peril!

So, does Dave think he's obsessed with running marathons?

'No, just running and keeping very fit.'

That's sort of an admission then.

'I have lots of other hobbies,' he adds.

Such as?

'Golf, gardening (especially growing my own fruit and veg), music, natural history, business and I sing in three choirs.'

How very Welsh.

'I'm also still working,' he reminds me. 'The trouble with working for yourself and owning your own company is that you just keep on at it – it's a way of life, not just a job.'

And what do other people think of his running exploits?

'I've been called brainless and a nutter, and they think what I've done is impossible.'

How rude.

'I don't care!' he declares, 'I do it for the friendship and the camaraderie, to achieve my own goals and raise the money for charity. I'm also writing a couple of books – one about accountancy, one about running – although I haven't actually started either of them yet.'

What about an ultimate goal?

'I'd like to run a marathon in every capital in the world,' he says. 'Otherwise, I just want to keep running till I look down on fellow runners.'

I assume he means Heaven, not the lofty heights of big-headedness?

'Of course,' he confirms, 'or maybe I should be saying, "Look up!" at them.'

Well, only he can know…

So, how about one tip for any virgins out there?

'Get your body and mind used to running and run every day.'

Hey, that's *two* tips, Dave – call yourself an accountant!

SUMMER SHORTS

It strikes me that if any justification for running multiple marathons or any race at all were needed, raising funds for worthwhile causes, as Dave does, must be the ultimate. Not only are you helping others, you are also helping yourself in keeping healthy and fit, as well as achieving self-set goals leading to increased self-esteem and personal fulfilment.

If running in Cairo, carry a water pistol to fire at any unruly urchins! This can double up as drinking water on the run. Just remember not to pack it in your hand baggage, though.

MILE 25

THROWING STONES

Steve Edwards is one of the most admired and distinguished members of the 100 Marathon Club, setting countless records and raising the standard of multiple marathon running to an unprecedented level.

STEVE EDWARDS

Born: 1962
570 marathons (updated since original interview):
• 1st marathon: 1981 – Coventry
• 100th marathon: 1990 – St Albans
Records – current and past:
• Fastest 500 Marathons Ever Run By an Individual
• Fastest Marathon for Veteran (Over-40)
• Most Marathons Run in One Year (87) and in Fastest Average Time (3:14)
• Youngest Male to Run 100 and 200 Marathons
• Fastest 10 Marathons in 10 Days Outright/Fastest Veteran Master

Having joined the 100 Marathon Club at the relatively tender age of 28 and now just shy of his 50th birthday, Steve Edwards is one of the longest standing (well, actually, his *standing* time is probably very little as he's run over 500 marathons so he's best described as one of the longest-*running*) members of the Club.

Despite this, I was lucky enough to catch up with him (not in any literal sense, you understand), in Malta, where he was running his 520th road marathon. With him was his lovely wife Teresa, Steve's mainstay and most loyal supporter.

It was clear as we stood chatting on the corner of the street opposite Malta's delightful little harbour, blocking the pavement so everyone had to take a great circuitous route around us, that this is one couple for whom marathon running as a way of life not only suits them both, but actually brings them closer together despite the fact that it's only Steve who does the marathon running, although Teresa runs for general fitness and health.

Their closeness is obvious in the way they talk together, one taking over easily from the other but never overlapping, their bright-eyed, bubbly enthusiasm about everything marathon, particularly the bonds they feel with the other 100 Club members, and last, but not least, their positive outlook on life as a whole.

All that remains for me to add is that they even look alike – but that would be an outright lie. Steve is 6'1", with a hairless pate upon which the early morning sun practises basketball while Teresa is 5'3", with a mass of gorgeous, curly-whirly, dark hair. However, both have blue eyes and perhaps not surprisingly given the running, both are healthily slim.

When we spoke Steve readily agreed to be involved in the book and to answer any questions I had for him and so the instant I got home, I emailed him a questionnaire. Strike while the proverbial iron is hot is my motto! Poor man, I thought as I emailed the 40 questions to him, as if he hasn't got enough to do – what with running marathons virtually every week, training almost every day and working full time.

But I should have known better even from our short-ish meeting in Malta for the questionnaire was duly returned quickly and answered so eloquently and comprehensively that I felt the only way I could give Steve's responses the justice they deserved was to simply reproduce them in this book exactly as he wrote them. So, here they are.

When did you become a member of the 100 Marathon Club?
In the very early days of the club you didn't become a member until you had run 100 official measured marathon races of 26 miles 385 yards. It was therefore a very exclusive club and I remember many of the members being much older than me.

I was introduced to the club in 1988 after running a marathon with Richard Bird, who at the time was not only aspiring to become a member but was also attempting to break the World Record for the most marathons run in one year. I was just looking to run one a month that year but after meeting others in the club, I ended up running 20. In December 1990, I ran my 100th official marathon race and therefore became a fully qualified member of the club. At 28 years old, I was also credited with the World Record as the youngest athlete ever to run 100 marathons.

What is your marital status? Children?
Married, with one grown-up son (from a previous marriage).

Does your partner run? Your children?
My wife Teresa also runs but mainly to keep fit and stay in shape. She has run many races including half marathons and the one marathon. She said it would be her first and last, just to see what

her husband put himself through! My son Jason did run at school and was more of a sprinter, but doesn't run at all now.

What do they think of your running?
Teresa is very proud of all that I've achieved and accompanies me to every race I attend. I know that I couldn't have achieved what I have without her love and support so I always consider everything I do in running as a team effort. When he was young, Jason came with us to most races and would sometimes run through the finish line with me. He was also proud of his dad and I suspect he still is, although he probably can't fully understand why I do what I do.

When/Where did you run your 100th marathon?
St Albans, December 1990. A great day, with every single member of the 100 Club present. A big celebration afterwards to toast a new member and a new World Record.

How long did it take you to get to the 100th? (date/place of 1st marathon)
I ran my first marathon in my then home town of Coventry in October 1981, aged 18. However, I only ran about a dozen or so marathons before 1988, which is when I got going properly after meeting the 100 Club.

How many have you run to date?
I am a bit of a purist when it comes to numbers and personally think that only official marathon races of accurate distance should be counted, so therefore my total is 545. However, if I include ultras and also off-road LDWA (Long Distance Walkers Association) type events, which aren't really races (or accurate in many cases), then it's nearly 570 (at the time of going to print).

What made you start running marathons?

My first marathon in Coventry was during the running boom of the early 80s when most towns and cities had a marathon/half marathon. I was drawn to a poster advertising the inaugural Coventry Marathon and it made me think. After a bet with some mates, that was my decision made. I was only 18 at the time and I'd never run a race of any other distance, the Coventry Marathon was my first ever road race.

Why so many?

After my first marathon I realised how good it felt to be very fit and be able to run freely without getting out of breath. I tried different distances – five miles, 10 miles, 10ks, half marathons, etc., but I didn't seem to get quite the same buzz out of these as running the marathon. I also seemed to be more geared towards endurance rather than fast speed and therefore had greater success at marathon distance than shorter distances.

Having talked to a coach about what time he thought I could run for the marathon with the right training, etc., he said around 2:30 based on what he saw of me and how I ran, my bio mechanics, etc. I thought that would be a fantastic time to have on my running CV and it would have been enough to win many of the low-key events, but I knew it was never going to win a major marathon. I also remember looking through an old Guinness World Records and coming across a record for the most marathons ever run. It was set by a gentleman by the name of Sy Mar, an American Indian who averaged between 3 hours 40 minutes and 4 hours for each one.

That's when I considered the possibility of becoming an extreme marathon runner and going about setting extreme marathon running records instead. This would still require the ability to run reasonable times for marathons but it also meant running reasonable times regularly and consistently. The Sy Mar record also sowed the seed in my mind about the possibility of running 500 marathons and whether it might be possible to run them all averaging under 3 hours 30 minutes, which would be a world first.

How often do you run a marathon?
Since 1988 I have run a marathon on average every 16 days. My average time for all 545 marathons is currently 3hrs 18min.

Do you have a pre-race routine?
Yes, I pretty much have it down to a fine art now. I'm big on preparation and plan everything meticulously, including nutrition and hydration, which I think, along with a good training regime, is crucial for longevity in this sport.

I make sure I eat more carbohydrate-rich foods from 48hrs before the race. I stay well-hydrated the day before and leading up to the race start. I always have a big cereal breakfast 3 hours before the race and sip on a carbo-loading drink up until race start. I have all my kit ready the day before and make sure I arrive early, leaving me plenty of time to powder my nose, grease up and get changed.

I use Vaseline on my armpits and groin – there's nothing worse than sore bits when you run! I also rub it on my feet as I find it helps to prevent blisters and keeps my feet softer and in better condition. I also use plasters on my nipples: I did use Vaseline many years ago, which worked but tends to ruin your running vest!

Then before I go, I make sure I have my gels (I usually take two during a marathon). I also wear a cap if it's sunny and warm to protect my head (the hair disappeared a long time ago!)

Any lucky charms, etc. you run with?
Not really, I'm very minimalist – don't even wear a Garmin [a

sports watch that measures distance, speed, altitude, heart rate, time and pace], just an ordinary stopwatch as I can pretty much judge my own pace.

Any superstitions in connection with marathon or racing? Why?
Again, not really: I always plan ahead and try to make sure I've thought of everything beforehand, perhaps I get a little hung up on making sure I get up on time so sometimes I'll set the alarm on both my clock and phone!

Did you start off with the intention of running so many marathons?
No, not at all! After I finished my first in 1981, I had to crawl down the stairs backwards the following morning as my legs were like gateposts. It took me nearly a week before I could walk normally and I swore I'd never run one ever again!

How did it happen?
A combination of things, really – the chat with the coach, the Sy Mar record, starting off with attempting the one-a-month in 1988, which was also a charity fund-raising exercise to raise money for Great Ormond Street. But I guess what capped it was talking to Richard Bird that day while we ran and meeting up with what was at the time the original 100 Club.

How many a year?
I've averaged 23 marathons a year since 1988. However, in 1992 I set a new World Record for running the most marathons in a one-year period: Richard Bird's record of 71 had been broken by an American athlete who did something like 74. So, after becoming the youngest athlete to run 100 marathons, I needed a new challenge – the Most in a Year was the next step. I also wanted to bring it back to the UK! In March 1992, I crossed the finish line of the Barcelona Marathon (in the Olympic stadium)

to record 87 official marathon races in 12 months. My average finish time for the 87 was 3hrs 14min, over an hour quicker than the previous record holder despite running 13 more marathons. This record stood for about18 years – I think it was broken in the year 2000.

Any marathon runners or others who have influenced you?
Personal to me, Richard Bird and Colin Green (original co-founder of the 100 Club) and also members of my first claim club Bourton Roadrunners, especially Dennis Walmsley who has certainly inspired me to run even quicker. Also, Ron Hill was a hero and of course pretty much a forerunner of running multiple marathons. However, it's my wife Teresa who supports me in all that I do, who has been really important.

I'm also in admiration of anyone who attempts the challenge of running just one marathon and it's a very humbling feeling to be told by others that what I do has motivated and inspired them to challenge themselves in some way.

Favourite marathon?
Many favourites, for many reasons: Stockholm, where I ran my PB of 2:51 in 1992. New York and Chicago because you can't beat the glitz, glamour and atmosphere of American big city marathons; Connemara in Ireland, not only because of the beautiful scenic course but also where I ran my 500th marathon in 2010.

But if I had to pick one, it has to be the Brathay Windermere Marathon. This is where I completed the first four Brathay 10 Marathons in 10 Days challenges from the first ever one in 2007 through to 2010. At the 2008 10-in-10, I set the first Guinness World Record for the fastest time (now broken) and in 2009, set the fastest Vet Masters (over 40) time, a record which still stands. It's also the marathon that Teresa chose to run as her first and last. Therefore, Windermere is indeed a very special place for us both.

Least favourite?
Hard to say as I enjoy running; obviously some aren't as spectacular as others or offer quite as much in the way of scenery, etc. but I think it would be unfair to name them!

Most unusual?
Midnight Sun Marathon in Tromsø, as you start at 11pm and run into the early hours of the morning; however it's light the whole time. Then you go to the pub afterwards to celebrate!

I also remember running a track marathon in October 1989, in Bracknell which started at midnight on the Saturday night when the clocks went back. The eventual winner did 2:57 but as the clocks went back an hour while we ran, he claimed a fun record of the first sub-2 hour marathon! For me it was the second marathon in a series of four I did over just three days. On the Sat morning I did Seven Sisters in Eastbourne, on Sat night it was the one I mentioned in Bracknell, Sunday morning it was Harlow (these three were within 27 hours with travelling and little sleep), then Dublin on the Monday morning.

Worst weather conditions?
For hot conditions it has to be Crete in 1991 – it was in the mid-1990s and I set off at a 3-hour pace only to fade badly at 14 miles. I was suffering jet lag as I had run the Auckland Marathon only a week before but I have never struggled so much over so long of a marathon course; the heat had literally drained every ounce of energy left in me.

For cold and wet, it has to be the Cornish Marathon when it was run from Rilla Mill. I've ran this event many times but in the year 2000, when we were running over the Bodmin Moor part of the course, it lashed down with large, freezing-cold hailstones. We were literally battered – sore head, ears, eyes… It was hard not to cry, you just had to keep going until you were out of the storm. I remember getting to Jamaica Inn and turning right, and the sun just appeared – it was like nothing had happened and we had just gone through a door to another room, strange. I'd never experienced anything like it before or have since.

Hardest course?

Has to be the Swiss Alpine Mountain Marathon, which is just under 80km, has some tough climbs and varying weather conditions, from hot at low levels to freezing when you get to the top. I ran it in 1991 and went over badly on my ankle as I was coming down from the top – I actually fractured a bone in my foot but managed to hobble the last 16km to the finish.

Easiest?

I wouldn't class any marathon as being easy – I've always raced them to the best of my ability and finished shattered. Every now and then, though I guess there are days when I've felt really good from the start and ran pretty much pain-free from start to finish. My PB in 1991 at Stockholm was one of those days. You can probably count on one hand how many times that happens. My second-best ever time of 2:52 in 1990 at Benidorm was another time.

Do you think you are obsessed with running marathons?

I wouldn't say 'obsessed' is quite the right word. 'Dedicated' is the one I prefer! Most athletes will admit that you have to be focussed and determined almost to the point of selfishness to achieve your goals. I have achieved many marathon endurance

World Records/Bests in my life so far and being determined and focussed has been the key to achieving those goals:

• Youngest Athlete to Run both 100 and 200 Marathons.
• Running the Most Official Marathon Races in a One-Year Period, Total of 87 (Average Time 3:14).
• First Official Guinness World Record for the Fastest Time to Run 10 Marathons in 10 Days Outright and the Fastest Vet Masters Time.
• Fastest 500 Marathons Ever Run By an Individual Athlete.

How do people react to you when they know you have run over 100 marathons?
Most people are shocked but I suspect that those who aren't sporty or don't run can't really comprehend the enormity of what's involved in doing this. In fact, many can't probably comprehend running a few miles let alone 100 marathons. When other runners talk to me about the amount I've run, they are shocked that I've been able to run them all in respectable times and for such a long period of my life. It's nice to be respected and recognised for that and I count myself fortunate I've been able to achieve that.

Do you do any other sport?
Not really – I used to play football and cricket when I was younger at school and also did martial arts. These days I do a little weight training and loads of core work to complement my running training. That alone takes up enough of my spare time (if there is such a thing!).

Injuries?
Up until the last two years none really to speak of that actually stopped me from running. However, with the workload of reaching 500 by 2010 instead of 2012, training for and

competing in four consecutive 10-in-10s and the ever-present hunger to ensure respectable times by training harder as I've got older has meant the inevitable. From July 2010 I was out of action for 6 months with a stress fracture in my ankle. During this time I also needed an overdue hernia repair. In December 2009, I slipped on the ice while out training and sustained a hip injury and didn't run for 6 weeks. In September 2008, I incurred an Iliopsoas [the combination of three muscles that join together from the abdomen to the thigh] muscular strain, which was so painful in my groin I couldn't run for about 6 weeks. My sports therapist now says I have to train smarter, not harder – good advice.

How long does it take you to recover from each marathon?
I normally go out for a gentle three- or five-mile run the day after and would say that I'm pretty much normal again within two or three days. However, on the whole I would say that if I had to, I could run a marathon the very next day.

What is your routine regarding food before, during and after a race?
See pre-race question. I'm very big on nutrition and take nutritional supplements to my normal food as I believe today's food quality in terms of the nutrients, vitamins and mineral contents is nowhere near as good as it should, or used to be. I also make sure I refuel within 10–15 minutes of a race with both food and a sports recovery drink.

Warm up/down?
I always do active stretching before a race and static stretching after. I also have an ice bath (legs only!) after a marathon or long, hard training run.

Do you have favourite running clothes/shoes?
I've worn neutral Asics Cumulus or Nimbus shoes for years and they've served me well. I tend to wear sprinter-type shorts rather than normal running shorts and a club vest.

Do you ache after racing?
I do, but try to mitigate this with good post-race recovery routine involving stretching, nutrition, ice bath, etc.

How long after each race would you rest before resuming training?
24 hours – I always try to get out the next day for a short easy run.

What is a typical week's training, if any?
I generally run between 50–60 miles a week, which may or may not include a marathon. Within this I usually include two or three quality sessions involving intervals, hill reps and a tempo run. I also do about four or five core work sessions a week, rotating between floor work and Swiss ball. I also do one weight training session a week.

How much time per week is taken up with training and racing on average?
Between 10 and 12 hours' training a week – racing a marathon adds another three-and-a-bit hours but then you need to add on travelling time, etc.

One piece of advice you would give to aspiring 100 Marathon Club members?
Get fit for your sport and maintain it – don't just let your sport maintain your fitness, i.e. do everything that's required to condition and maintain your body to run lots of marathons. Not just running training but also core work, body strength exercises, stretching, adequate nutrition and hydration, etc.

One tip you would offer to first-time marathoners?
Difficult to prioritise out of so many, so I will offer two: 1. Do the training – there's no shortcuts, you'll only get out what you put in; 2. Start off steady at the pace you are intending to try and complete the marathon. Don't think that by going quicker at the start, you'll have time in the bank – it doesn't usually work like that and will generally do the exact opposite. If you've done the training, you'll maintain the same pace and finish on time, perhaps slightly quicker. If you haven't done adequate training to run the marathon in that time, it was never going to happen anyway.

Do you have an ultimate running goal and, if so, what is it?
Not sure about an ultimate goal but my next goal is to try and improve on that 500 marathon record by 2012, by becoming the first person in the world to run 500 sub 3:30s. I have 43 to go! If I achieve that, I'll be close to 600 in total. From there, the 1,000 barrier has to be an option but only if I can continue to run them in reasonable times relative to age. As I say, for me personally it's the finish times that give these types of records credibility.

What about non-running goals?
My day job is in IT. I've done this for nearly 30 years and I guess it's fair to say it doesn't quite hold the same attraction as it used to and these days I consider it more of a means to an end rather than my career. Marathon running, on the other hand, has rewarded me with many things, including helping me escape from the daily stresses of the day job. The truth of it is that I often wish I could forge a new career from all that I have achieved in marathon running and to that end I would love to start doing motivational speaking. I've been asked to do the odd talk from time to time, but up to now it's generally been on a voluntary basis. It's something I know I would enjoy, apart from the financial aspect. For me the

greater enjoyment would come from inspiring people to follow their own dreams, which is very powerful. If that were to happen, I might then get a chance to do the other thing very close to my heart, which is to write a book. I know the title – in fact I have two in mind, both very apt but unfortunately that's as far as it's ever got!

We subsequently enjoyed a chat about some of Steve's favourite running stories…

'I'd just done a marathon in Germany and was travelling through the night on my way to do my second marathon in Switzerland when I was stopped by armed police for speeding. I told them I was tight on time and that I'd run one marathon and was on my way to my second one, but they didn't believe me. It wasn't until they saw my trainers and running gear in the car that they decided I must be telling the truth, but they still insisted I accompany them to the police station to get a penalty notice and pay the fine.

'The really strange thing was that I'd won the German race and some prize money – which turned out to be the exact amount of the fine. It was like it was meant to be!

'I've also run out of petrol twice whilst driving in Europe; the first time I had to park in a lay-by somewhere in Germany and wait until morning as the garages were all shut. The second time I had to push the car across the Czech/German border to a garage so I could fill up – and that was after running two marathons!

'And then there was the time I had to get changed in a telephone box after being bussed out to the middle of nowhere to start the one-off Rotherham Marathon!'

No wonder it was a one-off. All the locals complained they couldn't get to use the phone box for hours and when it finally became free, it stank of Deep Heat!

Steve's final funny story is my personal favourite and came about from something he hates: reporters who take what he says out of context. Uh oh! I've been warned. Maybe reproducing his questionnaire was a very, *very* good idea on my part.

'I once told a reporter that I ate a good, healthy balanced diet but could also get away with eating anything I liked, such as pizza/Chinese/junk foods. The article was given a full-page spread in the newspaper with a headline that suggested I lived off junk foods! I was livid, especially as I set so much store by, and spend so much time on proper nutrition.

'Shortly after that article was published I turned up in Holland to run my 499th marathon, only to find that the Dutch had picked up on this report somehow and when they interviewed me over the public address system, they made a huge thing about the fact that I ate nothing but junk food!'

Any other comments, Steve?
Why do I run? There are many reasons why I run – obviously because I enjoy running and it keeps me incredibly fit. But it's more than just that: running for me is a way of life. There's a great camaraderie and social side to running, which has meant my wife and I have made many new friends. We have also visited many wonderful places that we would not have otherwise visited, had it not been for doing a race there.

It's obviously been rewarding in terms of personal achievement but it's also been a great opportunity to put something back. Over the years I've supported and competed in hundreds of races, which has not only helped contribute to the grass roots of the sport but also enabled me to raise approximately £25,000 for various charities. I also feel that by setting and realising goals that my achievements as a non-elite athlete are incredibly inspirational. It's amazing just how many people contact me from time to time to not only acknowledge what I do, but to also say how it has inspired them to do something challenging themselves. When you reach into people's hearts like that, it's not only very humbling, but also very powerful.

As long as I can stay fit and healthy, I will always look for new challenges – it's in my nature. I already have some ideas of what I might do next but one thing's for sure: I will aspire to achieve as much as I can in running. The body is an amazing machine and just like they say the human brain is underused, I also believe that true of the human body itself. It never ceases to amaze me just how much the body can respond when tested and believe me, you haven't lived until you've experienced that feeling of pushing your body to the absolute limit! As I say, it's a way of life and I feel privileged to have been part of that life from a relatively early age. If I can continue into old age, then I will.

Could I define the marathon event? In 1992, after setting the new Most Marathons in a Year record, I was asked to define the marathon as an event. The marathon is widely known as the ultimate test of athletic endurance: 26.2 miles of running, a gruelling and punishing event that tests the limits of one's resolve to overcome fear with sheer guts and determination.

Thank you, Steve.

Now you would think after such a complete set of answers that I would have no requirement to bother Steve further, but three hours after I'd dialled his number, I came off the phone, exhausted yet jubilant. Here was a man so much after my own heart – I had to check it hadn't been surgically removed by some kind of new techno-wonder equipment!

Now, Teresa, don't get the wrong idea here: I'm merely talking about my running heart, not my romantic heart. You see, running and me go back a long way; back to the days when there were no heart monitors or Garmins. Indeed, nothing to tell you how you felt when you ran – except your own feelings. Sometimes you ran like the wind, like there was nothing to stop you running forever, your legs and body light and free. Then there were times when you felt like someone had driven a tractor over you, everything ached and hurt and nothing wanted to move in a forward direction. From that you learned that some days you could train hard and others not so much, and the more you ran the more you began to heed what your body was telling you. And the more times you ran the same distance, the more you learned what it felt like to run that distance in a certain time. All the time you were getting to know more about your own body, too.

So, you knew how good it felt to go out without a care for your time – just to run how you felt, something deep inside connecting with the natural world around you, the air you breathed, the way the body took in oxygen purified by the trees and aided your running. You, your body, nature, all working together… The way it was meant to be.

And Steve, along with most of the other 100 Marathon Club runners, knows these things too, despite running in a world full of technical know-how, shops and websites bursting at the seams with running must-haves and all the while magazine articles telling you how to do it (and how not to).

And here I must once more quote Steve directly:

'Life becomes very simple when all you have to do is get up and run, put one foot in front of the other. Life has become so complicated. I think running is a bit like what it was like for prehistoric man – you went out, got food and brought it back, the hunter/gatherer thing. Running taps into our instincts.'

So, apart from his funny stories, the importance of good nutrition, camaraderie and how running often reflects life, that is what we talked about for three hours.

293

Thinking about how far Steve has come since that first marathon, back in 1981 and what he said to me at the end of our conversation about not knowing what he could do until he tried and one thing leading to another, I can think of no better way to end this chapter than with a quote that Steve's father often used to say to him:

'Unless you throw a stone in the water, you'll never know where the ripples might end.'

SUMMER SHORTS

Run natural (run light) – leave your watch, your iPod, your Garmin, behind. Learn to listen to your body and enjoy the beauty of nature around you. Marvel at being a part of it.

And never trust a reporter.

MILE 26

CRAZY RACES IN CRAZY PLACES

Here's a round up of just a few of the 100 Marathon Club members' favourite races.

THE MEDOC MARATHON – LONGEST MARATHON IN THE WORLD

Rothschild, Beychevelle, Latour… Hunky hams, cheery cheeses, seductive oysters…

You might be forgiven for thinking you've stumbled upon some misplaced section on the best restaurants in France's southwest region of Medoc, rather than a chapter about places to run a marathon – but you haven't! Glee of glees, this is what you can expect if you elect to run in what's billed as the Longest Marathon in the World – the infamous Medoc Marathon. If the name of your marathon game is 'fun' rather than 'fast', you prefer fancy dress to running kit and your idea of a pit stop is a glass of wine rather than water, then this is the race for you!

According to the official website the event was created in 1984 by a group of passionate marathon fans, who believe that sport is synonymous with 'health, fun and conviviality' and who to this day insist 'spoilsports, thugs and record seekers are not invited'. Held every autumn, the organisers invent a different fancy-dress theme each year (one year it was Westerns, another comic book characters – although runners do have the option of choosing their own theme, if they prefer. Apparently construction workers and transvestites are among the most popular!).

As for the race itself, the journey begins at the small, relatively unknown town of Pauillac, about 20 miles from Bordeaux, and weaves its way alluringly through some of the most beautiful vineyards and châteaux in the area. The course is described as flattish, with some uneven pavements, dirt and gravel tracks.

However, with every water station en route also serving wine, you're more likely to have to concentrate on staying *on* your feet rather than noticing what's beneath them! Not only is there wine on tap but as you reach the last 4km, you are offered oysters, cheeses, hams, a barbecue and ice cream! Hence the race's reputation for being the world's 'longest' marathon, with most runners taking their time to savour the delights of France's hospitality at its bountiful best. Couple all this with around 80 live bands en route and you've got yourself a party on the run.

And should you be one of the few who actually manage to finish the race rather than dropping out (or even passing out) beforehand, you will become the lucky recipient of a finisher's medal, a rather useful rucksack and a bottle of surprisingly decent wine presented in a stylish wooden case to take home with you – or not.

Regardless of whether you make the finishing line, you will be invited to attend the after-race party held inside an enormous marquee, where they offer all sorts of refreshments, including sandwiches, beer and – yes, you've guessed it – wine!

Among the comments on the live2run marathon guide

CRAZY RACES IN CRAZY PLACES

website from previous participants are: 'It's not just a marathon, it's an experience' and 'One of the top 100 things to do before you die'. Which, if you haven't taken the advice of another previous participant quoted on the site to 'include in your training leading up to the race drinking a bit of wine each day, slowly increasing the dosage', I would suggest you do the other 99 things on your list first!

THE NORTH POLE MARATHON – LITERALLY THE WORLD'S COOLEST RACE

The North Pole Marathon claims to be the 'World's Coolest Marathon' – and you can take that whichever way you want.

Recognised by the *Guinness World Records* as the northernmost marathon on earth, this is also the only officially measured marathon to be run entirely on water (in the form of ice floes made from the frozen waters of the Arctic Ocean).

With just six to 12 feet separating you from 12,000 feet of unfrozen sea and in sub-zero temperatures, this is likely to be a running experience you will never forget – which in my view has to be a good thing because otherwise you might be at risk of repeating it!

The adventure, not to mention the testing of your nerve, begins before you even arrive – with a flight from Spitsbergen in Norway to an airstrip at the Pole, an airstrip that must be continually moved because of cracking ice. Indeed, as you circle above the airstrip at the Pole and look down at the frozen land below, you can actually see cracks expanding but luckily, expanding so little that it's still okay to land.

'It gives you that sense of stepping over the ocean – very exciting,' says 100 Club member Osy Wayne, who in 2006 ran the race (his 100th marathon) dressed as a polar bear!

Assuming your nerve holds you will now find yourself at the geographical North Pole Camp, 90 degrees north – the point exactly opposite the South Pole and where everywhere else on earth lies to the South, one of the most remote places on the planet. From here the excitement and anxiety can only build as you find yourself billeted in tents overnight in temperatures some degrees below freezing – and that's not including any wind chill!

Around you there's nothing but snow and ice and while the course is undoubtedly flat, there are still areas of snowy hillocks to be overcome. As for race kit, forget shorts and T-shirt, think skiwear, goggles and woolly hat.

Stepping out into the frozen silence on the day of the race, the sound of scrunching snow is pretty much the only noise you'll hear as you follow the small red flags marking out this multi-lap course around the Pole. And when you cross the line, your hat, scarf and eyelashes frosted white, you'll become one of the select few to have run a marathon on the top of the world – and by all accounts, that's exactly how you'll feel, too!

But it doesn't end here: as a reward for your efforts, you will be given an opportunity to go for a helicopter ride over some of the local sights in the polar region after the race. But don't expect any luxury. 'We were crammed into the helicopter, sitting on boxes down the middle,' was Osy's experience, 'but it was still worth every minute!'

COMRADES – THE LARGEST ULTRA MARATHON IN THE WORLD

Take approximately 50 refreshment tables, 14,000 litres of Coke and cream soda, five tons of bananas, a tonne of chocolates, 400kg biscuits, 400,000 plastic bottles, 2,500 litter bins, 750 tubes of Deep Heat... Whoa, what was that? *Deep Heat*? What kind of party *is* this?

Now add to the list: 16 ambulances, six rapid response vehicles, four quad bikes with paramedics, two helicopters and a partridge in a pear tree (I mean a public first aid tent) and you get a fraction of an idea of just what sort of organisation goes into the world's largest and most testing ultra marathon event.

The Comrades Marathon has been held every year since 1921, apart from the war years (1941–45), and must therefore be one of the earliest organised ultra-marathon events in existence, too. It was the brainchild of World War I veteran Vic Clapham from London (no wonder the English have a reputation for being eccentric!). After he and his parents had emigrated to South Africa in the late 19th century, poor old Vic got caught up in the Great War of 1914–1918, when he fought as a soldier with the 8th South African Infantry.

When the war ended, not only was Vic left deeply affected by the atrocities suffered by his comrades but he was also struck by the camaraderie evinced in the men in overcoming them. So it was that he came up with the idea of a 56-mile race as a living memorial to all those who had fallen in the War, aptly naming it the Comrades Marathon.

The race itself is a series of up and down hills – all named, many historically and each with a story to tell – and every year the start and finish of the race is reversed, alternating between Pietermaritzburg and Durban. In 1921, the event attracted 34 entrants; in 2010, there were over 12,000, although only 9,000 officially finished the race.

As if the race itself isn't tough enough with the heat, the hills and the distance, there is also a cut-off time at the 87km point. If you miss the cut-off, you are excluded from the race. In 2010, over 1,000 runners finished in the last 10 minutes of the race, with the first non-finisher missing out by one second. Now that is strict. Despite this, many runners return year after year – some of them like 100 Marathon Club's Dave Ross, who has completed seven races so far and seeks to attain one of the revered 'Green Numbers'. These are only attainable after completing 10

Comrades Marathons (one a year, rather than the 10-in-10 days of Windermere – but then Comrades is more than twice as far as Windermere and ten times hotter!). Once you acquire a Green Number, you have that number for life and nobody else can ever wear it.

So, if it's a bit of (Deep) heat, hills and history you're after, this may be one for your marathon to-do list. And if you have such a list, you should be aware that it's only a matter of time before you feature in a book like this!

SPARTATHON

Another race with strict cut-off times is the 'Spartathon', an ultra marathon that takes place in September of each year in Greece and carries with it a reputation as one of the most difficult and satisfying ultra distance events in the world.

The race itself began life almost 30 years ago when distance runner John Foden, who was in the RAF and had an interest in Greek history, wondered if it really was possible to cover the 250-kilometre route from Athens to Sparta within 36 hours, as Pheidippides was supposed to have done.

Not one to want to be left wondering, Foden did what any member of the 100 Marathon Club might do – he gathered a team of (presumably) willing men and together they planned the route as closely as possible to the description given in the history books. And then they ran it – obviously, because otherwise there wouldn't have been much point in planning the whole thing, would there? That wouldn't prove a thing. Remarkably, they managed to achieve their objective and finished within the time limit, proving the claims in the history books were probably true. Foden's curiosity was satisfied (and his loved ones most probably gave thanks he wasn't a cat!).

The race itself is conducted on a point-to-point basis, with the course's elevation ranging from sea level to 1,200m. It is run over a series of road, rough, muddy tracks and rugged mountain paths. Undoubtedly the most challenging part is the ascent and descent of Mount Parthenio in the dead of night (where it is said Pheidippides met the god Pan), although there have been no reported sightings of said god since Spartathon began.

With no proper pathway over the mountain, runners must follow a trail of coloured, flashing lights and trust the strong winds won't blow them off-course (the runners, not the lights, although I suppose that could happen but I'm sure the organisers already have this covered!) and the drop in temperature at the top of the mountain, which can go as low as 4°C/39°F, doesn't give them hypothermia.

Just in case they do run into difficulties though, there are regular aid stations with food, water and other refreshments as well as the runners' own personal supplies, plus police, doctors, physiotherapists and emergency vehicles on hand throughout the duration of the race. Apart from the distance what makes it even more demanding is the strict cut-off requirements, with each of the 75 control points having its own time limitation. If a runner is not there by the official closing time, they will be eliminated from the race and there are no exceptions.

Indeed, so tough is the race that it's said even the most experienced athletes can start hallucinating towards the finish (I don't wish to be a killjoy or change history or anything, but couldn't that explain Pheidippides' Pan?), losing all sense of time and reality (see what I mean?) and running on automatic pilot as completely and utterly exhausted, they force themselves to carry on.

It is reported only about a third of the runners who start the race actually manage to cross the finishing line at the statue of Leonidas and for those who do, having tested their physical strength and mental toughness to the limit and emerged triumphant, the sense of such an achievement renders many just too emotional to speak. As for the reward for such Herculean efforts, you'll receive an olive wreath and a goblet of water from the Evrotas River – apparently meant to replicate what victorious Olympians would have been honoured with in times of yore.

You know, it's still not tempting me.

THE BRATHAY WINDERMERE 10-IN-10 – 10 MARATHONS IN 10 DAYS

'The UK's Ultimate Endurance Running Event'

Often we hear of celebrities doing daft things like running 43 marathons in as many days or rowing across the Atlantic in a bucket, or even swimming the Channel while wearing a blindfold. We consider such 'achievements' merely entertaining, or maybe inspiring – or conversely, if we are celebrity cynics, we might take the view that they are only done as publicity stunts, although personally I'd rather pretend I was a cat and make mewing sounds on national television – but that's just me (and George).

But how often do we hear about the daft things that ordinary people get up to? (And I don't mean things like a fully (over)grown man riding a child's bike up a home-made ramp and being surprised when the front wheel comes off, or swinging from a frayed piece of rope across a muddy river which, unsurprisingly, snaps mid-mud.) Oh, no, I'm talking about something much dafter! By this I mean running 10 marathons in 10 days. If you want to find the 'crazy' in this book, surely that must be it. Why, oh why would anyone in his right mind consider doing such a... well, crazy thing?

For the 100 Marathon Club members it's obviously a quick way of building up their numbers but it is also incredibly tough, testing both physical stamina and mental strength. Indeed, so tough is this challenge that a training weekend is held a few months ahead of the main event to help participants prepare as fully as possible for the daunting task ahead.

Already billed as the UK's ultimate endurance running event despite only springing into existence in 2007, when founder Sir Christopher Ball, a fellow of the Brathay Trust, seemed to think it might be a tip-top idea to incorporate an endurance running event of, oh, say, 10 marathons run in 10 days within the Brathay Windermere Marathon. Or, to put it another way, runners would cover a total of 262 miles over 10 days, completing the same undulating marathon course around the picturesque Lake Windermere every day. Oh, and let's start the race with a shotgun – now that might be fun!

To be fair to Sir Christopher, he did actually participate in the inaugural event himself – when he was 72 years of age! Indeed, he has only just relinquished the record as the oldest competitor this year to 100 Marathon Club member John Dawson who is 73 and who only took up running at the age of 52 following a heart attack. In 2010, John also lost an eye to cancer but that hasn't stopped him running. To date he has completed 383 marathons, 318 of which were run as an OAP.

On completing the 10-in-10 (for the second time, the first having been in 2007) and taking the record, John said: 'I am proud of what I have achieved and hopefully it will inspire other, more mature people to get out and run, or just to become more active.'

In the same race another 100 Marathon Club member, Dave 'Foxy' Bayley, set a new Guinness World Record for running the fastest marathon dressed as a lifeguard. In the process he added his name to the list of other record-breaking 100 Marathon Club members such as Steve Edwards, who established the initial World Record accumulated time of 35 hours 20 minutes 45 seconds for the 10-in-10 in 2008, only to have it taken away a year later by the youngest member of the 100 Club (and the youngest male in the UK/world to have competed 100 marathons), 23-year-old Adam Holland, who knocked almost three hours off Steve's record and then returned the following year to reduce it by a further 2 hours 30 minutes, averaging an amazing 3 hours 02.05 for each marathon.

But for all the remarkable personal achievements that the 10-in-10 might bring individuals, there is a far greater reason for taking part – the reason why the event was started in the first place – to raise funds through sponsorship to support the Brathay Hall Trust's work with underprivileged children and young people in the UK, which the Trust does through targeted programs helping them to develop their skills, resilience, confidence and motivation to make positive choices in their lives.

It seems to me you couldn't get a much finer example of people putting all those skills into practise than those who take it upon themselves to run 10 marathons in 10 days, not only to test themselves but also as a means of helping others perhaps less fortunate. If you want to find out more, go to www.brathay.org.uk.

100 MARATHON CLUB SPECIALS

As well as taking part in races across the world, the 100 Marathon Club are also keen inventors of their own events. Here are a couple of the slightly more curious ones!

Greenwich Foot Tunnel

This one-off event was held in 2002 to mark 100 years of the existence of the tunnel, which runs for 1,217 feet and passes beneath the River Thames between Cutty Sark Gardens and Island Gardens on the Isle of Dogs. These days, the tunnel is widely recognised for being a good vantage point from which to watch the London Marathon as runners pass by the *Cutty Sark*.

Given the centenary and marathon connections, the 100 Club decided that running a marathon through the tunnel might be a jolly good way to mark such an auspicious occasion. However, the authorities were not so keen and refused to allow the tunnel to be closed to the public while the event took place. Undaunted, the 100 Club simply started the race at 2am!

Sid Wheeler, one of the participants, observed: 'The only other people about were drunks and tramps!'

As the tunnel was so narrow, the runners set off one by one on the 58-lap race in order of their anticipated finishing times. Hugh Jones, former British international and previous winner of the London Marathon in 1982, set off first and won the race in a somewhat remarkable time, given the circumstances of 2 hours 45 minutes.

Sid Wheeler told me that there were two lifts in the tunnel, one at either end. 'We used one to leave our kit in while we ran and the other served as a drinks station and toilet. Because of the lack of room in the tunnel, we were unable to throw down our drinks bottles when we finished drinking so we had to carry them until we reached one of the baskets that had been positioned especially for the purpose.

'The air became quite acrid after a while...' he decides to mention.

I feel an involuntary wrinkling of my nose.

'And with all the breathing causing humidity,' he continues, unperturbed by the state of my nose, 'the surface – which had been dry at the start – became wet and slippery.'

At the risk of sounding like a girl (which I am, so I don't suppose it matters really!), the whole experience sounds pretty disgusting if you don't mind my saying so. Give me fresh air, a gentle breeze and sunshine any time. However, one must not lose sight of the object of the exercise and I guess having people who have run over 100 marathons, who belong to a club called 'The

100 Marathon Club' running through a 100-year-old tunnel, does make sense in some weird and wonderful way!

From Windsor to White City – and Saying 'No' to HM the Queen

The year 2008 marked 100 years since London hosted its first 'modern' Olympic Games naturally featuring the Marathon itself. What better way to celebrate such an historic occasion than to gather some of the finest members of the 100 Club to replicate the marathon run in 1908 at those Olympic Games?

Well, you could just raise a glass of bubbly in a glass produced specially for the occasion (you know, one with the Olympic logo or torch engraved upon it), but I suppose that wouldn't be quite so challenging or as memorable as running a marathon along the exact same course as those Olympiads had passed along a hundred years earlier, would it?

So, on Thursday, 24 July 2008, at 14:30 hours precisely – the same day, date, month and time as the original Olympic Marathon – a large contingent of the 100 Club plus a few friends and guests did just that, setting off from the original starting point on the main street just outside Windsor Castle, following the same course (as near as possible, given 100 years of road changes) and finishing on the same line. Back then the finishing line would have been within the Olympic Stadium, but of course this no longer exists and is instead part of the BBC grounds. At least there's a plaque commemorating the 1908 Olympic Games, where incidentally the GB team won a bucketful of medals.

Indeed such was the resolve of the 100 Club to replicate the original 1908 event as accurately as possible that they even turned down an offer by Her Majesty the Queen to start the race because that would have meant changing the day it was run from the Thursday to the Saturday (the Queen being otherwise engaged on the Thursday) and it would therefore not have taken place on the exact date as the original!

The race was won by joint winners, Dave Ross and Ian Sharman, who were given the same time of 3 hours 36 minutes 30 seconds and in 1908 the same race was won by the Italian Dorando Pietri in 2 hours 54 minutes 46 seconds before he was famously disqualified for being assisted over the line by officials as he was on the point of collapse. Victory was instead awarded to second-place runner, American Johnny Hayes, with a time of 2 hours 55 minutes 18 seconds.

For the purists among you, you will be relieved to know that the course that was run in 2008 was measured by an accredited course measurer for accuracy!

I wonder if, in 2112, anyone will think to re-enact the 2012 London Olympic Marathon in the same way? Crazy as it might seem, I rather like to think that they would.

MILE 26.1

MEETING IN MALTA

Because members of the 100 Marathon Club live the length and breadth of the British Isles, the task of interviewing any or all of them proved something of a challenge. My preference was to meet them all in person as I wanted to write about them as real people, not just a voice on the telephone or as an email correspondent, so when I heard that about 20 of the Club were setting off to run the Malta Marathon, as well as to support 'wannabe' member 29-year-old Naomi Prasad in her bid to run her 100th marathon and in so doing become the youngest female in the UK, if not the world to do so, how could I resist? Besides, Malta had long been on my list of places to visit and what better excuse to go there than a marathon? (Is it me, or am I starting to sound like them?)

It all began at half past six on a Friday morning. Actually, to be precise, I got up at four o'clock in the morning, so technically it began then, but you probably don't want to hear about my early-morning ablutions, do you? The point is to recognise this was also the time it began for some members of the 100 Marathon Club, too.

I travelled to Gatwick to catch the 7.30am to Malta (the only cheap flight from Gatwick that day, obviously – otherwise I'd have caught a later one and had a lie-in). As soon as the gate number flashed up on the board, I was off and running – out of habit more than anything else. After all, I was flying on my own and so it didn't matter if I got on first or last, so long as there was a seat on the inside.

Having trotted the 10 miles from the departure lounge to the gate, I joined the short queue of six or seven sprinters who had somehow managed to get there before me and plonked my bag down on the floor, checking I had my passport and boarding card to hand. Satisfied all was in order, I took a moment to look around me and couldn't help but notice a very tall, slender man just in front of me. Runner, I labelled him straightaway, I bet he's going to do the Marathon.

By the way, I must confess to being something of an expert in this field, mainly due to my other job working with the running holiday company, Running Crazy Limited. Then I have to meet customers at the airport and take them to the hotel. Only once have I misidentified someone who wasn't a customer and nearly managed to take him back with me! Imagine his shock at finding himself incarcerated with 100 runners, all looking forward to running a marathon when all he'd been hoping to do was have a lazy time by the hotel pool.

However, I digress. Back to Malta – or at least Gatwick Airport. Having picked out my prey, I studied him carefully. He barely stood still, pacing backwards and forwards from his rucksack on the floor to the window, all of 50 feet. Definitely a runner…

I decided I needed to speak to him as he could well be a member of the 100 Marathon Club, someone I'd already spoken to over the phone and it would be rude of me not to initiate some kind of conversation.

'Excuse me,' I ventured, catching him just in time before he twirled around his bag to make a return trip to the window, 'are you going to Malta to run the Marathon?'

He smiled down at me from his lofty six-foot plus and tugged at his dark blue sweatshirt. 'I suppose this gave it away?'

Ah, okay, did I not mention he was wearing a top emblazoned with the words, '10-in-10 Brathay: 10 marathons in 10 days'?

'A little,' I admitted, offering him a full grin because I knew it was pointless pretending to be sheepish about it.

'I don't suppose you're a member of the 100 Marathon Club?' I bashed on, unashamedly.

'No, I'm not actually,' he said.

I tried to hide my disappointment.

'But I do know quite a lot of them,' he went on cheerily, as if he felt somehow responsible for alleviating my downheartedness and making it clear that my disappointment wasn't hidden at all. 'I'm always bumping into them at races,' he continued. 'Actually, there's quite a few of them on this flight,' he offered encouragingly, glancing around him at the much-increased queue now gathered behind us.

My disappointment was quite gone: this was great! Maybe he could point them out to me? But first I felt some sort of explanation on my part was due so I told him about the book and how I'd spoken to some of the 100 Club members, but never met them.

'In that case,' he said easily, 'I will introduce you to them. I know Roger Biggs is on this flight. And Gina Little…'

'Oh, I've spoken to both of them,' I told him, excitement building. 'Are you sure you don't mind?'

'Not at all,' he said, appearing to mean it.

A thought suddenly entered my head – unusual at that time

in the morning it has to be said, but there it was nonetheless. Maybe I should interview him? He may not have done over 100 marathons but he had obviously been around – in the running sense, I mean. So I asked if he would mind, and he laughed and said no, not at all. He really is a very nice, helpful man, I thought, rustling about in my hand baggage and eventually withdrawing notebook and pen with a triumphant flourish.

I had just established that the nice helpful man's name was Chris Heaton and that he had no idea how many marathons he'd run, but would stab at a guess of 'around 40', adding he doesn't run them for accumulation but does the UK ones, 'either because they're in beautiful places or as training runs, or to see people I haven't seen for years who live nearby; the foreign ones I do for travel and adventure.'

Naturally, it was at this point that the orange people arrived and decided to start boarding the plane and so I had to replace my notebook and pen in my bag.

I asked Chris if he would mind if I sat next to him, promising not to interview him for the entire flight. The nice man told me he didn't mind at all, which turned out to be a godsend because no sooner were we seated than he pointed out Roger Biggs, chairman of the 100 Marathon Club, coming down the aisle (but not in a bridal way).

'Roger!' I called out, unable to contain my excitement.

A man of average height with greying hair and glasses glanced quizzically towards me, as well he might, seeing we'd never met before and he had no idea who I was.

'Helen,' I said, by way of introduction, 'the writer,' I added as an explanation. The people in the row in front turned to stare, no doubt expecting to find someone famous behind them – they were disappointed.

But Roger, bless him, appeared not to be. He leaned across the seats and warmly shook my hand, introducing me to the attractive petite blonde behind him, who turned out to be none other than Gina Little, and then told me that there were quite a few more members of the Club following behind.

'I'll introduce you to some more people when we get off at the other end,' he promised, having been told to hurry up and move down the plane by a necessarily bossy stewardess.

What a pleasant, friendly, helpful man, I thought. And as for Gina, she looked stunning – all shiny-blonde hair and sparkling blue eyes. Why couldn't I look like that at quarter past seven in the morning? (Apart from the fact that I have brown – okay, greyish – hair and hazel eyes, that is.)

The three-and-a-half hour flight passed quickly enough with only just over half of it spent quizzing Chris (of course *his* recollection of events may differ), during which time I discovered that he was 51 years old, he'd run his first marathon when he was 35, having given up rugby, he trains most days and his advice to anyone aspiring to run 100 marathons would be: 'Take your brain out and keep running – it's a marathon and not a sprint!' Not, he added, that he was well placed to give advice as he hadn't done 100 himself.

One other thing I discovered about Chris before we disembarked was his rather dry sense of humour. Asked how he came to run so many marathons, he replied, 'By running so many marathons' and in response to whether or not he wears any lucky charms, 'No, I'm heavy enough as it is.' But the funniest thing he told me was the following true story.

'I was on a packed train, standing room only, with my wife,' he begins, setting the scene perfectly, 'when two middle-aged women started talking to me and asked if it was true that I'd run 10 marathons in 10 days – I was wearing the shirt at the time,' he pauses to explain. 'I told them it was true and one of the women remarked that she couldn't go shopping 10 times in 10 days. There was a brief pause, followed by one of them asking me if she could feel my legs. After checking with my wife, I agreed and the woman duly bent down and had a feel. "Ooh, Janet," she said to her friend, "have a feel of these. I haven't felt a man so hard in all my life!'"

I had just about managed to stop chortling and admiring Chris's masterful impression of two apparently northern middle-aged women by the time the plane landed. Thanking him for his contribution and wishing him well for a safe and pleasant (nay, peaceful) onward journey, I pulled in to stop the other side of Customs in the hope of catching up with Roger and Gina again.

And I was in luck: a few minutes later, they appeared and showed me the medal that was to be presented to Naomi when she had run her 100th marathon. Roger also showed me two pins that were to be presented to two other members, Dave Ross and Dave King, who were both completing their 200th marathons.

I then had the pleasure of being introduced to married couple Mel and Dave Ross (he of 200 fame), who had met through running marathons and told me that together they had run a combined total of over 300 marathons (you can read their full story again on pp.197-202). Dave actually proposed to Mel up a mountain prior to them both running in the Davos Marathon in Switzerland. And she still said 'Yes'!

Once outside the airport we went our separate ways but not before I had received an invitation to join them at their after-race party, which was to be held at a nearby wine bar on the Sunday evening.

The next time I saw any of the 100 Club runners was on race day itself, which, much to the relief of everyone, dawned bright and sunny following a night of seemingly unstoppable rain. The roads had been left slippery-wet and water still sloshed over the edge of an overfull harbour, but by the time the runners reached that part of the race, much of the road had dried out under a then baking sun.

I had positioned myself midway along the finishing straight in front of the harbour and my first sighting of a 100 Club runner was Dave Ross, followed by Steve Edwards. After Steve, it was impossible to say who finished where because runners of all shapes and sizes, in all sorts of conditions, approached the finishing line (about 200m from where I was standing). One poor chap (not a 100 Club member) actually keeled over almost in front of me, got up again, keeled over once more and was eventually helped to his feet but it was clear he could not continue and so he was taken to the side of the road and offered a drink. Sensibly, he took the drink but his eyes were still spinning in their sockets and it was plain he didn't have a clue where he was. This is not something I ever like to witness in any race and fortunately happens only rarely. Some 20 minutes later, I'm pleased to report that same man was back on his feet again, albeit shakily and was once more setting off in pursuit of the finish. Whether he got there or not, I don't know – I hope so, he certainly deserved it.

As for the 100 Marathoners, I watched them pass me by in their club colours and shouted encouragement to each one, not always by name but by club because of course at that time I didn't know who they all were. They, in turn, acknowledged me and thanked me for my support, even though most of them had no idea who I was either. I'm delighted to say not one of them showed signs of swirling eyes or shaky legs, even if they felt them! Indeed, most of them smiled and looked remarkably fresh considering they'd just run 26 miles.

I did spot one runner who I recognised, though: Martin Bush, who has run almost 600 marathons and who I met on a trip with Running Crazy Limited last year. He spotted me and called out cheekily, 'It's easy for you – you should be running!' I grinned back and told him that if he could chat, he wasn't running fast enough. He made some no doubt fitting retort, which I didn't quite catch (probably just as well) and disappeared on his way to the finish.

Watching the guys and gals running towards the finish, hearing Martin's jovial comments, there was a part of me that for a moment actually wished I was out there in the field, running with them, being a part of it, sharing the experience and all the while knowing that at the end, they would be waiting and cheering for me, hoping for me, happy for me… Also knowing that I, in turn, would be doing the same for them. There's something intrinsic in us all that responds to shared experiences especially difficult ones and the feelings they bring out in us demonstrate how much we need one another. It's a demonstration, too of all that's good in the human spirit. And I realised as I stood there on the sidelines, no matter how much it sometimes hurt, how much I used to hate it at times, I missed the days when I used to compete and was part of it. However, I console myself with the thought that I was lucky to have started running so early in life (at the age of 10), lucky that I'd been able to continue competing after the removal of my kidney at 21, and lucky that following a slipped disc at the age of 39, I found a physio who was able to get me back on my feet. Even today, although unable to compete, I can still experience the joy of running – albeit slowly and not very far.

But it wasn't over yet for the support and camaraderie continued well into the evening and all I can say is that it's a good job I'd spoken to Naomi over the phone before heading out to Malta and wasn't relying on interviewing her (or indeed anyone else) at the after-race party because it would have been nigh-on impossible to hear her above the noisy throng of well-wishers and supporters present. Not that I could mistake her for who she was, though. She looked just as I had imagined: tall, slim and elegant, with a burning passion for her achievement shining from her dark eyes.

The intelligence that I'd witnessed when we spoke on the phone was reflected in the eloquent acceptance speech she gave when Roger presented her with her 100 Club medal, deep-felt joy evident in the huge smile she kept on her face all evening.

The warmth and the camaraderie of that night will stay with me always, for it is rare indeed to witness such an assorted mix of people demonstrating genuine pleasure or sincere sympathy to others, depending on how their races had gone. Crammed together in a space at the back of the wine bar, they were like one big, noisy, happy family and I felt privileged to be a part of it. From the moment I arrived, they treated me like one of their own, offering me food and drink and inviting me to join in conversations all over the place.

It reminded me of when I first started out in athletics over 40 years ago. Those were the days when there was no money in the sport, when people did it for the love of it. My experience in Malta made me realise that whether or not running over 100 marathons is considered mad by others doesn't matter a jot because for those who choose to do them, it isn't just about the running, it isn't even about the travel (although that's a big attraction) and it certainly isn't about the money (there isn't any, except for the winners) – what it *is* about is friendship, camaraderie and a sense of purpose. And try as I might, I cannot find even a hint of madness in any of that.

MILE 26.2

SUMMER'S END

As we have seen throughout this book, there are myriad reasons why so many people elect to run 26.2 miles in the first instance. However, it would seem that almost without exception, they do not make a conscious decision to run 100 marathons: it simply happens over time, like evolution.

Man didn't set out to live his life sitting down yet that's what has evolved. Running 100 marathons is like an evolution revolution – it's like people making a stand, literally. They want to feel the ground beneath their feet, experience the exhilaration of being slapped about the face by the chill rawness of an early morning north-easterly, taste the sweat of their own endeavours after it has journeyed down facial contours, stinging their eyes and dripping into open mouths that gasp desperately for that sweet-tasting, life-giving oxygen.

People want, maybe need, to experience life at its most basic – raw, without sophistication and falseness. Running a marathon allows them to do just that. And running 100 or more marathons means they can savour the experience time and time again until it becomes, in the words of the 100 Club chairman, 'a way of life'.

If you want to find out more about the 100 Marathon Club or think you may qualify to become a member, please visit their website at www.100marathonclub.org.uk